Travels with Baby

The Ultimate Guide for Planning Travel with
Your Baby, Toddler, and Preschooler

Second Edition

Shelly Rivoli

Travels with Baby Books
Berkeley, California
www.TravelswithBaby.com

Travels with Baby Books is a division of Speckled Frog LLC.
ISBN 978-0-9831-2272-2
Second Edition / First Printing

Table of Contents

Preface... x

Acknowledgments ix

Part I: Good Choices Make Good Journeys........ 13

CHAPTER 1 Deciding When to Go 14
The Case for Traveling with Babies 14

How soon should you travel with your baby?..................................... 17

Anticipating Ages and Stages 19

CHAPTER 2 Deciding Where to Go 31
Beach Vacations 31

✓ Family Beach Vacation Packing List 34

Camping Trips 35

✓ Family Camping Trip Packing List 38

Urban Adventures 42

✓ Urban Adventures Packing List... 45

CHAPTER 3 Deciding Where to Stay... 46
Staying (Safe and Sane) with Friends and Family 46

Best Hotels and Resorts for Young Families 49

Best All-Suite Hotels for Young Families 52

Best All-Inclusive Resorts for Children Under 5 55

Condos and Other Vacation Rentals 59

CHAPTER 4 Deciding What to Bring 61
Preparing Your Child's Travel Kit.. 61

✓ Your Child's Travel Kit Packing List...................................... 62

Clothing Considerations for the Whole Family 64

Great Products and Gear for Travel 66

Finding and Using Baby Gear Rental Companies (a.k.a. Baby
Equipment Hire) 82

Baby Supply Delivery Services 83

Fifteen Things You Might Not Think to Pack 84

Part II: Tools for Happy Travels 87

CHAPTER 5 Preparing for Changes 88
Changes in Nighttime Sleeping Routines 88
Changes in Naptime Sleeping Routines.. 92
Changes in Eating and Feeding Routines.. 94
Changes in Potty Training Routines 98
Preparing Toddlers and Preschoolers for Travel............................ 101
Three Secrets to Stress-Free Travel with Kids................................ 104
✔ Ten Things to Do Before You Leave Home.......................... 106

CHAPTER 6 Travels with Your Unique Child 107
Temperaments in Transit 107
Activity Level: High Energy vs. Low Energy 108
Approach to New Things: Eager vs. Cautious 109
Physical Regularity: Very Regular vs. Unpredictable 112
Adaptability: Fast-Adapting vs. Slow-Adapting............................ 114
Intensity: Intense vs. Mellow 115
Mood: Positive vs. Negative... 117
Attention Span: Distractible vs. Focused.. 118
Sensitivity: High Sensitivity vs. Low Sensitivity 121
More Tools for Temperament.. 123

Part III: Special Considerations 125

CHAPTER 7 The Baby Abroad 126
When Does Your Child Need a Passport? 126
Your Child's First U.S. Passport... 127
Passports for Canadian Children... 130
Travels with One Parent, Grandparents, or Others 131
Parents and Children with Different Names 132
Convenient Conversions 134
At Least They'll Speak "English"... 135
Preparing for Cultural Differences... 135
Sightseeing with Private Guides and Escorts................................. 139

CHAPTER 8 Health "Ensurance" 143
Ten Pre-Trip Tips for Healthy Travels.. 143
Having Fun in (Spite of) the Sun 145
Managing Mosquitoes... 148
Using DEET-Free Insect Repellents... 149

Using DEET-Containing Products on Children 151
The Top Things You Should Know About Ticks 153
Four Big Reasons to Breastfeed for Healthy Travels..................... 156

CHAPTER 9 Going Farther Afield 158
Food and Water Safety... 158
Small Children Swimming Abroad... 162
Vaccinations and Travel Shots... 163
Malaria Prevention for Young Children 168

CHAPTER 10 In Case of Illness... 172
Medical Help Where You Need It 172
A Traveler's Guide to Ear Infections.. 173
Common Travel Ailments and Remedies 176

CHAPTER 11 Safety Concerns 181
Childproofing On the Go 181
Checking-In Safety Checklist:... 182
City Smarts for the New Parent 184
Great Products for On the Go Safety 188
Ten Important Steps for Safer Family Travels.............................. 190

Part IV: Travels by Automobile 195

CHAPTER 12 Before You Go by Car 196
Car Seat Laws Across State Lines 196
Car Seat Laws and Other Countries... 197
Advice for Driving with Children Abroad 202
Installing Car Seats with Confidence... 204
Seatbelt Specifics... 205

CHAPTER 13 On the Road.. 210
Pacing Your Journey... 210
Dealing with Diapers, Dining, and Such...................................... 211
Carsickness Survival Guide 215
Packing for a Comfortable Road Trip... 218
Roadside Emergency Checklist 220
Taxis, Kids, and Car Seats 221

CHAPTER 14 Renting a Vehicle for the Drive........................ 224
Choosing a Rental Car and Agency 224
Renting Car Seats... 225

Renting an RV 227
Renting a Conversion Van or Campervan 232

Part V: Travels by Airplane 235

CHAPTER 15 Before You Book Your Flight 236
Ticket Pricing and Options 236
Choosing the Airline... 238
Notes on a Few "Exceptional" Airlines 241
Table 1: Airlines Comparison Table... 244
Choosing the Flight... 258
Choosing Your Seats... 260
All About Airplane Bassinets for Babies...................................... 264
✔ Airplane Bassinet Checklist.. 266

CHAPTER 16 Countdown to Takeoff 268
Required Documents for Air Travel 268
Packing for Your Flight 270
Checking Bags and Baby Gear 277
Planning Your In-Flight Entertainment 282
Tips to Help Prepare Toddlers and Preschoolers for the Flight 286

CHAPTER 17 At the Airport and on the Plane 289
Clearing Security with Small Children (and a Small Mountain of Gear) 289
Tips for Swift Passage through Airport Security 293
Seven Easy Ways to Get Your Car Seat to the Gate...................... 294
10 Ways to Entertain Your Tot in the Terminal............................ 296
The Great Pre-boarding Debate 297
Using a Car Seat (CRS) on Aircraft... 299
Using the CARES Child Aviation Restraint 303
Lap Child Safety 305
What About All Those Germs?.. 306
Ear Pressure, Pain, and Relief.. 307
Changing Diapers at 30,000 Feet.. 309
Feeding Babies and Children on Airplanes................................... 310
Five Ways to Soothe a Fussy Baby in Flight 312

CHAPTER 18 Special Situations...315
Fifteen Ways to Ease Flying Solo with Your Child....................... 315
Flying with Twins, Multiples, or Multiple Children...................... 318
Flying with a Special Needs Child.. 319

Flying for an International Adoption 321

Part VI: Travels by Train 325

CHAPTER 19 Deciding to Go by Rail 326
Advantages of Taking the Train 326
Top Reasons to Travel by Train with Twins or Multiple Children . 328
Five Tips for Great Train Trips with Babies and Small Children ... 329
Get Started: Twelve Scenic U.S. Day Trips by Train 330

CHAPTER 20 All Aboard Amtrak 337
Why (and why not) take the "A" train? 337
Amtrak's Most Notable Routes and Highlights 339
Rates, Pricing, and Passes for Amtrak 345
Rail Pass Options and Multi-Ride Tickets 347
Seats, Sleepers, and Onboard Amenities 348
Amtrak's Baggage Policies 353
Airports Served by Amtrak 354
Required Documents for U.S. Rail Travel 356

CHAPTER 21 Catching VIA Rail in Canada 358
VIA's Most Notable Routes and Highlights 358
Rates, Pricing, and Passes for VIA Rail 359
Classes of Service, Seats, and Sleepers 361
VIA Rail's Baggage Policies 363
Airport and Other Connecting Services 364
International Travel and Travelers 365

CHAPTER 22 Train Travel in Europe 366
Riding Europe's Family-Friendly Rails 366
European Rail Travel Reality Check 367
Free Rides and Discounts for Children 369
Table 2: Children's Rail Discounts by Country 371
The Best European Rail Passes for Families 373
Other Family Discounts for Rail Travel 375
Classes of Service, Seats, & Sleepers 376
European Airports with Railway Stations 378

Part VII: Travels by Cruise Ship 379

CHAPTER 23 Before You Book Your Cruise 380
The Case for Cruising as a Family 380

Cruise Discounts for Infants and Children 382
Other Cruise Discounts 385
Minimum Age Requirements 385
Babysitting and Children's Programs 386
Family Dining Options and Opportunities 388
A New Parent's Guide to Cruise Lines 390
Table 3: Cruise Lines Comparison Table 391

CHAPTER 24 Booking Your Cruise 395
Stateroom Types and Configurations 395
Getting the Most Room for Your Money 398
Selecting Your Cabin's Location 399
Five Important Requests to Make in Advance 400

CHAPTER 25 Preparing for Your Cruise 402
Researching Your Ports of Call 402
Choosing Your Shore Excursions 403
Taking Taxis in Port 406
Packing for Your Cruise 407

Afterword: Five Reasons Travel Trumps the Other Gifts I've Given My Children 411
Index 414
About the Author 417

Acknowledgments

There might never have been a first edition of Travels with Baby were it not for the help of my mother, Polly Packard, who gave so generously of her time, patience, love, and cooking for our family throughout its gestation. Anyone who is helped by this book can be thankful for her contribution, as I will forever be.

I am also grateful to my husband and travel companion, Tim, who logged countless miles of his commute with those early manuscript pages in his hands, giving essential input and support for this project, and sharing my belief that if this book could answer our own questions, it could—and *would*—help other parents. (We were right!)

Also, special thanks to Rona Renner, R.N., for introducing me to the field of Temperament and The Preventive Ounce project, of which I could instantly see the value for traveling parents and am so pleased to address in this guide.

I would also like to thank Cynthia Harriman, author of *Take Your Kids to Europe*, for reading and providing valuable feedback on the first edition of *Travels with Baby* and encouraging me toward this next edition.

Additional thanks to my friends and family members who provided helpful feedback on earlier drafts and incarnations of *Travels with Baby*: Susan Bumps, Amy Kang, Cinzia Solari, Davide Cis, and Connie Anderson. A hearty thanks also goes out to Captain Jon and Barbara Rivoli for their airport anecdote included in this book, to Linda Geiser for the "McDrive," to Melissa Colby who helped Ziploc bags take up permanent residence in my suitcase, to Jutta Bauer for help with German car seats, and to the numerous parents who have shared their travel experiences with me through surveys, interviews, emails, chats in airport restrooms and café cars, and at www.TravelswithBaby.com.

Finally, I thank my family for living this book—and for letting me finish it two times over, even when there were plenty of other things to be done: Tim, who agreed that you *can* take a baby to Thailand; Angelina, who showed us the way; Rosalyn, who continues to remind us that each child is her own adventure; and Theodore, our delightful travel companion who joined us on the way to this second edition. I dedicate this book to each of you with all my love.

Preface

Before crossing the Pacific with our firstborn, we had braced ourselves for the worst, half-expecting a long-haul exercise in torture we would boldly endure to reach our destination: Thailand. To our surprise, flying overseas with our 7-month-old was much more fun than any other overseas flight we'd ever experienced. Instead of checking our watches as the airplane icon inched its way across the movie screen in between showings of second-run films, we were simply hanging out with our favorite little person in the world, having meals prepared for us and delivered right to our seats, watching movies which, for obvious reasons, we hadn't made it to the theater to see yet.

We quickly realized that we were already on vacation—free to enjoy our daughter's wonderful smiles and share her fascination with the reading lights and passenger safety brochures, free to cuddle her and cat nap at leisure with nary a load of laundry to fold, free to agree with the flight attendants and fellow passengers that yes, she is absolutely adorable. Even when she cries.

Whether you are gearing up for your trip because you *have* to travel with your baby, toddler, or preschooler, or because you simply *have to travel* and are ready to try it with your child, this book will help you lay the groundwork for successful travel of any kind: weekend getaways, lengthy road trips, international treks, family reunions, and virtually every reason you might have for packing up and heading out with the newest member of your family.

Rest assured, it is written by someone who has been there—inventing songs no one should ever sing in the eleventh hour on the road, pleading with the manager of the general store to let a helpless infant (and her numb-knuckled mother) come inside to warm up before opening hours, and sprinting behind the train caboose through the rain shouting, "Stop! You have our car seat!!!"

As you might suspect, there have been moments when even I have had to ask myself, "Who in her right mind travels with a baby?" But I will be honest with you; after trotting the globe with a small child in tow—and then two—and now three, the good times have by far outweighed the more challenging moments. By far. And much like the birthing of a child, I suspect you will find that even the roughest moments look much rosier in retrospect and have all proven to be well worth the effort.

Now don't get me wrong, I'm not saying that traveling with your baby or toddler will be easy. In fact, I can pretty much guarantee that, as with any trip you might take, with or without children, you will have some difficult moments. Yet, while many parents opt to wait to vacation until their children are older, or are old enough to be left behind with grandparents or friends, they are—sometimes literally—missing the boat. New parents need vacations. New families need bonding time. New people need stimulation, fresh air and scenery, and happy parents. Leaving the house together, if only for a day, can work wonders for a family.

As I stroll along our "wall of travel," the collage of travel snapshots plastering our hallway at home, I am often overwhelmed by feelings of nostalgia and a longing to not just go back to many of the wonderful places we've visited, but to feel the weight once more of our eldest daughter still in her sling as we visited the elephant farm, to hear the clatter of her stroller wheels on the cobblestones of Provence, to feel her small hand squeeze mine the first time she realized what it really meant to take off in the airplane as she shouted to all of the passengers on board, "Big Daddy Ay-pane! Up!"

Traveling with a baby; a toddler; then a baby *and* a toddler; and now with three young children, has certainly kept us on our toes. We have grown and bonded so much through our adventures in ways that seldom happen when keeping up the busy schedule at home, and we count ourselves so lucky to have had these chances to see so much of the world already—by long tail boat in Thailand and a glass bottom boat in Jamaica, from an SUV in Costa Rica and the top of the Eiffel Tower.

Wherever our adventures take us, in our own backyard and abroad, I count myself luckiest for the chance to see it through the eyes of my children. Here's wishing your family many memorable and pleasant experiences traveling together.

Safe journeys,
Shelly Rivoli

Part I:
Good Choices Make Good Journeys

CHAPTER 1

Deciding When to Go

The Case for Traveling with Babies

Who could use a vacation more than a couple in the trenches of new parenthood? Sleep deprivation, mounting laundry, visits from gift-bearing guests, and a return to the workplace can leave Mom and Dad with little energy or time to enjoy the marvel of the newest twig on the family tree. But when you travel with your child, far afield or close to home, it allows for a refreshing change of scenery for both of you. Better yet, it is an escape from the other responsibilities of home that too often get in the way of enjoying quality time together. So why wait?

Top 3 Reasons to Travel While Your Child Is Still a Baby

1. **You can choose a destination and activities that interest you.** For now, your child is equally content to visit the Metropolitan Museum of Art as the aquarium or zoo, so long as she's with you. In a couple of years, however, you can bet that you'll all be finding Nemo.

2. **Jetlag won't faze you with your already sporadic sleeping routine.** Or more importantly, your baby adapts to new time zones more easily when she still sleeps multiple times per 24-hour day. Later on, when she naps only once a day or not at all, it may take longer to adjust to a difference in time zones. For now, you can also

look forward to her naps to help catch extra winks for yourself during your vacation, should you need them.

3. **Your child will never be cheaper to travel with (hurry!).** Your heart may skip a beat the first time you price airfare for THREE to your extended family's festivities or your favorite vacation spot. Until she turns 2 years, however, your child can fly free on your lap for domestic flights or for 10% of your ticket on most international flights, or for 50% in her own seat with some airlines (more details in Chapter 14). Plus, some cruise lines, all-inclusive resorts, and tour operators will not charge fees for infants—though they will for "children," which is sometimes defined as 1 year or, most often, 2 years and older.

Big Sur, California: First family camping trip in the redwoods.

Taking That First Trip...Together

As we prepared for our first getaway as a family, a weekend camping trip, it seemed much less overwhelming when I realized this: For the next few days, I will change just as many diapers, stop for just as many feedings, and sleep just as many (or few) hours, whether I'm at home or not. So why not do it all somewhere incredibly beautiful? And so I found myself nursing our infant daughter under a canopy of redwood trees, her little eyes shining up at the patches of bright sky overhead, her little ears perked for the sounds of birds and the trickles of a nearby stream.

I began to rest in a way I had not been able to at home, with the never-ending laundry, thank-you notes still to write, and other hovering responsibilities on top of the simple biological rigors of new motherhood. And as my husband took over meal preparation (a vacation in itself for me) and the details of our camp, I was free to focus entirely on our daughter and the wonder of her presence in our lives. We came home from that long weekend refreshed and recharged, and with a renewed sense of confidence in ourselves as parents, and as partners.

Traveling with a child younger than 6 months old may sound overwhelming at first, especially when you are a first-time parent and are as new to the world of parenthood as your child is to the world around him. You may be overwhelmed by questions, such as:

- **What do you pack** (see Deciding What to Bring, pg. 54)?

- **How do you plan** (see Deciding Where to Go, pg. 31)?

- **How do you physically transport the child** (see Great Products and Gear for Travel, pg. 66)?

- **Where will he sleep** (see Travel Beds and Sleeping Solutions, pg. 76, and All About Airplane Bassinets, pg. 264)?

- **How will you deal with all of those diapers—and how many should you pack—and in what** (see Perfecting Your Carry-On Diaper Bag, pg. 273)?

- **What about exposure to germs** (see What About All Those Germs?, pg. 306)?

- **What if he catches a cold** (see Common Travel Ailments and Remedies, pg. 176)—**or worse** (see Medical Help Where You Need It, pg. 172, and A Traveler's Guide to Ear Infections, pg. 173)?

I've faced all these same questions myself—at least once—and now you'll have a tremendous advantage over my own family in its early days of travel: this book, chock full of answers.

How soon should you travel with your baby?

If your child hasn't yet arrived on the scene, it may be a little early to start planning, though I know in some situations it may be important or even necessary to do so. If that's you, keep in mind that the exact time of arrival may vary in weeks from what you originally expect (a friend and I with the same due date had our babies 5 weeks apart!). Your personal recovery time may start or end later than expected, as well— and during a road trip or lengthy flight in your early postpartum weeks, your comfort spending hours sitting may prove less than ideal.

Many doctors advise against flying with newborns in their first two weeks as they adjust to life outside the uterus, and some airlines simply won't allow it, while other airlines will let infants in good health fly early with a doctor's letter. If you are adopting your baby as a newborn or will need to fly soon after birth with your own child, be sure to see Airlines' Minimum Age Policies, pg. 322.

However, if you'll be traveling far afield with your infant, especially to developing countries, it may be wisest to wait until after your baby has received all of his vaccinations (usually around 6 weeks) because cases of whooping cough, measles, and polio, for example, which may be rare or nonexistent in the U.S., are still seen in many parts of the world (and even large international airports can help to bridge those worlds, where microbes are concerned). You will definitely want to discuss your destination(s) with your child's physician and address any possible concerns, including a possible modified schedule of vaccinations (more in Vaccinations and Travel Shots, pg. 163).

Yet, once your child has made the transition and gets your doctor's go-ahead for travel, there are really no reasons you shouldn't travel with your infant, provided that:

- The baby is in good health.
- You are feeling well enough and are in good health yourself.
- You are reasonably comfortable with the idea of traveling with your child.

In fact, there are many health and safety advantages to traveling with your child while she is still an infant as opposed to waiting until she's older, dexterous—and mobile. In all honesty, traveling with your child may seldom be as easy as it is in the months before he eats solid foods or crawls.

Ten Reasons Traveling with Your Infant May Be Easier than You Think...

1. **The infant is better protected from germs and illness than older babies, toddlers, and preschoolers,** because she has very limited access to the surfaces, including the railings, turnstiles, airplane armrests, and floors, that older kids encounter.

2. **She puts far fewer things in her mouth than do her mobile counterparts,** leaving whatever may have been overlooked under the hotel bed by previous occupants, thankfully, still under the hotel bed.

3. **You have control over virtually everything that comes in contact with her,** and so long as you keep your own hands clean and washed frequently, you'll have a tremendous advantage over offending germs.

4. **If she is breastfeeding, she has additional immunity benefits from her mother's milk,** which includes white blood cells (leukocytes) activated by microbes the mother is exposed to (see Breastfeeding for Healthy Travels, pg. 156).

5. **The infant's needs may be frequent, but they are few.** With enough diapers, breastmilk or formula, and the comfort of your arms, she can be happy pretty much anywhere.

6. **The infant still spends a good deal of time napping—while you may do what you please** (strolling museums, eating in restaurants, flying overseas, or driving down the coast). Take advantage while you can!

7. **The infant is also easier to feed on the go than are older babies and toddlers,** without the need to pack strained or finger foods, or deal with the inevitable mess generated by each meal.

8. **Breastfed infants are, of course, especially easy to feed** while traveling, though it may take a little time to master the "public feeding" with grace (see Nine Tips for Nursing on the Go, pg. 97).

9. **The infant is also incredibly portable.** You can pretty much strap her on and wear her to the ends of the earth, conquering stroller-prohibitive terrain like the stairs of the Paris Metro or the ruins of Carthage with ease.

10. **Infant carrier car seats are significantly easier to travel with** than the car seats that will follow, allowing you to transport baby from taxi to stroller frame without disturbing her sleep—and providing a convenient place to set her while eating in restaurants.

Anticipating Ages and Stages

As the saying goes, there is a time and place for everything. For example, a trip to New York City may be much easier while your child can still travel in her infant carrier car seat, popping in and out of taxis and a lightweight stroller frame (infant car seats that can be used without the base, see pg. 66). And a beach vacation may be infinitely more relaxing once your child knows not to eat the sand or run headlong into the surf. But predicting the right time and place for trips with your child can be a tricky business. Especially since each child marches, crawls, and rolls over to the beat of his own drummer.

While keeping in mind that each child will develop at his own perfect pace, and with his own distinct temperament (don't miss Temperaments in Transit, beginning on pg. 107), here are some general guidelines for the various ages and stages of development your child may experience from birth through four years, and tips for how you might best plan your travels together.

Birth to 3 Months

Once you begin to feel you have your sea legs as parents, it may do you a world of good to get out of the house. You may also want to take advantage of maternity or family leave time to do some traveling.

Where to go: Weekenders not too far from home, or visits with family and friends, can be great places to begin; just be sure to read the tips and advice in Staying (Safe and Sane) with Friends and Family, pg. 60.

Sleep tips: Since your baby sleeps more hours of the day now than she will in the months to come, it's an ideal time for trips that require long hours spent in the car seat—or in an airplane (ideally with an airplane bassinet or skycot; see pg. 264). She also requires little space for sleeping, and may be fine sleeping next to you or in a space-saving infant travel bed (see Travel Beds, pg. 76), leaving you with many options for lodgings, including smaller and more economical hotel rooms, economy train sleeper compartments (roomettes), or basic cruise ship cabins.

Other tips: Gear and feeding needs are minimal, though you will want to take into consideration that she'll need to be breast- or bottle-fed and diapered frequently. The travel wardrobe couldn't be simpler. No shirt, no shoes, no problem—just pack plenty of footed cotton playsuits, and some extra layers for warmth.

Be aware: Mosquito repellent and sunscreens are not recommended for infants this young, so choose a suitable destination or plan carefully if sun or mosquitoes will be a concern (see Managing Mosquitoes, pg. 148, and Having Fun in [Spite of] the Sun, pg. 145). You may want to delay travel to underdeveloped destinations until after two months, since her first complete round of childhood immunizations may not take effect until around eight weeks, during which time her immune system and natural defenses are also still establishing themselves (more in Vaccinations and Travel Shots, pg. 163).

Big help: If "the evening fussies" or colic are concerns, consider renting a baby swing (and/or other gear) at your destination (see Baby Gear Rentals, pg. 82).

Best bet vacations: Home stays with family and friends (see pg. 60), overseas travel (see The Baby Abroad, pg. 126), car trips (see Travels by Automobile, pg. 195), train trips (see Travels by Train, pg. 325), short cruises (see Travels by Cruise Ship, pg. 379).

Yosemite National Park, California: Snoozing through her first hike up to Inspiration Point.

3 to 6 Months

Your baby is in his prime for riding—and napping—contentedly on laps and in an infant carrier or sling, while sharing early smiles, all making travel together a true delight. He takes a new interest in his surroundings, and enjoys seeing the sights from the comfort of your sling or frontpack carrier—where he still has the comfort of staying close to the people he knows best.

Where to go: You are still relatively free to choose a destination and schedule the itinerary to suit your adult selves, but because your child's skin is still very thin and sensitive, sunscreen and repellents are not recommended (see Having Fun in [Spite of] the Sun, pg. 145, and Managing Mosquitoes, pg. 148). Consequently, you may lean toward destinations where extreme sun and biting insects are not a concern. Urban adventures in cultural capitals may provide the right amount of stimulation for all of you (MOMA for mom, baby swings in Central Park for Junior), balanced with climate-controlled interiors when and where needed.

Sleep tips: His sleeping arrangements may require more attention through these months as he becomes more active, quite possibly rolling over at some point. A travel bassinet or infant travel bed will give him a comfy place to snooze and play with his toys (see more about Travel Beds on pg. 76), or a portacrib may also be available on request at your hotel or for your cruise ship cabin. Now that he's becoming more aware of his surroundings, a white noise machine or soundtrack of waves can be extremely helpful in recreating the familiar sounds of sleep from home (more in Nighttime Sleeping, pg. 54).

Other tips: Most children in this range do not yet eat solid foods, which helps keep things simple and relatively tidy in transit. In particular, you won't need a complete clothing change after every meal as you may in the following few months. You can still take advantage of airplane bassinets on long-haul flights with most carriers (see Airlines Table, pg. 244), before your baby is too big and too easily distracted by the noise and traffic around the bulkhead area (see All About Airplane Bassinets, pg. 264).

Beware: Often during these months, babies experience a sudden heightened awareness of their surroundings, including other people, which can make it challenging for some to focus on breastfeeding in public places (e.g., airplanes), where they don't want to miss anything. For help, see tips for Nursing on the Go, pg. 97.

Big help: Using binder clips to attach an extra blanket to the canopy of your stroller can help shield snoozing babies from harsh sun and also minimize distractions during a nap on the go.

Best bet vacations: Urban adventures (see pg. 42), overseas travel (see pg. 126), and car trips (see pg. 195).

6 to 12 Months

Baby becomes an accomplished explorer anywhere she can touch down as long-distance rolling, scooting, crawling, cruising, and possibly walking become part of her physical repertoire.

Where to go: If you plan to travel overseas with your child, this may be an ideal time to go since it will be much easier to manage a long-haul flight before your child starts walking well, and while you can still take advantage of an airline bassinet where available (size and age restrictions become a factor with some airlines during these months; see All About Airplane Bassinets, pg. 264). If you want to visit a destination where food and water safety are a concern for most travelers, this can actually be a better time to go—while your child is eating jarred baby foods, and breastfeeding or drinking formula—rather than later, when she'll be eating more of the same table foods you do (see Food and Water Safety, pg. 158).

Sleep tips: Hopefully your child will have a fairly established sleeping and napping schedule at this point. Consequently, you may be nervous about disrupting a good thing during travel. If so, be sure to read the sections addressing sleep in Preparing for Changes, beginning on pg. 88, and pack (or download) your copy of *Take-Along Travels with Baby* for sleep tips you can use on the go.

Other tips: Since the floor is where it's at during this stage, and everything goes in the mouth, choose your accommodations accordingly. You'll want to plan a trip that includes a suitable space and time each day where she can exercise and explore in a safe environment. You may find it well worth paying the upgrade for a larger room or to stay somewhere you are confident will be clean. Consider bringing or renting any gear she is especially fond of at this time if it could make a tremendous difference in her enjoyment of the vacation (and yours).

Bring a play mat or baby quilt for play time on the floor. Also, a "jumper" that mounts in an open doorway (possibly your bathroom's or a closet's) will easily fit in most suitcases and can help keep her out of harm's way while you ready yourselves for the day.

Be aware: Consider remote destinations carefully, as well as longer cruises, as you may have to pack along your entire supply of diapers and baby food (or see Baby Supply Delivery Services, pg. 83). Urban adventures, on the other hand, allow you to pick up your baby essentials at markets and pharmacies as needed.

Best bet vacations: Urban adventures (see pg. 42), overseas travel (see pg. 126), and car trips (see pg. 195).

12 to 18 Months

Your child may look more like a "staggerer" than a toddler through much of this phase, and even though he is on his feet, he may be very unsteady and prone to falls. He will likely want to spend every chance he gets perfecting his walking skills, whether he is still cruising from object to object or sprinting off in sheer delight, and he may also be reaching new heights as a climber.

Where to go: If you hope to relax on your vacation, it may be more important than ever to look for accommodations that are prepared—and safe—for small children. Rethink exotic retreats with hard tile floors, or sleek hotels with "edgy" furnishings. Look for a family-friendly hotel or resort that anticipates small children, where you won't have to spend all the time in your room distracting your child from the AC controls, or steering him away from a glass coffee table (see the Checking-In Safety Checklist, pg. 182). You are now entering the window of time when it can feel like a charming vacation rental or the homes of extended family members can have many more safety concerns than you've bargained for (see Staying (Safe and Sane) with Friends and Family, pg. 60). If you truly want to relax on your vacation, this is an especially good time get acquainted with child-friendly resorts or cruise lines that may have a play room for toddlers, a playground, and/or a kiddie splash pool where your child can be active in suitable surroundings.

Sidi Bou Said: Learning to walk on a rooftop in Tunisia.

Sleep tips: If he will still nap in the stroller, this may provide you with opportunities to enjoy some attractions and activities during his naps that he might lose patience with in his waking hours. A travel bed, travel cot, or Pack 'N Play with tall enough sides to keep her contained when she wakes from a nap can be very helpful and important for her safety. See recommended Travel Beds, pg. 76, and at www.TravelswithBaby.com. More tips for naptime sleeping and nighttime sleeping during travel begin on pg. 92.

Other tips: He may now be eating more of the foods you do, which could help simplify things so long as there are not concerns of food or water safety for your destination (if there are, see pg. 158).

Best bet vacations: Beach vacations (see pg. 31), camping trips (see pg. 34), shorter trips by airplane, and family-friendly cruises (see pg. 379).

18 to 24 Months

These are the final months your child will be able to fly as a lap child—free on domestic flights and for around 10% of your ticket price on international flights. On very long flights, however, you may prefer to purchase a seat for him, and some airlines will provide a special discount for infants in seats (you'll find them beginning on pg. 244).

Where to go: Since it can very difficult for children at this age to grasp that there is a worthwhile payoff for sitting still hours at a time, your child may not have much patience for long hours spent in transit, especially in the car seat or in airplanes. Train travel, which allows for greater physical freedom and more face time with Mom and Dad, may be preferred (see Travels by Train, pg. 325). It's an ideal time for camping trips or beach vacations close to home, but be careful in choosing campsites as your child is highly mobile but does not yet understand dangers such as campfires, creeks, wildlife, or poison oak. You might also enjoy a family-friendly cruise, with flexible dining options, a playroom, and family-friendly entertainment.

Sleep tips: It may be getting more difficult to convince your child it is time to go to bed when you are sharing a hotel room or cruise ship cabin, and are not ready to do so yourselves. It may be worth the upgrade to a 1-bedroom suite at hotels or resorts to give you some separation of space, or to get a ship cabin or room with a balcony where you can step out and enjoy quiet conversation once Junior hits the hay.

Other tips: It will be important to break up long drives when possible (see tips for Pacing Your Journey, pg. 210), and walk laps around the airplane together. Talk about your trip plans ahead of time so that the events and activities, and particularly the transitions between them, will come as less of a surprise to your child.

Big help: Whether you have a long flight or a long car ride (or just a long wait in a restaurant), it can be very helpful to keep a "Bag of Discovery" in your day pack or diaper bag during these months. See more in Planning Your In-Flight Entertainment, pg. 282.

Best bet vacations: Beach vacations (see pg. 31), camping trips (see pg. 34), shorter trips by airplane, family-friendly cruises (see pg. 379), and train trips (see pg. 325).

2 to 3 Years

No more "free rides" for your child on domestic flights, most cruises, and rail travel in the U.S. and Canada, though kids continue to ride free on trains throughout Europe. Most child-oriented attractions will charge admission for your 2-year-old as well (although Disney Parks and Legoland Parks don't charge for children under 3 years). We all have our favorites, and that goes for your child now, too. She begins to express her own opinions about everything from food, to wardrobe, to activities, to whether or not she approves of getting into the car seat. The more involved and empowered you can help her feel through this phase, the more smoothly your travels are likely to go. Small steps along the way, like choosing which books to put in the carry-on, or which pajamas to wear at Grandma's house, could help her feel much more in control of the changing situation.

Where to go: Since tantrums may erupt for even the best-behaved little travelers when stretched too thin, you may all be happiest in vacation settings where these can be managed as safely and effectively as possible—and avoided as much as possible. A vacation that allows for flexible daily schedules, regular meal times and snacks, and physical freedom and activity for your child can be critical at this stage, so most beach vacations and camping trips will fit the bill nicely. Urban adventures, where parks and playgrounds are easy to come by between other sightseeing activities (e.g., New York and Paris) can also be helpful. This could also be a great year to travel by train, with your child free to explore the train cars with you, not constrained in a car seat. Since she rides trains for half the adult fare in the U.S. and Canada, and for free in Europe, it may be less expensive for your family to travel by train than by airplane on some routes (see Travels by Train, pg. 325).

Sleep tips: Some children give up their afternoon (and final) naps this year, making it all the more important to have an early bedtime. During travel, however, with the help of a physically active morning (e.g., swimming in the hotel pool or romping on the beach) followed by a ride in the stroller or long drive, these kids may still catch some winks. Plan your itinerary accordingly.

Other tips: Potty training may be a big theme for your household this year, so be sure to plan your itinerary accordingly, and be prepared for surprises (see Pottying on the Go, pg. 98). Longer flights become a little easier for most children as the year passes and your child's attention span allows for more reading time, some basic games, coloring, and other pastimes.

Best bet vacations: Beach vacations (see pg. 31), camping trips (see pg. 34), and train travel (see pg. 325).

3 to 4 Years

For many families, this is the year when travel becomes significantly easier, especially with the completion of potty training and the child's improved ability to express himself. Your preschool-age child may also crave more social interaction than ever before, so trips to campgrounds that are popular with families and stops at playgrounds and parks where other children may be can help provide this outlet. Also, "3 years and out of diapers" is often the magic formula for children to qualify for most kid's programs, clubs, and activities at many family resorts and on cruise ships, giving them supervised creative playtime with their peers while you get a chance to snorkel, shop, visit a museum, or take a nap by the pool. Home stays with friends and family also get a little easier now as your child has a better understanding of some basic safety concerns (e.g., we don't eat the Christmas tree ornaments).

Where to go: Although the largest theme parks may still be overwhelming this year (few children this age have the patience to wait in one line after the next), your child will likely enjoy visits to aquariums, natural history or science museums with children's displays, and zoos. Your load lightens as less gear is needed, though you may end up having to carry an exhausted child if he begins to refuse his stroller this year. San Diego offers a good mix of toddler-friendly activities, with built-in beach fun, a zoo, an aquarium, and the fun of fountains and kiddie rides in Balboa Park (and of course Sea World, if your group is up to it).

The British Museum, London: Don't rule out visits to big museums on your urban adventure—my preschooler could have spent a solid hour in just this "clock room" alone.

Sleep tips: Your child may no longer take a regular nap at home, but you may find he desperately needs one to keep up with all the excitement and activity of fun-filled family vacation. Be sure to schedule some down time throughout your vacation, whether that results in an actual nap or just a restful retreat.

Best bet vacations: Cruises (see pg. 379) and resorts (see pg. 49) with kids' camps for 3 years and older—as long as you're sure your child will be potty trained, beach vacations (see pg. 31), camping trips (see pg. 34), urban adventures (see pg. 42), and visits with family and friends (see pg. 60).

4 to 5 Years

Your child becomes more of a travel partner at this stage. He's able to better grasp the concept of your trip from start to finish, and has the patience required at times for sitting still or standing in lines. He may take pride in packing (and rolling!) his own suitcase or packing his backpack with toys and books for the flight, and he may also enjoy being in charge of his own camera (we've found a $10 digital camera from the drug store is much preferred over a disposable camera they may use up in the first 10 minutes). Gear needs are at a minimum now, enabling you to travel lighter than you have since becoming a parent.

Where to go: If you want to do an extended trip overseas and/or take advantage of cost savings of travel in shoulder seasons, this is your last chance before the complication of the school calendar and need to make up schoolwork during travel (Hurry! Go far! Go wide!). Your child may be ready for his first trip to the big amusement park this year, but make sure he understands he will spend some time waiting in lines for rides, and forewarn him about minimum height and age requirements that may prevent him from enjoying some "big kid rides." He is also reaching an age of awareness where some background may be appreciated when traveling to or through areas of interest (e.g., when the pilgrims came here a long time ago…). For travel abroad, he may enjoy learning some words or phrases ahead of time to use at your destination, and may also take more of an interest in the local customs and modes of transportation.

Sleep tips: Your child is getting too big for most toddler travel beds, and you'll have to start getting accommodations with an extra bed or the option of a rollaway (usually around $10 extra, though you sacrifice a lot of space in the typical hotel room for it). An easy solution may be to use a sleeping bag on the floor, though this all depends on where you will be staying. If your child is still an active sleeper (a.k.a. fall risk), an inflatable bed rail may be very helpful in taking advantage of existing beds where you stay (see more in Travel Beds and Sleeping Solutions, pg. 76).

Other tips: Collecting souvenirs as you travel (pine cones, coasters, wildflowers, ticket stubs…) and creating a travel scrapbook for your trip may be a fun project and creative outlet for your child.

Best bet vacations: From here on out, your best bets for family vacations will be based on your child's individual temperament (see pg. 107) and your own family's interests. Enjoy!

CHAPTER 2
Deciding Where to Go

Beach Vacations

Advantages:

Beaches are one of the few vacation destinations that can completely appease the desires of a toddler: exploration, discovery, exercise, fresh air, and loads and loads of sand. Hit the beach during naptimes and, with baby lounging in the shade, you can enjoy a good book, a snooze, or taking turns with your partner dipping in the surf. Older babies thrill at their first discovery of sand—and miles and miles of it.

Where to go:

When choosing your beach destination, keep in mind what your little beachcomber might find in the sand; some beaches are much more likely to have litter or fishing hooks, for example. Also, consider the shoreline carefully—will it be relatively safe for splashing and wading, and if not, will you be able to relax and watch the waves or will you have to spend most of your time keeping your child out of the surf (keep in mind your child's temperament; see pg. 107)?

For calmer conditions, look to destinations like Cape Cod, the Caribbean, or sandy-shored lakes, and beaches along seas rather than the vast oceans. Keep in mind seasonal differences, as well, such as Maui and Kauai where the north shore beaches have some stretches of incredibly gentle shoreline in summer months, but take a pounding and are favored by surfers in winter months.

Where to stay:

It can be well worth it to choose a hotel, resort, or vacation rental that is walking distance to the beach to avoid the hassle of loading and unloading your car on each end, each day, and finding parking. Since most beaches feature little or no sources of shade, you may favor beachfront resorts or private beaches that provide sun umbrellas for added comfort and protection. Depending on your destination, the higher price for a beachfront resort may also make up for the cost of a rental car and gas—and time lost in coming and going from your main attraction.

However, at expensive beach destinations, a vacation rental apartment or condo just a block or two from the beach may prove the most convenient and cost-effective, saving you on daily resort (and possibly parking) fees, while giving you the flexibility to cook and dine outside of expensive restaurants in the area.

What to avoid:

With crawlers and early walkers, aim for beaches where odds are the sand won't be littered with trash from lazy picnickers, and try to avoid rocky or pebbled shores for now as they may feel to you more like miles on end of choking hazards at this stage. Also, be wary of destinations popular with sailors and windsurfers as the winds and waves they favor may be unfavorable to your tiny beachcomber.

What to bring:

Bring sun block, a blanket, a bucket of toys, and a soft-sided cooler, and you're set for days and days of fun. Infants are easy to keep clean and well shaded with help from a pop-up shade tent, which can also provide much-needed shade breaks for the whole family, and remain fun for kids well through the preschool years (even in the living room on a rainy day at home).

For kids ready to explore at the water's edge, invest in a good life jacket or swim vest that will last through the preschool years, and for extremely sunny locations, consider UV-protective swim attire as an extra measure of protection. Some swimsuits that are made to look like

Kauai, Hawaii: The sheltered, shallow waters at Poipu Beach Park make it one of the most baby- and toddler-friendly beaches you could hope for.

surfer suits have special appeal for small kids and cover them to their knees, which is also helpful in keeping sand out of the diaper zone. "Rash guard" UV-protective shirts with mock turtleneck collars are also helpful and an easier combination with swimsuit bottoms for those hurrying to get to the potty in time, or needing frequent diaper changes.

We've also found it very helpful to bring along an oversized plastic shopping tote (my favorite is a giant blue tote from IKEA) that we can fit all of our lightweight, bulky items into, including a bucket of sand toys, swim vests, Neat Sheet picnic blanket, snorkels, and more, and we can shake water and sand right off of it.

Extra help:

To help avoid the "sandpaper syndrome" that results from rubbing baby wipes on sandy behinds, keep an extra water bottle handy for rinsing off. The bicycling and sports variety that you squeeze and squirt are ideal.

✔ Family Beach Vacation Packing List

Here are some very helpful items to remember for your beach vacation.

- ☐ Pop-up shade tent
- ☐ Soft-sided cooler or ice chest (hard-sided okay for road trips)
- ☐ Neat Sheet or lightweight picnic blanket
- ☐ Beach towels or 1-2 microfiber travel towels if flying
- ☐ Swim vest or infant life jacket for kid(s)
- ☐ Sun hats for all family members
- ☐ Sunglasses for all family members
- ☐ UV-protective rash guard or swim "suit" for kid(s)
- ☐ Swim suits for parents
- ☐ Quick-dry "cover-ups" for all family members
- ☐ Flip-flops, Crocs, or other easy-on-off shoes for everyone
- ☐ Waterproof/sweatproof sun block for all family members
- ☐ If needed: Swim diapers, diaper kit, and squirt water bottle
- ☐ Beach toys (can always be purchased/borrowed or improvised at your destination if needed)
- ☐ Other suggestions: Waterproof and sandproof camera—using your regular camera at the beach with small kids can be...risky.

Camping Trips

Advantages:

Camping can be one of the most satisfying and affordable vacations for families with young children. Babies could stare contentedly up at tree leaves and limbs against the sky for hours, while toddlers and preschoolers could spend just as long studying what's on the ground below: pine cones, frogs, beetles, furtive chipmunks... And while the kids are busy enjoying the outdoors, parents have a chance to literally unplug—something sorely needed by most of us these days. If and when you are ready to really get back to nature, be sure to read the Tips for Back-country Camping with Babies and Toddlers, pg. 37.

Where to go:

For an easy entrée into camping with a baby or very young kids, head to a drive-in campground not too far from home, where you can arrive early enough to set up by daylight (much preferred with small children than by car headlamps, in my experience) and for everyone to have plenty of time to get familiar with the new surroundings, the tent, and, for those old enough to use them: the restrooms.

Since infants and babies can't snuggle down with their faces into their sleeping bags like the rest of us, your biggest concern camping with an infant or baby may be choosing a camping destination where (and when) the nighttime temperatures will not dip too low.

Also, because doctors don't recommend using DEET-containing insect repellant or sunscreen on babies younger than 6 months, look to camping destinations and seasons with more favorable conditions like areas of shade and no standing water from snow melt for trips in your child's earliest months. (Be sure to read Managing Mosquitoes, pg. 148, for DEET-free ways to help prevent mosquito bites.)

Where to stay:

For best results, look for the "overlooked site" at the edge of the campground with shade, well-defined boundaries between it and the other campsites, and great potential for toy dump trucks. Also, until you are very sure your child understands the importance of water safety, you'll probably be more relaxed and able to enjoy time in your campsite when it is not right at the water's edge.

A lightweight Peapod travel bed may be as useful inside your tent as it outside on camping trips with baby (more on pg. 37).

What to avoid:

When possible, get an overview of the campground before choosing your site, so you can steer clear of campsites near creeks that may still have standing pools of mosquito habitat, those right beside restrooms where squeaking and slamming doors may continue through your child's bedtime, and where an overly bright light may keep you awake all hours.

In the first few years, for simplicity, you may also prefer to steer clear of tent camping in popular bear country campgrounds, where even keeping an ice chest in your car is strongly advised against and every rogue Cheerio or sticky dribble in your campsite could be a call to the wild (though be sure to read my tips on "What to do with car seats at Yosemite National Park" at www.TravelswithBaby.com, if it happens to be on your list). Campfires are fascinating at this stage, but since small children have little comprehension of the danger, you may want to wait until after dinner clean-up to build yours, when you can sit down and enjoy it together.

What to bring:

A play yard or bouncer seat can be helpful outside of your tent as a safe, clean place for baby to play while you set up camp, prepare meals, and play cards or strum your guitar. The Peapod travel bed pops up like a mini tent with a zip-tight screen and may be quite useful both inside your tent and out. If you have a large enough tent, you can use a play yard with a fitted mosquito net to help (nets are available to fit standard models), or use the Phil&Teds Traveller travel bed with a sturdy aluminum frame and zipping mesh cover (more details in Travel Beds, pg. 76).

Even if your child is potty trained, you may be glad to have a training potty in the tent when nature calls at night, or if the camp facilities are a little crude or unnerving for your child (e.g., ye olde pit toilet).

Toy trucks or train cars, sand toys, and children's garden tools can all be good toys to bring along from home—and for preschoolers, do not forget a butterfly net and "bug house." If you have room, a six-panel Superyard keeps toddlers corralled while you set up and break down your camp or cook. Also, a pop-up sun tent gives your toddler his own tent to play in without wearing out the zippers on yours.

Extra help:

If it will be much colder than home at night, you can help keep babies warm by making a "tent within your tent" using a travel bassinet or play yard that can be safely draped with a light blanket to hold the warmer air around your baby, but leaving a gap for good ventilation (always use common sense and your own good judgment).

✔ Family Camping Trip Packing List

Here are some helpful items to remember for your camping trip with the Junior Ranger.

- [ ] Mosquito repellent, including a DEET-free variety for babies or those who prefer (more on pg. 54)
- [ ] Glow sticks, bracelets, or necklaces for a nightlight in the tent (and to attach to your free-range child in the evening)
- [ ] Hands-free headlamp or wearable light such as the Beam N Read
- [ ] Travel bed or bassinet to create a "tent within a tent" in colder regions
- [ ] Camp kitchen kit with bowls, spoons, and cups for your new addition(s)
- [ ] Easy-prep meal in case rain rules out cooking in your campsite (e.g., extra sandwich fixings, bagels, cereal, pre-cooked pasta)
- [ ] Dining booster with tray for baby meal times in camp
- [ ] Thermos (with hot water) for keeping a "midnight feeding" or early morning bottle warm and ready in your tent
- [ ] Water reservoir with tap with plenty of drinking water
- [ ] Warm hats for the whole family
- [ ] Sun hats for the whole family
- [ ] Two thermal suits for babies (backup in case one gets wet)
- [ ] Swim suits for the whole family and swim diapers (where appropriate)
- [ ] Child-size swim vest or life jacket (where appropriate)
- [ ] Bucket and scoop for frogging or crawdadding
- [ ] Butterfly net and bug house
- [ ] Toy dump trucks, sand toys, garden tools
- [ ] Pop-up sun tent for entertainment or shade by the lake
- [ ] Training potty (if currently using at home)
- [ ] Anti-itch cream in case of bug bites or rashes (add to Travel Kit, pg. 61)
- [ ] Children's antihistamine in case of bee sting or other allergic reaction (ask pediatrician for advice and current dosage for your child)

Point Reyes National Seashore, California: Back-country camping with an infant and a toddler—and, thankfully, a lot of friends.

Twelve Tips for Back-Country Camping with Infants, Babies, and Toddlers

Car camping allows you to bring many helpful comforts along: an ice chest, more toys, more gear, a bigger tent, camp chairs, the play yard... But back-country camping is also possible with babies, toddlers, and preschoolers, with good planning and a few modifications. Here are some tips to help you get an early start.

1. **Breastfeed.** Nothing to pack, mix, wash, or sterilize for baby to drink. With the frontpack or sling adjusted just right, you can even do it as you hike!

2. **Bring shelf-stable boxed milk** for weaned toddlers and preschoolers. It isn't always easy to find (check the baby food section and baking sections if you don't see them with other dairy products), but cow's milk can be purchased in individual serving boxes that need no refrigeration, packaged with straws like juice boxes. Many children are just as happy with boxed soy or rice milk for the trip, which may be easier to come by. This is a great option

for shorter trips and trips where the water supply may be questionable or taste unpleasant.

3. **Mix evaporated milk with powdered milk**, if you go that route instead. Powdered milk is typically skim (or .05% milk fat at best), and you will still need the water to mix with it. Evaporated milk (whole milk with 50% of the water removed from it) can be added to improve the flavor and consistency.

4. **Go light on baby food.** This is no time to weigh down your pack with glass jars of pureed foods. Shelf-stable packaged applesauce and mixed "berry sauce" servings and baby foods packaged in plastic tubs are a much lighter-weight alternative. Bring along some rice cereal flakes or other grain cereal in a baggie to serve up straight or mix in with other food for extra nutrition and substance. Freeze-dried fruit and veggie puffs made for babies and toddlers are quite helpful, too.

5. **Don't skimp on clothes.** In your pre-parent life, it was easier to calculate the bare necessities you might need for your trip. But chances are that didn't account for the occasional diaper blowout, spit-up, potty training accident, or spontaneous romp in the stream. One puffy thermal suit for your baby won't be enough if her diaper leaks and soaks it your first night. So be sure to figure out a backup as you pack up.

6. **Choose destinations accessible by jogging stroller.** With babies and toddlers, it may be easier to carry your child on your back and put your pack and gear in the stroller. Once you arrive at your campsite, the stroller works as a make-shift bouncer seat, dining booster, and camp chair. With a weather shield, it also becomes your child's rain gear!

7. **Invest in a good backpack carrier.** If you will spend much time hiking with your child on your back, plus some gear, you'll need a very sturdy, supportive backpack carrier like the higher end models by Kelty. Attachable sun/rain/wind hoods can be especially helpful, and a fitted mosquito net is also available.

8. **Start small.** Even for the accomplished backpacker, back-country camping with kids may present new and unanticipated challenges. Start with shorter treks close to home where the weather and climate

are easy to predict. You may even want to plan a "reconnaissance mission" ahead of time—a daytrip to check out the trails and site before you stay overnight. A site that offers potable water and garbage service will help keep things simple as well. The National Park Service website, www.nps.gov, gives helpful descriptions of trails and back-country campsites for its parks. Your state and regional park services may offer this information as well.

9. **Divide and conquer.** Camping with a group may help all of you lighten your loads as some food and gear can be shared, particularly for cooking. If your group has other babies and small children, the kids will keep each other entertained and one lucky adult can carry the designated "diaper pack."

10. **Pack diapers—in and out.** If you'll have to "pack out" dirty diapers, consider your trip length carefully. Seal away soiled diapers in a large slide-lock storage bag, with one designated for each day. At day's end, squeeze out all the excess air and add it to your garbage sack.

11. **Update your first-aid kit.** Make sure you have appropriate contents for your child and your trip, including child-size bandages, infant or child pain reliever/fever reducer, and antihistamine (in case of a bee sting).

12. **Simplify.** The fewer pots and pans and dishes to pack and wash and carry...the more you'll be able to relax and enjoy the journey and time with your child. If you can, splurge on the freeze-dried meals you simply add boiled water to in a sack. Single-serving applesauce and puddings are an easy treat for all ages and need no refrigeration. Instant oatmeal is an easy breakfast for babies accustomed to thicker textures as well as for their parents; for extra appeal, add dried cranberries for those who can chew them.

New York City: On a play break outside of the Metropolitan Museum of Art, thoroughly enjoying the Group of Bears *by Paul Manship.*

Urban Adventures

Advantages:

An overdose of the Teletubbies? Elmo on the brain? Look to "the big city" for emergency CPR (cranial parental resuscitation). Whether it's a short drive from home or a long flight overseas, an urban adventure can provide the enlivening and enlightening experiences you crave, with plenty of stimulation for your child as well.

Most toddlers unaccustomed to city life will find much to marvel at just being out and about—like pigeons, mimes, street musicians, elevators, and streetcars. With preschoolers, you can also visit many sites that have special appeal to them, like natural history museums with dinosaur fossils and bug exhibits, or aquariums, and zoos. And while your child is still a baby? Enjoy art museums while he cruises along in his stroller.

Where to go:

Choose a city with great public transportation—subway, light rail, efficient buses—and a centrally located hotel, and you've got the makings of a car seat–free vacation. Cities like Paris, New York, and Washington, D.C., also offer an ideal mix of several cultural attractions within a walk of each other, with many playgrounds and kid-friendly parks in between, making it easy for small kids to burn off energy before snoozing through an art museum.

Where to stay:

Renting an apartment with all the amenities of home can be more than a convenience; it can also help your family experience the city more like a local—and help you cross paths with more local families who can provide invaluable tips on finding nearby playgrounds, kid-friendly restaurants and cafés, and more (see Condos and Vacation Rentals, pg. 59). However, if you're only going for a short stay, you may prefer to stay in a centrally located hotel, where you'll lose no extra time in getting to your main attractions and may even be able to enjoy the luxury of room service delivering your dinner to your door after a busy day.

What to avoid:

The parent juggling an upset toddler on a crowded street while consulting a guidebook, or taking 236 pictures of his child chasing pigeons may appear to the unscrupulous an easy target for pickpocketing. Carry only the things you'll need with you (cash, ID, a credit card) in a slim travel wallet you can wear beneath your shirt or trousers so you can focus on keeping track of your child and enjoying your vacation. (See more tips in City Smarts for the New Parent, pg. 184.)

What to bring:

Even if you are using your stroller less at home, a good travel stroller may be a much-needed safe way to transport your baby, toddler, or preschooler through busy streets and crowded stations, and for covering long distances on foot. It can also provide seating for your child at sidewalk cafés and city restaurants—and with a built-in recline, you've got a great place for on-the-go naps while you sightsee. One that folds compactly and has a shoulder-carrying strap to help keep your hands free when needed can also be a necessity when you'll be using largely "inaccessible" public transportation systems with your child, such as the New York City Subway or the Paris Metro (see tips for using the New York City Subway, Paris Metro, and Paris bus system with strollers at www.TravelswithBaby.com). For children small enough, also bring a frontpack carrier or sling for wearing your child on and off crowded public transportation.

Extra help:

If you need to catch some grown-up opera or theater while you're in town, check the Directory of Hotel Babysitter and Vacation Nanny Agencies at www.TravelswithBaby.com for your destination. Also, Hop on/Hop off bus service is available in most major cities around the world, and can be a good option for families with lengthy sightseeing agendas and babies or small children in tow. With a simple pass (24 hours or 48 hours), your family can ride this dedicated bus route to most of the major attractions at your own pace, getting off when and where you please without need of a car seat or climbing up and down subway steps.

Paris, France: Making a post-Louvre pitstop at this playground in the Touileries (and several other playgrounds we found) was a great way to mingle with Parisian parents, grandparents, and children.

✔ Urban Adventures Packing List

- ☐ Compactly-folding lightweight travel stroller (preferably with shoulder carrying strap and a reclining seat; more on pg. 71 and recommendations at www.TravelswithBaby.com)
- ☐ Sling or frontpack carrier for babies and toddlers who can still use them (preferably one you can store beneath your travel stroller when needed)
- ☐ Travel wallets for parents
- ☐ Rain or weather shield for stroller
- ☐ Binder clips and blanket to clip to stroller canopy for extra shade or distraction-free napping while sightseeing
- ☐ Your child's converted weights and measurements if you'll be traveling abroad (see Convenient Conversions, pg. 133)
- ☐ Pocket-size folding map of the city, including metro, subway, or other major transportation system (plastic-coated is best)

ON THE WEB:

Find planning tips and advice for several of the recommended travel destinations mentioned here and get tips for travel to many other popular travel destinations with your child (including family travel tips from local moms living around the globe) in the **Destinations** section at www.TravelswithBaby.com.

CHAPTER 3

Deciding Where to Stay

Staying (Safe and Sane) with Friends and Family

Staying in the home of friends or relatives is by far the most common first trip new parents make with their child, and for many, it's likely to be a repeat occurrence through the baby, toddler, and preschool years. Yes, having access to all the comforts of home, including a full kitchen, laundry facilities, separate quarters for your napping child, and of course, the loving presence (a.k.a. help) of your friends or family, can be a wonderful, relaxing way to vacation with your child. It *can* be, in many cases, with some good planning.

First, you will need to get grounded in reality. As a guest in someone else's home, you will be obliged to observe their daily rhythms and routines. Enthusiastic pets, light-saber-wielding children, steep staircases, toxic houseplants, precariously perched lamps, thimble (a.k.a. choking hazard) collections, and more may await your little family at the well-intentioned relative's home. Just establishing a safe place for your child to sleep or play during your visit could prove challenging. Add to that the possibility of delayed bedtimes, extended meal times, and noisy visiting hours and you may find yourself wishing for a night off at the local motel.

As well, take your hosts' lifestyles into consideration—in spite of their best intentions, would having a baby or small child under their roof full time prove a major inconvenience to them? Try to get your hosts on the same page before you arrive in their home. Describe a typical day with your child at home, when he usually rises, naps, how often he eats, and what his sacred rituals are. Tell them how much you are looking forward to seeing them, but be honest about your concerns—including upsetting their own routines (like, perhaps, sleeping). Share your ideas of how you can help with childproofing concerns and other details about having a baby or small child in their home. Especially where friends and family are concerned, it could be well worth spending a little more to stay nearby and come for visits if it means safeguarding the integrity of your relationship.

That said, here are some friendly suggestions for how to avoid some common pitfalls and have a safe, sane visit with those who are near and dear to your heart.

Dining

Your hosts may not be as prepared as they think they are for dealing with the thrills and spills associated with baby and toddler dining. If your child is using a portable dining booster, ask your hosts for an extra bath towel you might use to protect their chair from any overboard spills or splats. Pack a vinyl tablecloth (like those used outdoors) to spread beneath your child's seat to protect your hosts' floor during meal times. Afterward, you can simply shake off the crumbs and wipe the surface clean. Also, bring along your child's own plate or bowl to save your hosts from searching for suitable dishes or risking breakage of their own.

Diapering

As Benjamin Franklin said, "Guests, like fish, begin to smell after three days." Guests in diapers, however, may smell upon arrival. Be sure to check with your hosts early on to see where they keep their outdoor trash so that you may use it when needed. Bring your own supply of plastic bags and export any stink bombs straight away. Also, be thoughtful on disposing of wet diapers; some people bristle at the sight of perfectly harmless puffy Pampers in their bathroom wastebasket. It may be simplest to bring your own sack or trash bag for collecting these in your quarters rather than filling up your hosts' wastebaskets.

Sleeping

I'll say it until I'm blue in the face: Earplugs can make a thoughtful and humorous hostess gift. If your child isn't likely to make it through the night without a vocal interlude, give your hosts fair warning. They can take any precautions to help ensure a restful night for them (using aforementioned earplugs, closing their doors, indulging in a nightcap, and so on). This will also help prevent them from worrying if your child is feeling well or if you need their assistance or intervention—Uncle Larry's "Get Happy!" clown dance could prove disastrous at three a.m.

Household Hazards for Young Children

Anywhere you stay (a hotel, a campsite, a sleeper car) you will have to size up potential dangers to your child and deal with them the best you can. But when you stay in someone else's home, the number of potential dangers may actually increase. In addition to the more easily anticipated risks like stair steps, sharp corners, and electrical outlets, you may also face a few surprises that come with staying in an active household of friendly folks who may not be accustomed to playing "What's Under Grandpa's Easy Chair?" or, with toddlers, "Look What I Found in the Kitchen Trash!" Just make sure you don't overlook these potential hazards while in the throes of visiting.

- Pet foods, snacks, and grooming supplies
- Excitable, defensive, or aggressive pets
- Prescription drugs and other medications, including those not kept in childproof canisters like ointments or drops
- Craft projects and knitting baskets
- Candy dishes and nut bowls
- Decorative fountains
- Holiday ornaments and decorations
- Floor lamps and cords
- Table lamps within reach
- Unsuitable toys from older children

- Party favors or decorations (including latex balloons, which can be a choking hazard)
- The "junk drawer"

Child Hazards to the Household

Also, don't overlook the hazards your child might pose to your hosts' home. Other adults may not be as tuned in to the potential consequences of leaving some items within a child's reach, or the lightning speed with which a child can perform magic tricks with table cloths (swoosh!) and car keys (flush!). Especially if you'll be visiting with a curious toddler, you will need to stay two steps ahead of your child where these items may be accessed.

- Purses with pens and lipstick inside
- Books and magazines
- Cell phones or regular phones
- Stereos and entertainment equipment
- Remote controls
- Car keys (especially with remote control key fobs)
- Cameras
- Computers and PDAs
- Toilet paper
- Music CDs and DVDs
- Musical instruments
- Table cloths

Best Hotels and Resorts for Young Families

If your child has trouble napping on the go (in the stroller, in the car), you may want to choose a resort that includes as much of your entertainment and recreation as possible—especially if you may end up taking turns with your partner while one stays with the child and the other hits the pool or sauna, or gets a much-needed massage. Having a restaurant (or several) on site, though it is rarely a bargain, can also help to keep things simple at the end of long days.

If your child goes to bed much earlier than you and your partner or tends to sleep through your dinner time, it may prove very practical to take some meals in your room. Room service may also come to the rescue if dinner at the diner was not all your child had expected, or if jetlag finds your family awake and hungry at an inconvenient hour.

Many large resorts now offer children's clubs as well, where children (usually 3 years minimum and out of diapers, though often 5 years) can be registered for group activities and events to enjoy while Mom and Dad gear up for scuba lessons or trek to the tops of magnificent ruins. Private in-room babysitting is also often available for babies and toddlers on request, usually with a minimum 24-hour notice. Check the hotel's website and/or call for details if this is a deal-breaker for your trip, or arrange your own childcare through an agency listed in the Directory of Hotel Babysitter and Vacation Nanny Agencies at www.TravelswithBaby.com.

With any luck your hotel room will have a mini-refrigerator that, in spite of being fully stocked with overpriced treats and refreshments, will have enough space left for your leftovers or snacks and, perhaps, a bottle or a sippy cup. But there are some stages when travel with a child is much easier if you can just have a kitchen of your own (see next section).

Although the specific amenities will vary by hotel property, here are a few of the major hotel and resort chains where you can expect to find family-friendly perks and conveniences.

Disneyland Resort Hotels, California

All three hotels provide free cribs and in-room refrigerators, plus themed swimming pools and restaurants, and children's play areas. Children 5 years to 12 years can attend Pinocchio's Workshop with special activities offered evenings from 5 p.m. to midnight at Disney's Grand Californian Hotel at a rate of around $13/hour per child, optional dinner included for $5. In-room babysitting is available for an additional fee (with signed waiver). http://disneyland.disney.go.com or 1-714-520-5060.

Four Seasons Hotels and Resorts, International

Worldwide, Four Seasons Hotels and Resorts are equipped for young families with cribs, diaper pails, and childproofing items, and can even provide strollers on request. The Four Seasons Maui even provides complimentary car seats and diapers for your stay. Their "Kids for All Seasons" supervised kids club is for children 5 to 12 years, though 4-year-olds are welcome at the activities with a parent. Check individual properties for availability and times. Babysitters for children of all ages can be arranged through the hotel. www.fourseasons.com or 1-800-859-5053.

Hilton Worldwide Resorts, International

While several of these are labeled "family resorts," and may have kiddie pools, playgrounds, and kids clubs, not all will have amenities or activities specific to children less than 5 years. While the hotel does arrange babysitting by outside contractors for other ages, most Hilton kids camps and Kid's Night Out programs are for children 5 to 12 years only, and the Hilton San Diego Resort & Spa, for example, states: "All children ages 3 and under, or children who are not potty trained, are required to wear swim diapers and must play in our children's pool only." Be sure to check specific locations for details that may be deal-breakers for you. www.hilton.com or 1-800 -HILTONS.

Holiday Inn SunSpree Resorts, International

Children 12 years and younger stay and eat free in the hotel restaurants (with paid adult). Select SunSpree Resorts have supervised (drop-off) activities for ages 4 years and up (check individual resorts for details and times). Many resorts have kiddie pools, play areas, and other special perks for children. Check for details for the resort you're considering at www.sunspree.com or 1-888-465-4329.

Holiday Inn Full-Service Hotels & Resorts, International

Most full-service hotels and resorts feature a swimming pool and a full-service restaurant on site where children 12 years and younger eat free from the children's menu (with paid adult). www.holidayinn.com or 1-888-465-4329.

Omni Hotels & Resorts, International

Several US Omni Resorts offer kiddie pools and water play zones, and both the Omni Amelia Island Plantation Resort and the Omni Orlando Resort have kids clubs for children 4 to 12 years old. The Omni Barton Creek and Omni La Costa offer supervised childcare and kids clubs for children 6 months to 12 years. Select properties in California, New England, and Texas offer Omni Kids' Suites with kids' furniture, art centers, games, and books, with a connecting room for the rest of the family.

Hyatt Resorts, International

Numerous resorts worldwide feature kiddie pools and restaurants with children's menus. Camp Hyatt is available for an additional fee at many resorts worldwide, with supervised activities for potty trained children from 3 years to 12 years. Partial day, full-day, and some evening sessions may be available, depending on the destination. www.hyatt.com or 1-800-233-1234.

Best All-Suite Hotels for Young Families

Booking a suite with a kitchen or kitchenette could save you money and possibly your sanity. But think twice if your child is at a stage where an un-childproofed kitchen may be more of a nuisance than a convenience. As well, ask yourself: How much of your vacation time do you really want to spend in the kitchen? And how much will you spend on groceries? And how much might you end up eating out anyway?

Yet there are times the advantages will far outweigh the luxury of eating out. For example, would it make a tremendous difference to have access to a carton of milk and other essentials all hours of the day or night? Would formula preparation and bottle washing be more manageable with a kitchen of your own? Does eating in restaurants with your child at this stage wear you out—or overstimulate your child? Would the savings from not having to eat every meal in a restaurant more than make up for the cost of lodgings that include a kitchen? Is your child a picky eater, or will you be staying somewhere that food safety is a concern?

One-bedroom suites also give the advantage of a separation of space, which can also make a tremendous difference for families when a child needs naps or goes to bed much earlier than the parents would like to. Often, parents enjoying a one-bedroom suite will put their child to bed in the bedroom, then enjoy the rest of the suite for themselves. When ready to retire, they can tiptoe into the bedroom.

Here are some of the best all-suite hotels for travelers with young children.

Candlewood Suites

Studio, 1- and 2-bedroom suites include complete kitchens with full-size refrigerator, stovetop, dishwasher, and microwave. A 24-hour convenience market, free self-serve guest laundry, CD and DVD lending library, and outdoor dining area with barbecues are available on site. www.ihg.com/candlewood or 1-877-CANDLEWOOD.

Embassy Suites

One-bedroom suites include a sleeper sofa in the living room, and TVs with in-suite movies in both the bedroom and living room. Instead of a kitchen or kitchenette, Embassy Suites includes a wet bar, microwave, and refrigerator in each room. Complimentary hot breakfasts are "cooked to order" for all guests, and most properties have a swimming pool. Kids are welcome at the nightly reception, which includes beverages and snacks for all. www.embassysuites.com or 1-800-EMBASSY.

Georgetown Suites

Studio and 1-bedroom suites in Washington, D.C., have fully equipped kitchens (including full-size refrigerators, oven/range, and dishwashers). Children under 12 years stay free. Self-service laundry, free crib on request. Complimentary continental breakfast bar daily. www.georgetownsuites.com or 1-800-348-7203.

Hawthorn Suites

Spacious studio, 1-bedroom, and 2-bedroom suites available with complete kitchens including two-burner stove, full-size refrigerator, and microwave. Convenience store, guest laundry room, and swimming pool on site. Children up to 17 stay free. Complimentary hot buffet breakfast daily. www.hawthorn.com or 1-800-833-1516.

Homewood Suites by Hilton

Studio, 1-bedroom, and 2-bedroom suites with full-size refrigerators, dishwashers, microwave ovens, and twin-burner stove tops. Free crib on request, self-serve laundry facilities, and convenience store. Swimming pools at most locations. Complimentary hot buffet breakfast daily, and complimentary light dinners served Monday through Thursday evenings. www.homewoodsuites.com 1-800-CALL-HOME. Complete review of the San Diego Liberty Station location at www.TravelswithBaby.com.

Residence Inn by Marriott

Studio suites are designed with a distinct sleeping area and sleep 1 to 4 people in beds (including sofabed), with living and dining areas, and complete kitchens with full-size refrigerator, stove, and microwave. Complimentary hot breakfast served daily, 24-hour market on site, and free grocery delivery service. Dry cleaning and laundry on site. Free cribs may be available, though it is first-come first-served. www.marriott.com or 1-888-236-2427.

Staybridge Suites

Studio, 1-bedroom king, and 1-bedroom with two queens (both in bedroom), and 2-bedroom/2-bathroom suites all have complete kitchens with full-size refrigerator, stove, dishwasher, and microwave. Complimentary hot breakfast served daily, 24-hour market and guest laundry room on site. www.ihg.com/staybridge or 1-800-439-4745.

ON THE WEB:

These sites will help you search and book according to your needs:
Ciao Bambino lets you search and book upscale properties with suitability by age / amenity (inc. kids club) – www.ciaobambino.com.
Six Suitcase Travel lets you search and book hotels suitable for big families of 5 or more – www.sixsuitcasetravel.com.

Franklyn D Resort, Jamaica: Our personal vacation nanny for the week, one of the all-inclusive perks for families staying at the resort (see pg. 58).

Best All-Inclusive Resorts for Children Under 5

All-inclusive resorts can help keep things simple on a family vacation—really simple. However, the perks for families with small children can vary widely, and just because a resort advertises itself as a "family resort" doesn't mean you won't need to do a little homework about those details.

For example, some all-inclusive resorts will let children under a certain age stay free with two paid adults, whereas others will charge the same rate for any additional people in the room, regardless of age. And where some all-inclusive resorts offer free children's programs and childcare—even personal nannies—others will charge for any and all children's activities, and the majority do not offer any type of supervised care for children in diapers.

If you're vacationing with a toddler or preschooler, you should also be sure the resort offers children's menus and/or buffet items that will be of interest. Some all-inclusive resorts offer dining in one or more restaurants that—by the way—won't serve children under a certain age; good to know before you sentence yourselves to a week of dining at the resort snack bar.

At the other end of the spectrum, fortunately, there are some all-inclusive resorts that go beyond that extra mile to help families with babies, toddlers, and young children have vacations that are fabulous for all members of the family. Here are some of the best all-inclusive resorts for vacations with children under 5.

Beaches All-inclusive Family Resorts

- **Locations:** Jamaica and Turks & Caicos
- **Free for:** Under 2 years
- **Childcare for:** Newborns and older

Includes daily drop-off childcare by professionally certified nannies in the price of your vacation. Newborns through toddlers up to 24 months are cared for in the nursery, and 3- to 5-year-old children who are potty-trained can attend the daily Kids Kamp for toddlers. Complimentary cribs are available on request; strollers are available to rent for your stay. Kids Camp Groups for older children are also available. Nannies are available for additional childcare after hours at around $15/hour, which covers up to three children per family (rates vary by resort). www.beaches.com or 1-888-BEACHES.

Club Med Resorts

- **Location:** Select destinations worldwide
- **Free for:** under 4 years in Florida, Mexico, and Caribbean
- **Free for:** under 6 years at other destinations worldwide
- **Childcare and kids clubs for:** 4 months to 3 years for a fee at fifteen destinations worldwide, and for 4 years and older for free at many destinations

Club Med Resorts vary from one property to the next in what they offer families with the youngest of children, so be sure to research the resort destinations you have in mind to make sure they'll accommodate your family's needs. While most Club Med resorts offer daily kids clubs for children 4 years and older for no additional fee, select properties also offer childcare for younger ages for an additional fee. Baby Club Med childcare is now available for children 4 months to 2 years at fifteen resort properties from Sandpiper Bay, Florida to Sinai Bay, Egypt. Petit Club Med childcare is available for children 2 years through 3 years at additional properties (you can search for properties with Baby Club Med and Petit Club Med on the website). Many of these resorts also offer an area in their main restaurants with assorted baby foods and toddler meals. A baby feeding room is also open 24 hours, where guests can access bottle warmers, a microwave, refrigerator, and other items helpful in preparing bottles and baby meals. When available, guests staying at these particular resorts with a baby up to 23 months old may also receive a "Club Med Baby Welcome" package, including a baby bed, baby bath, changing table, and other items such as a high chair and stroller by request. Private babysitting is available by request. www.clubmed.com or 1-888-932-2582.

Country Kids

- **Location:** Octon, France

- **Childcare and kids clubs for:** 3 months to 12 years

Set on 30 acres in a protected region of southern France, Country Kids provides luxury all-inclusive vacations for families with children 12 years and younger during the months of July and August (and self-catering holidays with childcare and activities available a la carte in May, June, September, and August). The resort features its own "petting farm," where children can help collect eggs and enjoy the animals, heated swimming pools, spa services, canoeing, horse and pony rides, tennis, boules, wine-tasting, and more. The historic accommodations range from 2- and 3-bedroom apartments, each with its own entrance and outdoor terrace, to a 2-bedroom cottage and 5-bedroom farmhouse. All accommodations include king-size feather beds for the parents, kids rooms stocked with books and toys, hand-built stone and timber full kitchens, and washer/dryer. Included in each stay: unlimited time for children in the Creche and Kids Club, baby equipment, two nights of private babysitting in your accommodations, one massage or beauty treatment for each adult. www.country-kids.fr or +33 4 67 97.

Franklyn D Resort

- **Location:** Runaway Bay, Jamaica
- **Free for:** Under 6 years old
- **Childcare and kids clubs for:** Newborns through teens

All-inclusive rates include a personal "Vacation Nanny" assigned exclusively to your family who will help look after your children each day from 9:00 a.m. to 4:40 p.m., whether accompanying your family during your activities or watching the children while the adults go on their own, or any combination. She is also available after hours if needed at around $6/hour. Some families may be interested in hiring an additional Vacation Nanny at $20/day to help tend to children of different ages and activity levels (e.g., one to keep up with your infant's routine, one to keep up with your busy toddler). The guest to staff ratio is 1 to 1, and toddlers and younger children can attend the daily children's activities with their vacation nannies. Children under 6 years old stay free. www.fdrholidays.com or 1-800-654-1FDR. Complete review, video tour, and "Meet the Vacation Nannies" video at www.TravelswithBaby.com.

Grand Palladium Resorts

- **Recommended locations:** Riviera Maya, Mexico; and Punta Cana, Dominican Republic
- **Free for:** Under 1 year old
- **Childcare and kids clubs for:** 1 year old through 19 years in Riviera Maya and up to 21 years in Punta Cana

Boasting the largest children's activity centers at resorts in Mexico/Caribbean and the Dominican Republic, these two Palladium resorts not only offer acres of children's play spaces both indoors and out, but also offer supervised kids clubs welcoming children as young as 1 year old. The resorts have recently launched a "Play at Palladium with Raggs" program, with the five characters from the Raggs international children's TV show giving musical performances, attending private breakfasts with families, reading at story times, and more. These resorts will also provide cribs and diaper pails, and can arrange for other special requests for your children (e.g., snacks, video games) with advance notice. Some other Palladium resorts offer kids clubs for children 3 years and older as well; check individual properties for details. www.palladiumhotelgroup.com or 1-800-961-7661.

The Tyler Place Family Resort

- **Location:** Highgate Springs, Vermont, USA
- **Childcare and kids clubs for:** Newborn through 15 years

Since 1933, this lakeside all-inclusive resort has catered specifically to families. Graduated day rates for child guests include morning childcare and kids camps for nine different age groups, beginning with newborns to 12 months, 12 to 18 months, 18 to 30 months, and on through 17 years. Children's dinnertime and evening programs are also available, when Parents' Helpers may also care for infants and toddlers for additional fees. Infants can be cared for in the infant care center and/or in your accommodations. All-inclusive rates include cribs, high chairs, strollers, individual bikes for each family member, baby bicycle seats, and helmets. All of the Tyler Place cottages and suites include a separate bedroom for parents. www.tylerplace.com or 1-802-868-4000.

Condos and Other Vacation Rentals

For many parents, a vacation rental is the ideal home away from home. Many not only include a helpful separation of space in the form of bedrooms and common areas, but they also include kitchens and often other homey amenities. Not to mention, it can be really fun to feel like your family has its own home for a week at your destination.

In large cities, a vacation rental apartment may also place you in a more residential area, where you are more likely to cross paths with local families and be closer to a park or playground. Grocery shopping and restaurants may also be much less expensive away from the main tourist strip in town.

At beach destinations, your vacation condo may even come stocked with beach towels, sand toys, boogie boards, and sun umbrellas or beach chairs that can make all the difference in your enjoyment of your location. It may also be easier to borrow or rent baby gear—and have room to use it—when staying in an apartment rather than a hotel room.

The important thing to remember when looking for your ideal vacation rental is that some properties may pose more risks for the mobile baby or young child than the average hotel room, especially if the property has unique features or extra items you won't find in the typical hotel room (stereo equipment, cleaning supplies, balcony or stair railings that are a few centuries old). Always review as many photos of the property as you can before choosing to help rule out major safety hazards for your tot, and read customer reviews with an eye toward other families who have stayed there with young children. The Checking-in Safety Checklist can also be helpful on arrival (on pg. 182 and in *Take-Along Travels with Baby*).

Because vacation rentals usually require a non-refundable deposit and often full payment in advance of your stay (and can be nearly impossible to reschedule for alternate dates if you have to delay your trip for some reason), it's a good idea to get travel insurance that will reimburse these expenses in case you need to cancel or make any changes to the timing of your vacation.

ON THE WEB:

Here are some helpful sites to get you started in your search for the ideal vacation rental for your family.

Euro Relais – Properties throughout Europe. www.eurorelais.com

FlipKey – Worldwide vacation rentals. www.flipkey.com

Home Away – Worldwide vacation rentals. www.homeaway.com

House Trip – Worldwide vacation rentals. www.housetrip.com

Internet Holiday Ads – Worldwide vacation rentals. www.iha.com

Rentalo – Worldwide vacation rentals. www.rentalo.com

Vacation Rentals by Owner – Worldwide. www.vrbo.com

CHAPTER 4
Deciding What to Bring

Preparing Your Child's Travel Kit

Your child's "travel kit" is more than what simply goes into the diaper bag or carry-on. It's comprised of basic products and items that can help your child through a wide range of difficulties that might crop up in your travels, but could be hard to come by while en route, on a day trip, late at night, or in faraway destinations. Some contents will change as your child grows, and you'll want to check through your travel kit periodically to replace anything that has expired or is no longer appropriate or necessary for your child.

I recommend storing these items in a clear plastic slide-lock food storage bag that will contain any leaks and make it easy to find items inside. I have also learned from experience it's very helpful to keep your child's "travel kit" intact at home, both for organization's sake and in case you suddenly need to travel unexpectedly for a family emergency. (If you'll be traveling frequently, it helps to keep it ready too, of course!)

As you create your child's travel kit, keep in mind that those cute little travel-size tins you may see with certain ointments for babies are not necessarily great for traveling—they can be virtually impossible to open at sea level once they've been used in an airplane or at very high elevations due to the change in air pressure.

✔ Your Child's Travel Kit Packing List

Note: For a TSA-ready version of the travel kit that can be carried into the airplane cabin, see Your Child's Travel Kit for Carry-On on pg. 272.

☐ **Saline nasal spray** (non-medicated) – For infants, just a drop or two in each nostril can help clear passages, soothe dryness (especially from flying), or loosen debris for removal with the aspirator.

☐ **Aspirator with guard** – The guard not only helps parents use these with confidence but it can be a bit safer when in motion on airplanes, in trains—and while tending to an animated child.

☐ **Emery board or baby nail clippers** – A simple emery board may be all you need when traveling with an infant, but child-size nail clippers can be indispensible in preventing self-inflicted scratches by the older baby or toddler (whose fingernails always grow with surprising speed, and tend to harbor all the grit and germs of those places they explore).

☐ **Thermometer** – While the accuracy of a rectal thermometer may be very important if an infant falls ill, I favor a reusable forehead thermometer over the digital variety for travel because it does not rely on specialty batteries (that always seem to be "LO" when needed), it gives quick results on even squirmy or sleeping children, and it can be shared by the whole family without need of sanitizing.

☐ **Quicklist of current dosages** – A quick reference list of your child's current correct dosage for any over-the-counter remedies you may need to use during your trip, some of which follow here. Your doctor's office can provide this info at your appointment or possibly over the phone.

☐ **Acetaminophen drops or liquid medicine** (e.g., Infant's or Children's Tylenol) – Helpful for teething and reducing fevers when they strike. Confirm current dosage with your child's doctor.

☐ **Children's chewable acetaminophen or ibuprofen** – Once your child is old enough to use these instead of the liquid form, be sure to make the switch—it will help lighten your travel kit.

☐ **Antihistamine drops** (e.g., Children's Benadryl) – Helpful for spring allergy-type symptoms as well as some allergic reactions like bee stings. Confirm indications for use and correct dosage for your child with his doctor.

☐ **Tummy drops** (e.g., Mylicon) – To soothe upset tummies and relieve gas.

☐ **Measuring dropper/medicine spoon** – You may prefer to use one purchased independently of the medicine that is easier to use and wash.

☐ **Baby vapor rub** (e.g., Vick's Baby Rub) – This kinder, gentler version of the vapor ointment for adults can be rubbed on your child's chest and neck to help her breathe easier during bouts of congestion. If there is a safe place to leave the open jar near your child's bedside (but where he cannot access it) it can also work as a makeshift vaporizer at night.

☐ **Antibiotic ointment or spray** (e.g., Neosporin) – Treat scrapes, scratches, nicks, and cuts right away—and that goes for all the travelers in the family. Cover scrapes with a bandage to keep clean and protected, and to help prevent babies from ingesting the ointment. You may be able to find a travel-size combination antibiotic and pain-relieving spray, which can be very helpful when you need to treat an upset child.

☐ **Band-Aids** – Waterproof Band-Aids will far outlast the other varieties, especially when any swimming, water play, or sand will be a part of your vacation. Bring a variety of sizes, from "tiny finger scratch" to "giant goose egg scrape."

☐ **Tea tree oil or other antiseptic** – Cleans scrapes and wounds.

☐ **Protective skin cream or balm** – A mild, soothing cream for chapped cheeks and tender bottoms (particularly those due to sandy swim diapers). Burt's Baby Bee or similar product works well.

Nerja, Spain: Our trusty tiny washer. Throughout much of the world, even where washing machines are commonplace, clothing dryers are often still few and far between. Don't assume that "laundry" at your vacation rental will include a dryer unless the description specifically says so, and pack at least one quick-dry outfit for each family member.

Clothing Considerations for the Whole Family

When you travel with a baby or small child, there is no right number of onesies, socks, or this-and-thats for X number of days' vacation. Your travel trousseau will be as individual as your child, her age, and the trip. As you contemplate the variables for your upcoming adventure, it may be more helpful to meditate on these certain truths about types of children's clothing—and a few items of parents' apparel—as applied to travel.

Playsuits – Footed playsuits offer some definite advantages: no socks or booties will be lost along the way, ankles and lower legs will not be exposed to sun or cold as they might be with pant legs that can ride up, there is no elastic to bind at the waist or trap heat, and they always match themselves. Those with numerous snaps to align and close can be a drag, however, especially when racing to board an airplane on time or get back to your seat before a bout of turbulence. For greater ease and speed of changing, look for those made with a zipper instead; you may be able to find some in cost-effective 3-packs by Gerber or other familiar brands.

Two-piece outfits – Top or bottom? With babies and small children, you never know which will be the first to soil (and this goes for the clothing on the parent holding the child as well). One-piece outfits and playsuits require a total change either way, but a shirt is easy to replace in transit, as are pants when you're already changing a diaper. By only replacing one half at a time, you may also reduce your laundry load. During the baby food months, there may even be times you elect to simply remove your child's shirt before feeding—much less laundry!

Overalls – For older babies and young toddlers, overalls provide one fantastic advantage over other two-piece outfits: the straps provide the perfect place to link a toy.

Shirts – It's hard to go wrong with a lightweight cotton, long-sleeve T-shirt. It's a great basic layer in changeable weather, adds warmth in cold climes, and provides lightweight, breathable sun protection in hot weather. Just remember that, unless your shirt specifies a level of SPF protection (as some do), it will not provide total sun protection in extreme situations.

Hats – A good hat protects its wearer from sun, rain, or cold weather, but a better hat does so while providing a strap to help keep it in place. While Mom and Dad need hands free to carry children, hold smaller hands, or push strollers, a gust could make off with either of their hats. And at some stages, children will simply try to remove their own hats themselves, unless they have that indispensable chin strap.

Hooded sweaters and jackets – These offer the built-in advantage of having no extra hat to keep (or lose) track of.

Zipped jackets and sweaters – Parents who will be wearing children in frontpack carriers will want to avoid wearing jackets and sweaters with zippers that could scrape or irritate the child.

Shoes – Parents will want especially supportive, comfortable shoes for traveling if they'll be spending any amount of time carrying a child—especially if they'll be using a sling, frontpack carrier, or backpack carrier during sightseeing. Shoes for toddlers and older children should provide adequate protection from gravel, rocks, and pinecones if they'll be exploring that sort of territory.

Quick-dry clothing – Whether you need to quickly clean up your shirt or your child's between flights or your faced with the prospect of air-drying your family's laundry indoors in typhoon season, it's wise to have at least one top and bottom for each family member that can air dry quickly if needed. Fleece and other travel-friendly fabrics reign supreme.

Great Products and Gear for Travel

Having the right products and gear for trips with your child can make all the difference between a relaxing, comfortable trip and, frankly, a logistical nightmare. If you err on the side of over-packing, you may be bogged down with too much gear and too many suitcases to fit in your taxi or rental car, or to make it through the airport without enlisting an army of skycaps. Pare down too much and you may suffer through every meal of your vacation with your child in your arms, or end up financing your chiropractor's next sailboat from having left your stroller behind.

Following are some of the best products and gear available to help streamline trips with babies and small children, from truly portable travel beds and safe alternatives to car seats, to mini waterless vaporizers and portable safety gates. Thanks to their lightweight properties, and space- and sanity-saving conveniences, many of these items may also be preferred for use at home. For a closer look at many of these products and current category recommendations, be sure to visit www.TravelswithBaby.com.

Car Seats, Accessories, and Alternatives

Infant carrier car seat – Car seats for infants and babies that can snap in and out of a base in the car and can be carried by a handle. Many are designed to be used without the base during travel. Virtually all include a shade canopy and can also be used with a stroller as a "travel system," or with a Snap N' Go or universal-type stroller frame. Available from Britax, Graco, Peg Perego, and all of the major car seat brands.

The Sit 'n' Stroll converts from car seat to a light-duty stroller and includes a canopy to shield children from sun, rain, and reading lights.

Sit 'n' Stroll – A car seat that converts to a stroller and buckles easily into airplane seats, taxis, and other vehicles (the seat belt goes around it instead of through it). Rear- and forward-facing, from birth up to 40 lbs. The Sit 'n' Stroll now comes standard with a sun/rain canopy, which can also be quite helpful for keeping sun off your child in the car. The Sit 'n' Stroll is especially well suited to cruise vacations, where space is at a premium, but a lightweight stroller, car seat, and dining booster (and just a safe seat for your child in the cabin) may all be quite helpful. (More photos with detailed review at www.TravelswithBaby.com.)

Radian RXT convertible car seat + booster – This convertible car seat folds in half to only 6.5" thick, and with its steel alloy frame, it is one of the safest car seats to consider checking through the airport baggage system (more on checking car seats on pg. 278). The Radian RXT seats children from birth or 5 lbs up to 80 lbs in rear- and forward-facing positions, and later converts to a belt-positioning booster. It is FAA-approved for air travel in the car seat mode, and at only 17" wide, it is one of the best candidates for fitting in between armrests on a variety of aircraft and fitting three across a back seat.

Safety 1st Go Hybrid car seat + booster – This forward-facing car seat also folds to fit in its own carrying case (included) and has an innovative design that eliminates the need for a "shell" through the body of it, making it another safer candidate for checking through the airplane baggage system. Compared with the steel-framed Radian, it is lighter weight and therefore easier to carry. Unlike the Radian, however, the Go Hybrid relies on an upper tether for installation and therefore cannot be used on airplanes or in vehicles that are lacking a tether anchor. The Go Hybrid can be used as a car seat from 1 year and 22 lbs up to 65 lbs, and then converts to a backless booster for children up to 100 lbs. (See photo on pg. 276. Complete review with more photos at www.TravelswithBaby.com.)

Ride Safer Travel Vest – The "wearable booster seat" that meets or exceeds all standards of the FMVSS 213 (Federal Motor Vehicle Safety Standard). Available in two sizes: small, from 35 lbs to 60 lbs, or large, 50 lbs to 80 lbs It weighs 3.5 lbs and the deluxe model, which comes with an optional upper tether strap, can be used with shoulder or lap-only belts (a new version is also now sold without the tether, but it must be used with shoulder belts only). Unlike regular booster seats, this provides the protection of a 5-point safety harness. Like booster seats: it's not approved for use in aircraft. (See photo on pg. 223. Detailed review with photos at www.TravelswithBaby.com.)

Baby B'Air lap child safety vest – A flight safety vest for lap-held babies and toddlers that attaches to a parent's seat belt to help protect against turbulence. FAA-approved for use in flight, but not for use during taxiing and takeoff. Available in two sizes. (See photo on pg. 305.)

Testing out the original FlyeBaby en route to Jamaica.

FlyeBaby air travel hammock – The FlyeBaby can be a great convenience when flying with a lap-held infant, especially on flights where bassinets will not be available, or when you prefer not to fly on the bulkhead row. A small hammock is created by attaching one end to your folded tray and the other to your waist. Your baby rides facing you and buckled into the hammock with a 5-point harness. The FlyeBaby is not considered a safety product, and is only approved to use during cruising portions of your flight. Best to approximately 9 months with most babies and in most airplanes. Detailed review with photos at www.TravelswithBaby.com.

CARES aviation restraint – The FAA-approved flight safety harness for children over 1 year old and weighing 22 to 44 lbs. Straps attach to both the airplane seat back and airplane lap belt to create a 4-point safety harness for a child sitting in his own (paid) seat. Not approved for use in automobiles. While it has definite advantages over flying with a car seat, it can have its drawbacks, too, especially with children who are "escape artists" and can more easily remove themselves from the harness/airplane safety belt than they would from their car seats, and for children who need to sleep on long flights and may be more comfortable doing so in their own car seats. Read more about the pros and cons of using CARES on pg. 303, and see my detailed review of our experiences using CARES with more photos at www.TravelswithBaby.com.

Backpack carrier for car seats – Attaches to your car seat for easy hands-free carrying of your car seat. Great for parents flying with seated toddlers and preschoolers. The Pac Back provides padded straps with extra support from hip and chest belts. Some other models include a cover for the entire car seat, like the J.L. Childress Ultimate Car Seat Carrier and Brica CoverGuard.

Traveling Toddler car seat strap – This simple, cost-effective solution (around $15 US) combines a rolling carry-on suitcase with your child's car seat to become an airport-worthy travel stroller. The strap connects to the car seat's LATCH and tether points, allowing your child to ride strapped in to his car seat by its 5-point harness as you push the carry-on through the airport in front of you. The car seat quickly detaches for its ride through the X-ray at security. The Traveling Toddler car seat strap can be used with virtually any car seat that can be used forward-facing and rolling carry-on suitcase with a locking handle.

GoGo Kidz TravelMate and Brica Roll 'n Go – Adds wheels and a height-adjustable handle to your car seat, making it possible to wheel your child clear to the gate and even down the aisle of larger aircraft in most major brand car seats (airplanes larger than a 737). You can leave it attached to your car seat while flying, but it must be removed before installing your car seat in an automobile. While many tout this accessory combined with car seat as an alternative to a stroller during travel, you may be glad to have your real stroller (checked through to your destination for free by most airlines in a protective travel bag) or to rent a full-feature stroller for use at your destination (see Baby Gear Rentals, pg. 82).

Car seat shade canopy – If you've enjoyed the shade canopy on your infant carrier car seat, you know how nice it is to be able to adjust it and keep the sun off your child and out of her eyes. While the Sit 'n' Stroll convertible car-seat-stroller (see pg. 67) now comes standard with a sun canopy, which can be used in the car or airplane as well as when it's in stroller mode, you may also be able to find a "universal" car seat canopy for toddler car seats as well. Brands and available models have varied over the past few years, so for the latest models and brands available, check www.TravelswithBaby.com.

Strollers and Accessories

Snap N Go, SnugRider, or other infant carrier car seat stroller frames – Far lighter than the strollers included in most so-called "travel systems," these stroller frames work with your infant car seat to give you the benefits of a stroller with the convenience of keeping your baby in her car seat through multiple phases of travel (through airport, onto airplane, into taxi). Lighter weight basic models are available from Graco and Baby Trend. See these and other recommendations at www.TravelswithBaby.com.

Umbrella strollers (see also Travel strollers) – Lightweight, inexpensive, and often the first consideration for travel, these bare-bones strollers fold compactly just as their name suggests. Since they offer little to no recline, they are usually not suitable for children younger than 6 months old, and even older babies and toddlers will often slump forward in these when napping. If you'll need your child to do much napping on the go, or if you plan to check your stroller for a flight or use it on challenging terrain (uneven sidewalks, curbs, cobblestones), I strongly recommend you invest in a lightweight "travel stroller" instead.

Travel strollers – Travel strollers are also designed to be lightweight and fold compactly, while better handling the needs of travelers and rigors of traveling. In fact, a good travel stroller may be as useful at home as it is abroad. Seats may recline partway for children 3 months and older, or recline completely for use with newborns or help with diaper changes. Other helpful extras may include a bumper bar (great for attaching toys or a travel tray), sun canopy with storage pockets, storage basket, or a carrying handle or strap. A few models are also compatible with infant car seats. Good economical options can be found from One Step Ahead and Chicco. Other popular models are available from Combi, Maclaren, Britax, and UPPAbaby, to name a few.

See current recommendations for single and double/twin travel strollers at www.TravelswithBaby.com.

Stroller shade nets – They go over your stroller just like rain shields but offer UV protection and shade instead. Look for one with a UV-protective mesh for the best ventilation combined with UV protection, and one that also offers a snug fit for insect protection for the best value.

RayShade or other stroller canopy shade extensions – Strap on to your stroller for wider coverage than what's provided by your stroller's canopy alone. Look for one with a UV rating to ensure you're getting what you expect here. The RayShade fits over your stroller's canopy to create a much larger shade canopy that extends further out above your child and offers some side protection as well. It blocks 99% of harmful UVA and UVB rays. Available for single and side-by-side twin strollers, both with small storage pockets (including one for a cup). Folds to 10" x 10" and fits in its own storage pouch.

Stroller UPF parasol – These clip right on to your stroller side bar to provide additional sun protection from the front or sides, changing as needed. It can be very helpful with travel and umbrella strollers that have small canopies and leave little legs exposed. Bugaboo makes one that fits its models of strollers, and Eckert of Germany offers a universal stroller parasol with UPF 50 that is made to work with both strollers and joggers.

Child Carriers, Wraps, and Slings

Slings and wraps – Most slings and wraps allow you to wear your child in multiple positions, and can be used from infancy into toddlerhood. Simple, across-the-body fabric slings like the New Native and Maya Wrap slip easily over the head with one hand, ensuring easy passage through airport security scanners even if you are asked to remove your sling in the process (tips on clearing airport security begin on pg. 289). The classic Moby Wrap is perhaps the most versatile of the wraps, allowing you to wear your child in a snug sling position (even twin infants, if you've got 'em), and also forward-facing, outward-facing, or even on your back, plus it uses wide bands of fabric crossing both shoulders and your back to help distribute the weight—though it is not so easily removed for security screenings at the airport, should you be asked to do so (as I once, very memorably, was). Most slings and wraps can also help mothers nurse discreetly on the go. Recent years have seen an explosion in the number of baby-wearing wraps and slings available, though as travelers you may want to look for size-adjustable models that can be shared between parents.

Soft-structure child carriers – Most of these can be used with infants from their earliest weeks, provided they meet the minimum weight and length limits outlined by the manufacturer (Baby Björn specifies 8 lbs and 21" minimum), and are used following the instructions and using any extra inserts or leg straps for infants. With frontpack models, such as the Baby Björn, children may face inward with head and neck support until they are ready to face forward—which can be very helpful when your baby likes to see what you're looking at, when you are hopping on and off of buses or subways and needing to sit brief periods with baby "on your lap" (she's facing the right way), and in posing for those many great travel photos along your way. By the time baby reaches 15 lbs, however, you may be ready for a more supportive carrier. The Ergo and its many new cousins allow you to wear your child on the front facing you, and on your back facing you as well, and can support a higher weight limit (up to 35 or 40 lbs depending. However, the back-carry mode with any soft-structure child carrier can be difficult without the help of a second adult, until your child is old enough to help. As you shop, keep in mind that carriers with thicker fabrics and dark colors can be very warm for children if you'll be visiting hot destinations, and as you travel, keep in mind that the TSA might ask you to remove an infant sling or baby carrier and run through the scanner at airport security (even if it is only cloth, and even if you weren't asked to do so on your previous flight). Average max weight for child is 25 lbs. See current recommendations of child carriers at www.TravelswithBaby.com.

Granada, Spain: A child carrier that allows you to move your child from back to front comes in handy when taking crowded public transportation or lining up for your tour of the Alhambra's Nasrid Palaces, where you discover backpacks of any kind are not allowed...but frontpacks? ¡Sí!

Framed backpack carriers – A framed backpack carrier can provide much-needed support for hours of carrying your child upon your back, and can accommodate children of higher weight limits than the other carriers. Most are created for children at least 6 months of age, who can sit up comfortably unassisted. Framed models range in quality and features from those designed for afternoon outings to week-long treks in the wild. Accordingly, many include optional add-ons like sun/rain hoods, comfort stirrups, storage bags, and removable daypacks. For your travel purposes, however, a framed backpack carrier may not need to be large to be useful. Small models like Deuter's KangaKid and Kelty's Junction models offer the 2-in-1 convenience of a backpack carrier with an internal frame and a small daypack compartment for storage—and is not much larger than a daypack overall (two birds with one carry-on). The KangaKid is also designed to conceal the "child cockpit" when not in use. Average maximum load for these packs (child + toys + snacks + water + diapers, etc.) is 40 lbs, though some, like the Kelty Tour, may be rated to 50 lbs. One unique carrier for this category that accommodates children 2½ years to 60 lbs is the Nomis Piggyback Rider, which offers a standing ride-on bar for kids that like to be on their feet most of the time, but need an occasional lift. Rather than a bulky frame, the 3-lb Piggyback Rider features a streamlined harness for the parent with optional add-ons of a storage pack or hydration pack, a basic safety harness and grab handles for the child, and the standing ride-on bar. See more on these and other recommended framed backpack carriers for travel at www.TravelswithBaby.com.

Hip carriers – Child hip carriers are ideal for shorter-use periods of carrying older babies and toddlers, when you want a very simple way to slip them in and out of a supportive carrier such as when you're sightseeing by public transportation or sightseeing with a group on a shore excursion. Note that some soft-structure carriers that can be worn on the front and back also offer a hip-carry mode for older babies and toddlers, though it can be complicated to achieve with the various buckles and straps. The original Hip Hammock simplifies the process and can be used with children from around 2 months up to 3½ years. The Sidekick is a diaper bag that looks much like a lady's purse, is worn cross-body, and features a fold-out hip carrier to use when needed (Dad may be shy about wearing the purse, however). One of my favorites in this category is the Combi Urban, a lightweight no-frills hip carrier that folds into its own waistpack; it has been discontinued, though some units can still be found for sale online for the moment. (More details on these and others at www.TravelswithBaby.com.)

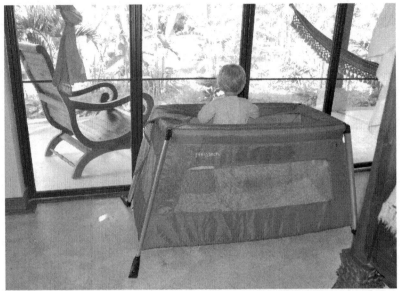

Playa Hermosa, Costa Rica: The Phil&Teds Traveller offers a sturdy but lightweight aluminum frame with the advantage of a mesh screen cover for the top (good for parental peace of mind when you're not sure who else might pass through your room in the night...). Read more on pg. 77.

Travel Beds and Sleeping Solutions

Play yards/Pack 'n Plays – Sometimes called a play yard, play pen, Pack 'n Play, or even a portacrib, these soft-sided cribs not only make a safe play space for your baby or toddler when visiting un-childproofed settings, but they can serve as a bed as well. Some play yards come with attachable changing stations, bassinets, shade canopies, mosquito nets, and other accessories as well that may also be helpful, depending on your destination. However, while you can fold them for travel and even check them on airplanes (usually for an extra checked bag fee), many parents find them too cumbersome and heavy for travel except by automobile. On the bright side, a "pack 'n play" may be available on request at your hotel or on your cruise, so be sure to ask when you make your reservation.

Travel beds – Most similar to play yards, with raised sides and rigid structures to help keep little ones contained, are the Baby Bjorn Travel Crib Light (11 lbs) and the Phil&Teds Traveller Full-Size Traveller Crib (6 lbs, now with full mesh sides). The Phil&Teds earlier model (still available at time of writing) includes a mesh top that may be left open or zipped closed, while the newest model features a UV-mesh net that stretches over the top. Both offer a side panel that may be unzipped while your child plays on the beach or when he's old enough to come and go as he pleases. The Peapod works like a small pop-up tent, converting from a 14" disc in its travel bag to a 48"L and 18"H sleeping tent, with UV protective mesh sides and air-cushion mattress (see photo, pg. 36). It works well for babies and even preschoolers, though babies first learning to stand and walk may be frustrated by the low ceiling. The Peapod Plus opens to 52.5"L and 25"H, accommodating children up to 6 years, and comes with its own lightweight sleeping bag.

Infant and toddler travel "trundles" – Another option for sleeping, though not so much for playing or childproofing (once your child can climb out). They are very lightweight and fold to nearly flat. Some will fit inside a large suitcase or may be worn over the shoulder with a carrying strap. Available brands include Small Fry, Eddie Bauer, and Graco.

Co-sleepers/infant bumper beds – Compactly folding co-sleepers or "bumper" beds like the Snuggle Nest or Wee Sleep can be used for infants sleeping between Mom and Dad in a shared bed. These are a fantastic option when staying in tight quarters with an infant as in cruise ship cabins and big-city hotels.

Inflatable toddler beds – For car trips to Grandma's house and camping trips in a commodious tent, an inflatable toddler bed, such as the Tuckaire or Aerobed for toddlers, offers cushy comfort, insulation from cold/hard floors, and have raised sides to prevent "roll off." The Tuckaire also features a removable inset mattress that makes tucking in sheets and blankets—and keeping them there—a snap. Tip: When vacationing at a hotel with your toddler or preschooler, you may be able to rent one of these from a local baby gear rental agency, which could provide that extra bed for your child while you all enjoy more space in your room with one king-size bed, rather than two queen-size beds.

Portable bed guardrails – Indispensable when traveling with toddlers and preschoolers where grown-up beds are available, but keeping active sleepers in them may be a problem. Some models include SleepTite and Regalo, though the BedBugz inflatable bed bolster packs the lightest and smallest of them all, and can be used with twin or full-size mattresses.

Products for Eating and Feeding

Travel trays – Various folding and flat trays are designed to be attached to strollers (with bumper bars), car seats, and the standard-issue trayless square high chairs you'll find in many restaurants. The best are created with a raised lip around the edges to keep snacks and crayons from rolling away, and help not only with dining on the go, but can prove invaluable in helping kids entertain themselves during flights and even long car rides. The flat Taby Tray is the largest of travel trays and works with most car seats as well as strollers, with a depression just for crayons or markers and a built-in cup holder. The best travel tray available for all-purpose travel is the Snack 'N Play, which has nice, high edges, storage pockets on the side, and rolls up to stuff beneath your stroller or in your travel carry-on. (As we found on one memorable road trip, it also works well as an impromptu sled.)

Portable dining boosters – Available in a wide variety of styles, including ones that can be strapped and secured to virtually any adult chair and offer 3-point safety harnesses to keep escape artists in their place. Most folding travel boosters work for babies as soon as they can sit up (around 6 months), and grow with them through toddlerhood. Those featuring snap-on trays will help keep little hands from raiding the table, and the trays can be removed once your child is ready to pass the peas. If you'll be traveling mostly by car, the booster with tray from Safety 1st may be the most useful (you can simply set your mobile baby in it with some toys on the tray while you babyproof your motel room) and it wipes clean with ease since it is molded plastic. But for streamlined travel by airplane, consider ultra-compact folding models like the Brica Fold 'N Go booster that you can slip into the outside pocket of your suitcase if needed. More on these and other dining boosters for travel at www.TravelswithBaby.com.

Hook-on booster chairs (ones that clamp to the table) – Make sure to get one that will accommodate the many different table thicknesses and "skirts" you will likely encounter in your travels. These have the advantage of packing down very small for your daypack or diaper bag, but consider that your baby will have easier access to the table and you may not be able to use it for as long as some other dining boosters. One Step Ahead and Phil&Teds both offer hook-on chairs that fit thicker tables and accommodate children up to 37 lbs and 40 lbs respectively, and work well for toddlers. However, one restaurant I visited had banned use of this type of child seat since a customer had cracked a glass tabletop when tightening his child's chair, and it should be noted that the instructions do advise against use with glass tabletops or tablecloths. Nevertheless, if space is tight at home, this seat may also be a wonderful solution to bulkier high chairs and you needn't sacrifice an extra chair (or the space one would take up) for a booster seat.

Dining chair "harnesses" – There are a number of dining harnesses available now, which simply secure child to chair, and work with most sizes and shapes of dining chairs. Some of these may serve other purposes as well, such as the FlyeBaby, which starts out as an air travel hammock for infants, then continues to serve as an on-the-go dining harness for babies old enough to sit up through young toddlers (read more about the FlyeBaby on pg. 69).

Reusable pocket bibs – In the interest of generating less dirty laundry and waste during your travels, I strongly recommend getting a wipe-clean bib that will guard your child's clothing and most of the stroller and car seat straps from dribbles, splats, and spills. One with a built-in pocket to catch crumbs and run-off is particularly helpful here. While there are several waterproof/water-resistant cloth options out there, I've found they can start smelling unpleasant after a day or two without laundering. The Baby Bjorn scoop bib solves this problem, but most find it is a better fit for older babies and toddlers. The Rinse-and-Roll Bibbity Bib is available in three neck sizes, rinses clean, and rolls into its own pocket. Either of these last options can be wiped clean with a handy sanitizing wipe when needed as well.

A SippiGrip can help babies and toddlers keep a handle on their hydration during hot road trips—and keep you from constantly searching the floor for where it went this time.

The BooginHead SippiGrip or Drink Deputy – Bottles and most sippy cups (without handles) can be kept within reach and off the floor with help from these inventive strapping devices that attach to car seats, strollers, and high chairs.

Insulated and freezable cups – It's often a good idea to add some ice cubes to your child's sippy cup before heading out with a beverage, but an insulated sippy cup will help keep his drink even fresher even longer (some commonly available by Playtex). Munchkin even makes a cup that freezes to help keep drinks cool, though you will need access to a freezer during your travels to get the full benefit. As soon as your child is ready, however, an insulated stainless thermos with pop-top and built-in straw will become a very sound investment, used for road trips as a toddler, filling with water at the airport before boarding the plane as a preschooler, and still using in the school lunch pail years later.

Fleece blanket – If your child tends to conduct himself at lunch as some would the symphony, consider using a light fleece blanket to line the stroller back and headrest when high chairs or boosters aren't available. The mess will cling to the fleece, which will easily wash in the sink and dry in a few hours at your hotel.

The Snack Trap or Snack Catcher – They keep little fingers busy and mouths munching while keeping crackers and Cheerios from spilling across the floor. These two-handled cups with cleverly split lids are ideal for the diaper bag or daypack. Tip: Load one with Cheerios and dried cranberries and use a carabiner clip to attach it to your child's stroller strap to help distract your toddler as you wait in boring lines.

Travel bottle and food warmers – Various models use your vehicle's cigarette lighter to power warmers for bottles or both food and bottles. Models by Diono, Munchkin, and The First Years are most popular, but many parents complain these warmers take too long to heat to be practical, so advanced planning will be helpful on your part (i.e., don't wait until your baby is hungry). Overheating can also result in melted bottles, so follow the instructions carefully. For no-electricity-needed options, Dex and Prince Lionheart offer warming systems with a neoprene or insulated sleeve to surround the bottle while a warming pack heats the bottle inside. These also may take longer to warm bottles than you're accustomed to at home, and it will definitely help if you don't start with a chilled bottle. Also, the warming packs must be boiled to "reset" after use, so bring extras to get you through long days of travel, and work the boiling into your travel itinerary. Tomee Tipee has simplified the hot water warming method for travelers with a stainless thermos for storing hot water, and an insulated canister which fits most bottles and food jars. For tips on warming bottles and baby food during air travel, see pg. 270.

San Diego, California: Baby gear rental companies sometimes rent more than baby gear. Here, Toddler's Travels outfitted us with beach toys, chairs, a sun umbrella, and even a wagon to pull them with.

Finding and Using Baby Gear Rental Companies (a.k.a. Baby Equipment Hire)

Strollers, swings, bouncy seats, bassinets, high chairs, full-size cribs, and play pens can all help you have a much more comfortable, and even a safer stay wherever you are bound. But of course you can only lug so much to—and through—the airport, not to mention the miserable gas mileage you will get while crossing the country with an exersaucer strapped to the roof of your car.

If you would like to have a framed baby backpack carrier for hiking in Hawaii, for example, or a heavy-duty buggy for touring the Old

Country, it can be well worth the rental fee to avoid checking yours, risking damage, or juggling one extra item in transit.

Throughout the U.S. and in many other countries, it's now possible to rent everything from exersaucers, safety gates, beach toys, full-size cribs, wagons, double jogging strollers, and rocking chairs to baby swings and slings—even breast pumps and steam sterilizers.

Some baby gear rental companies offer additional services as well, such as delivering your preferred diapers, formula, or groceries with your gear rental. You can imagine what a huge help that can be in some situations (see Baby Supply Delivery Services on pg. 83 for more on that theme).

Typically, a baby gear rental company will deliver your desired equipment and gear to your accommodations, be it a hotel, condo, vacation rental, or all-inclusive resort. Some companies will also meet you at the airport or train station with your rented car seat and gear, or provide discounts for twins or package deals for multiple items.

ON THE WEB:

The Worldwide Directory of Baby Gear Rental Agencies at www.TravelswithBaby.com now includes baby gear rental companies (a.k.a. "baby equipment hire") throughout the U.S. and Canada, in Mexico and the Caribbean, South America, Asia, Australia, New Zealand, Europe, and Africa.

Baby Supply Delivery Services

Once you start packing, it isn't hard to see you could fill an entire suitcase just with the essentials for your beach vacation or adventure abroad. However, it isn't always practical to plan on spending your precious vacation time hunting down the extra things you'll need for your child—assuming you can find them once you reach your destination. If you will be renting gear for your child, the agency may also deliver essentials like diapers, wipes, formula, and baby foods along with your equipment rental, so check when you make arrangements.

- **Babies Travel Lite** can deliver all manner of goods in popular destinations worldwide, including baby and toddler sunglasses, swim diapers, sun block, toddler snacks, baby foods, bath and beach toys, and beverages (including boxed milk!). www.babiestravellite.com or 1-888-450-LITE.

- **Jet Set Babies** ships orders of diapers, sun care products, baby and toddler foods, formula, and more to locations throughout the U.S., in Puerto Rico, and in the U.S. Virgin Islands, as well as to U.S. military bases around the world. www.jetsetbabies.com or 1-888-570-0811.

Fifteen Things You Might Not Think to Pack

1. **Large binder clips** – Fantastic for clipping blankets to stroller canopies and infant car seats for extended shade coverage. These also help keep bags of chips and crackers closed tight.

2. **Old blanket or "Neat Sheet"** – Create a sun canopy from your tail gate (with binder clips, above) or drape over your car windows for shade when pulled over for a nursing break or rest stop. Also useful for beach outings, impromptu picnics en route, and emergency roadside repairs. Use binder clips at the corners as weights or to secure to your car or other objects as shade. You may prefer the Neat Sheet as a lightweight, waterproof alternative to blankets, as it sheds sand and shields against boggy lawns.

3. **Pillow** – Helpful on road trips for nursing, napping, and creating a level surface over bucket seats during diaper changes.

4. **Spare sun hat** – It would be interesting to know how many times the average sun hat falls off (or blows off, or gets thrown off from) a child's head. Be prepared, and try to use one with a chin strap.

5. **Small flashlight or wearable light** – Not just for camping! A small (pen-sized or slightly larger) flashlight can be very helpful in searching through the glove box, diaper bag, carry-on, or suitcase

without turning on additional lights that may disturb your child's slumber. I've also found the Beam N Read adjustable LED lamp you wear around your neck and can angle as desired for the task is great when traversing the hotel room post bedtime or when holding the hands of two children looking for the campground restrooms at night (and unlike headlamps, you don't blind everyone you look at in the dark. More at www.TravelswithBaby.com).

6. **Extra pair of shoes** – We've all seen it, the lone child's shoe, kicked off or slipped off, in the parking lot or along the park trail. And now that you're a parent, it could happen to you. Whether you are going away for days or a day, you may be glad you brought a back-up pair.

7. **Stationery box** – The ½" deep boxes that résumés or special papers are packaged in can be indispensable in traveling with toddlers and preschool-age children. Fill with scratch paper and a few crayons and you have an art station that's ready to roam. Just open the lid and let them go—the edges of the box keep artwork from getting onto other surfaces and the crayons from rolling off the edges.

8. **Facial tissue/Kleenex** – If you are all perfectly healthy before you set foot out the door, runny noses may be the furthest thing from your minds. In case of cold or allergies, you might be grateful to have some travel-size tissue packs or a handkerchief for your daypack or diaper bag.

9. **Tampons/maxi pads** – If you are a breastfeeding mother who has not yet resumed her cycle, guess what? It could happen at any time, so be prepared.

10. **Breast pump** – Even if you are not planning to pump or have any need for bottles, it may be a comfort to express milk at some point in your trip. Restless flights, long nights spent suckling a growing babe, or traveling with a baby that sleeps more than usual (and feeds less than…) due to the hum of the car or airplane engine may find you painfully engorged at some point.

11. **Your laundry detergent** – In case you decide to do a load of laundry after all…it may be hard to find your preferred detergent for your child's clothing (baby-friendly, low-odor, etc.), especially

without purchasing an entire box or bottle of the stuff. Pack a baggie with just one load's worth in your suitcase's inner pocket.

12. **Velcro bands** – At home, you'll find them in your fabric store and possibly on the goodies and gadgets aisle of your supermarket. As you travel, you may find them bundling up window blind cords, attaching toys or shopping bags to your stroller, or wet clothing to the balcony rail of your vacation rental.

13. **Rubber drain cover** – The wide, flat variety could help hold a baby's bath or a small load of laundry in a leaky sink, or even convert some shower stalls into a pint-sized pool for bathing toddlers.

14. **Inflatable beach ball** – Think lightweight, soft, and safe for rolling around the hotel room on rainy days or at the airport when you're grounded in a haze. Sure, you can use it at the beach, too.

15. **Glow sticks** – Even if you travel with a nightlight, there may not be a suitable outlet (or any outlets at all in the case of a tent) where you can use the nightlight. Emergency glow sticks can be used instead, and older children may even be comforted by carrying theirs with them to the bathroom in the night. Most stay illuminated up to 12 hours and can usually be found at hardware stores.

Part II:
Tools for Happy Travels

CHAPTER 5
Preparing for Changes

Changes in Nighttime Sleeping Routines

Hitting the Hay:

Snuggling a beloved blanket, reading stories, or humming a song is easily accomplished in tents, in hotel rooms, and even in row 27 of coach. But giving a bath, rocking together in a chair, or plugging in a favorite nightlight may present some serious logistical challenges when it's bedtime during your trip. As a traveling parent, it will behoove you to make your routines at home as portable as possible, especially bedtime routines.

My husband and I have found it helpful to have at least one bedtime story and a poem committed to memory—they travel with us wherever we go and take up zero space in the suitcase. Better yet, we can recount them as needed, even when pacing up and down the aisles of a crowded airplane or traveling in a dark car. And in moments when your child is overtired and out of sorts, it may be more effective to softly whisper a poem or story in his ear than to pull out a stimulating book or toy. Stories and poems with simple rhyme schemes are often the easiest to memorize. If you're not sure where to begin, you might take a look at Sandra Boynton's *The Going to Bed Book* and Robert Frost's poem "Stopping by Woods on a Snowy Evening"; both have helpful rhyme schemes and are especially well suited to both bedtime and travel (and both have ending lines that can be repeated as needed, and repeated as needed).

Co-sleeping families accustomed to sharing "the family bed" may have the easiest time of all catching zzz's while traveling. When you and your children are already accustomed to sleeping side by side, you will feel right at home shutting eyes on airplanes, trains, in foreign hotels, in tents, and anywhere space or beds are limited. Co-sleepers may find some challenges, however, when traveling in Europe where twin beds are quite common in smaller hotels, or on trains where most beds are bunk-style.

For families that are more accustomed to having space to sprawl and even rooms to separate early sleepers from those with later bedtimes, travel can pose some interesting challenges. Some parents have found it helpful to try one (or all) of the following:

- Observe a family bedtime when sharing a single room, tent, or compartment.

- Ask your hotel if a portacrib is available or a rollaway bed for older toddlers and preschoolers. If not, consider bringing your own travel bassinet or travel bed.

- When sharing a bed with an excitable child, put the child to bed first as per your routine so she is soundly asleep before joining her on the mattress.

- Create a "safe zone" for infants and young babies at the head of the bed where the blankets will not interfere, in a gap between parents' pillows. Always be certain the child cannot slip between mattresses (as when two twin beds are pushed together) or between the mattress and the wall. Your best bet may be a "co-sleeper" such as the Snuggle Nest, which folds up for travel and provides safety bumpers for the baby in the bed between Mom and Dad.

- Get creative! Past generations often used a drawer on the floor as baby's temporary bed (but in strange places they may come with splinters or bugs, so inspect them thoroughly first). Look around, consider your resources, and be sure to use common sense.

The National Bardo Museum, Carthage: If your tiny traveler wakes for a playdate with you at 2 a.m., just remember that she'll have to make up for it at some point—and that's where your nice, quiet visit to the museum comes in...

Keeping the Peace:

You may also want to bring along your own source of white noise to help muffle any strange new noises, including those of crisp hotel sheets as you roll over in the night, and of course, less desirable interjections of street or hotel noise, a banging furnace or air conditioner, elevator traffic in the hallway, an ice machine, or perhaps a crying baby. (Wait—that one came with us.)

But what do you do when the sleeping conditions are wildly different from those of home, and even recordings of ocean waves or TV static can't help? First, I recommend having a good chuckle in recognition of the absurdity of your situation; e.g., it's not every couple with an overtired infant that gets to share the wall with newlyweds. After you laugh heartily about the parade of Vespas outside cracking the plaster on your ceiling with their baritone bravado, ask about changing to a quieter room—most hotel staff will recognize that all of their guests are more likely to sleep like babies if the babies among them are asleep.

And don't be afraid to use your bedspread or a beach towel, or ask for an extra blanket if needed, to help block out bright lights or block drafts—or help muffle hallway noise that may come in from under your door.

Conquering Jetlag:

To help overcome jetlag, try to set your internal clocks to the new time zone as quickly as possible. While you can try moving bedtimes and wake-up times gradually in the days leading up to your trip (15 minutes a night/morning is very doable for most young children), it won't do much for major changes in time zones.

Getting the whole family out of doors and into the sunlight during daylight hours, no matter how exhausted you may be, can do a world of wonder for getting your biological rhythms in synch with your new surroundings. When possible, plan to arrive at far-flung destinations during daylight hours to make the most of this. Even with a much earlier bedtime than usual on the day of arrival, we've been stunned at how quickly we find ourselves and our children waking up at the same time as usual in the morning.

As for daytime naps and jetlag, don't deprive an exhausted child of a nap if she needs one, but try to keep it to a reasonable length of time for a *nap* (whatever is the norm at home if that helps). This will also help her get back into her routine on the new schedule.

And finally, if your child wakes up raring to go in the middle of the night, you may need to simply allow her to burn off some energy she didn't get to use during long hours of travel, or consume some extra calories to make up for a meal she's missed, or even have a bowel movement (yes, even poop can experience jetlag). Once the need appears to be met, gently return to your same bedtime routine.

Naptime in Phuket, Thailand: Push a couple of seaside lounges together under a shade umbrella.

Changes in Naptime Sleeping Routines

When it's easy:

Perhaps the greatest incentive of all for traveling with an infant is the incredible ease with which most will nap—and how often—while parents are on the go. Consider the soothing effect of car travel, stroller rides, and even simply being carried around in the infant carrier or sling for most babies.

In some cases, traveling babies and children may nap a little *too* much during daytime outings. While it may make your long drive or visit to MOMA all the more peaceful, you may pay for it later. If your child is a likely candidate for napping too many hours on the go, be sure to build in some breaks for exercise and physical activities that will be more stimulating for your child, whether that's tummy time for an infant or a stop at the local park for older babies and children.

When it's tough:

As babies get older, however, they not only nap fewer hours of the day, but they tend to respond more to their surroundings as well. Some locations and settings, including airplanes, may simply be too exciting for some babies and toddlers to sleep in no matter how weary they (and their parents) may be. As I caution in the section Choosing the Flight (pg. 258), planning a flight at exactly your child's naptime may backfire (with sometimes painful results).

To help with napping while you are out and about, whether by choice or necessity, you might:

- **Bring along a favorite small stuffed animal, blanket, or other lovey** to present each time it's naptime (another sleep routine that travels), whether it's during your sightseeing, on the plane, or in the car.

- **Plan a walk with the stroller away from exciting scenery** (e.g., through the rose garden rather than past the carousel) to help get snoozing underway.

- **Use a blanket and binder clips** to help keep sun or bright lights from disrupting peaceful slumbers and to block out other distractions.

- **Make waves: Broadcast music or white noise** from your digital player or phone (ocean waves work well for us). Some strollers are even equipped with speakers or portable speaker pockets to assist with this "sound method."

- **Choose an aisle seat for your child away from the bulkhead row** if your flight includes nap time (more tips in Choosing the Flight, pg. 258, and Choosing Your Seats, pg. 260).

If your child is very sensitive to changes, you may need to plan more structured breaks for napping where the conditions are closer to those at home. Just remember that even if your child needs to nap at your hotel room most days of your vacation, you can still take turns with your partner, with each of you having a chance to catch up on rest, a good book, or email at the room, while the other lounges at the pool, goes on a photo safari, gets that pedicure there wasn't time for before leaving home, or visits that obscure museum nobody else in the family wants to see (more tips on planning travel with your unique child—and spouse—in Temperaments in Transit, pg. 107).

Changes in Eating and Feeding Routines

Strange new foods and the unfamiliar places in which they are eaten are not always as enjoyable for babies and small children as they are to adults, though you may be pleasantly surprised when your child discovers she likes something from the new menu—a lot (all hail the pineapple). Bringing along some favorite foods and snacks to mix in with the new could make a tremendous difference during the initial adjustment, and what doesn't go well with Cheerios?

If your child has just begun eating solids, you may simply want to plan a trip to the market at your destination to stock up on jarred baby foods. But in more exotic or remote destinations, you may find yourself packing a heavier suitcase to accommodate jarred baby foods from home. For toddlers and older children, you might be glad to have along several of these portable foods.

Ten easy foods to pack for travel with young children:

1. Cheerios or similar breakfast cereal

2. Favorite crackers

3. Graham crackers

4. Small jar of peanut butter

5. Finger-friendly pasta

6. A few canned vegetables or fruits (don't forget a can opener)

7. Instant oatmeal packets

8. Applesauce in individual, sealed servings

9. Fruit leather or dried fruit bars

10. Dinner rolls or mini bagels (stay fresher and travel more easily than a whole loaf of bread)

Breastfeeding on the "Balcony of Europe": My older daughter's souvenir fan with bullfighters provides both shade and privacy. Olé!

Breastfeeding during travel:

If you are breastfeeding your child, you will have a ready supply that requires no refrigeration, special storage, preparation rituals, or paraphernalia. For more travel benefits of continuing breastfeeding through your travels, see pg. 156. For tips on breastfeeding during travel, see Nine Tips for Nursing on the Go, pg. 97.

Formula feeding during travel:

If your child takes formula, you may find it well worth packing some bottles of ready-serve formula even though it is heavier in the suitcase and more expensive than powdered mixes. To help keep things as simple as possible, particularly for the traveling segments between destinations, you may also want to use disposable bottle liners. Tommee Tipee offers a dry formula insert for its bottles that stores pre-measured dry formula mix and water in separate sections of the bottle until you are ready to mix and serve.

For more tips on preparing and warming bottles during travel, see Travel Bottles and Warmers pg. 54, tips for clearing security with bottles and excess liquids for your child pg. 270, and tips for bottle feeding on airplanes pg. 310.

Finding and using regular milk during travel:

For most toddlers and preschoolers, simply ordering a glass with a meal at a restaurant will not cut it. Having a refrigerator in your room with your own carton ready to go at all hours can be a tremendous help, whether it's for washing down graham crackers at bedtime or preparing in-room cereal at dawn.

We've found it helpful to travel with insulated sippy cups, like those made by Playtex, with a few ice cubes added from the hotel ice machine or restaurants—and when the ice cubes stop clinking, we know the milk has started to warm up. An insulated baby bottle storage bag that fits your child's sippy cups may still be very helpful during travel, or possibly an insulated diaper bag. And if your hotel room doesn't have a mini fridge, it may still have an ice bucket you can use to keep milk cold through the night.

For extended stays where refrigeration and milk may be a challenge, consider bringing along (or shipping ahead; see Baby Supply Delivery Services, pg. 83) shelf-stable boxes of milk, rice milk, or almond milk, which don't require refrigeration.

Dining in restaurants:

Since high chairs are rare in restaurants outside of the U.S., and even those in the U.S. often lack safety straps or adequate support, not to mention the basic sanitation required for the surfaces where the adults eat, you may want to bring along a portable dining booster or other alternative for your baby or toddler (more suggestions in Products for Eating and Feeding, pg. 78). Having a clean, comfortable, escape-free perch from which to dine, your child will also recognize that the seat means mealtime.

Nine Tips for Nursing on the Go

If you are just beginning to breastfeed, it may be hard to imagine doing so with any sort of style or grace, let alone without the help of a nursing pillow or stripping to your waist. But it does get easier with practice, and as your baby grows and begins to take up more space in your lap. In the meantime, here are some tips to help you nurse more comfortably as you travel.

1. Think bottom-up as opposed to going over the top. Wear knit shirts cut just wide enough to drape over the cheek of your child as she nurses and still keep you covered to each side (your shirt needn't be ridiculously oversized, just a loose-fitting T-shirt should do).

2. Use a sling to help position your baby and provide privacy while nursing. With practice, you may eventually be able to nurse hands-free, and quite privately, while taking in the sights at your destination!

3. Avoid aisle seats on airplanes and trains for fewer distractions to your child and greater privacy. If there are armrests, you'll be able to make use of them without getting bumped by passersby.

4. If you need breast pads, avoid the disposable variety that contain plastic and will make it difficult for your skin to breathe. The cotton variety can be sink-washed and will dry in a day in most climates.

5. Strategically place your child's stroller or diaper bag to create a privacy barrier.

6. Wear a nursing tank top or camisole underneath a shirt to keep your midriff covered and cold drafts out.

7. When dining out or attending dressy events, wear a wrap, scarf, or shawl of some sort that can drape over your child's cheek and help give privacy while nursing. (You can also use a cloth napkin.)

8. Wear a nursing bra that you can easily open and close with only one hand. This will make it much easier to fasten up with your baby still on your lap.

9. While your child is still very small, use the diaper bag or a folded jacket on your lap to help keep from hunching over, and use armrests where you can find them. (In airplanes and cars you may be able to use a pillow.)

Changes in Potty Training Routines

There are some very lucky parents out there whose young children look forward with much anticipation to visiting new restrooms. For them, discovering the uncharted territory of facilities at the aquarium, zoo, or back storage area of the supermarket are opportunities not to be missed. And a Turkish or pit toilet may provide a solid hour's worth of entertainment for—and questions from—some eager children. But for most of us, potty training can become even more challenging when restroom availability is unpredictable and the facilities are clearly not those of home.

Changes in time zones and diet can also affect a child's regularity, which can lead to unpleasant surprises and diminished confidence. And then there is the fear that may strike in any potty-training child's heart the moment they discover—too soon—the automated power-flush of an airport toilet. Yes, potty training regression is not unheard of during travel, and with good reason.

If your child is just beginning to work on toilet training, it may be easiest to continue diapers through your trip, and I can assure you that's not the end of the world. I've found it's a lot more fun changing diapers in France, or Thailand, or Costa Rica than it is changing diapers at home, and I wouldn't trade the memories we made on those trips together for anything—not even for an earlier finish line for potty training (which we have crossed now with all three children, in spite of our travels!).

Yet, if your child is well on his way or has already conquered potty training at home, there should be no stopping you now. Here are some tips to help in your travels with potty-trainees and those recently potty trained.

Ten Tips for Travel with Potty-Trainees

1. **Paint a clear picture for your child** – While it's easy to focus on the details of the family adventure that lies ahead, don't forget that bathroom breaks are a big new part of his world already. Let him know what to expect in the way of aircraft lavatories, rest areas, or campground facilities, and introduce any new travel potties or equipment in the weeks before you leave home to ensure that he's as comfortable with these items, and the options, as possible.

2. **Watch your watch** – New facilities may bring on performance anxiety, and exciting days packed with sightseeing and activities can make it hard for small children (and sometimes their parents) to remember to take potty breaks in a timely manner. Some parents find it helpful to set a reminder chime on their watch or phone, which can not only help them remember to do a "potty check" but can also help by putting an objective and neutral third party in charge of potty breaks (not Mommy or Daddy who want to interrupt the fun).

3. **Take the fear out of auto-flush toilets** – If you struggle to hold your hand over the sensor *and* keep your child balanced on the toilet, carry a small pad of sticky notes to place over the "magic eye" before you put anything or anyone near the seat. In a pinch, you can also use a Band-Aid, moist toilet paper, or used chewing gum. When your child is finished, let her get as far away from the toilet as she likes before removing it.

4. **Bring a travel-friendly potty** – If your child is nervous about public restrooms in general, or they may not always be available when needed (as on a road trip), it will be helpful to have a folding or inflatable travel potty she can practice using at home and continue to use during travel. Multiple brands are available,

including the Potette Plus 2-in-1, which folds flat and can be used both as a potty with disposable liner and inserts, and also as a child-size seat on top of a regular toilet. More on this and other options at www.TravelswithBaby.com.

5. **Rent a training potty or child-size seat for your stay.** If you'll be staying in one place for most of your vacation (at a resort, relative's home, etc.) and already plan to rent baby or toddler gear, you might be able to rent a potty or potty seat along with other gear for your stay for a very minimal fee (see more about baby gear rentals, pg. 82, and find an agency at your destination in the Worldwide Directory at www.TravelswithBaby.com).

6. **Offer rewards** – One of my children was especially sensitive about using noisy and unfamiliar restrooms during potty training. She was, however, very receptive to mini marshmallows, which I kept in a plastic baggie in my purse for each victory along the way. Animal crackers or stickers can work well, too.

7. **Prepare for delays** – On a turbulent flight or road trip, or in a ridiculously long line at customs, your child may spend more time than expected between visits to the toilet, challenging even the greatest masters of continence. To help with on-the-go "uh-ohs," use training pants or pull-ups in transit even if you've stopped using these at home. For one trip involving long flights and lines, I bought a colorful design of disposable training pants from a brand my daughter had never used before and called them "travel panties."

8. **Prevent wet beds** – For nighttime, disposable-training-type pants like Pull-Ups will do the trick for most toddlers. For the older child who has only occasional accidents, you could pack along the same waterproof sheet and bed pad you may already have at home, if you will be able to do laundry during your stay. If you won't be able to do laundry on your trip, consider purchasing hospital-issue disposable bed pads for your vacation. Also called "underpads" or "chux," there is a variety to choose from that fit the width of a twin-size bed, complete with wings that tuck in to help it stay put. Also, be sure to pack an extra set of pajamas, even if you're only going away for a night or two. Wetting the bed can be upsetting enough for some sensitive children, but to have a dry pair of regular

pajamas to slip into—and wake up wearing in the morning—can help lessen the upset.

9. **Use swim diapers every time** – Even if you feel pretty certain you're in the clear, don't take a chance. One accidental poop in the pool can shut down the resort swimming pool for four hours or even longer. You don't want to be that parent.

10. **Make peace with possible regression** – While some books and DVDs promise potty-training success in as few as 24 hours, they probably don't advocate taking a family vacation in the Caribbean, traveling to Grandma's big family reunion birthday party, or cashing in the frequent flyer miles for a long weekend in San Diego during this time—or any time soon after. Well, I do. Some children actually experience no setbacks in their potty training during travel, and it's hard to say what will happen for yours until you try. If your child does experience a temporary setback, know it will likely be overcome upon your return home.

Preparing Toddlers and Preschoolers for Travel

As parents, juggling the daily responsibilities of home and work while simultaneously grappling with the logistics of travel with car seats and safety boosters, airport transportation or parking reservations, rental car reservations, and so on, it can be easy to neglect that most important part in planning family travel: including the kids!

Set their courses for success, not frustration.
Like most of us, our toddlers and preschoolers like to know what is in store for them on an upcoming trip and to feel that they have their upcoming travel plans under control. But if you only mention the great payoff at the end of the rental car rainbow—a beach, a theme park, a favorite relative—you might be setting them up for a world of frustration on the way to it.

Help your toddler or preschooler form realistic expectations for the trip. Will there be a lot of time spent in the car, airplane, or train? Will there be a lot of other passengers sitting in rows around you as in a movie theater? Will you all need to ride buckled into your seats, including him in his car seat? Discuss it ahead of time and let him help plan ways you will pass—and *enjoy* the time together (see Planning Your In-Flight Entertainment, pg. 282, for ideas). Do what you can to help put it in his terms, too. For example, a three-hour car ride may be difficult to imagine, but explaining that "We'll need to drive the car the same amount of time it takes to watch three episodes of *Sesame Street*," may help put things into perspective and even prevent a few rounds of "Are we there yet?" (See also tips for Helping Toddlers and Preschoolers Prepare for the flight, pg. 286.)

Let them own a piece of the plan.
As well, when children feel involved in the process of travel and better know what to expect, they are much more likely to relax and enjoy the adventure. One of the best steps you can take toward easing travel with your toddler or preschooler is to help empower them to make good travel decisions for themselves. Will she need to sleep on the airplane for her regular naptime so she'll have energy to play with cousins when you arrive? Or will all of you spend the night on the aircraft? Let your child help figure out what all will be required—toothbrushes, bedtime books, pajamas or at least comfortable clothing, or a favorite blanket. And if you're really swimming in details you still need to nail down before your departure, let her "practice pack" a carry-on suitcase or her backpack for later inspection as you finish your work.

Broaden their horizons before leaving home.
There is no time like the present to help your small traveler become aware of customs and traditions—starting with your own right here at home. If there will be a special event, such as a wedding or holiday meal, discuss the details and customs that go along with an event of that nature and how to best participate. Will there be a special time when we'll be quiet and listen to music and poems? Will we sit around the table and put cloth napkins on our laps? Will there be a blessing given? Will it be appropriate to offer some help to our hosts—and what kinds of things can we do that might be helpful? Your child might even enjoy practicing some of these rituals at home, or staging a fun mock-version of the event (especially a Cautious Child or Slow-Adapting Child. See more on Travels with Your Child's Unique Temperament beginning on pg. 107).

Remember, the young child who feels empowered by travel is much more likely to enjoy traveling—both now and her whole life through. This is your opportunity to lay the foundation for success.

Tips for Raising a Happy Traveler

1. **Start traveling as soon as possible (before they know any better).** Babies get used to what they get used to, so think hard about how and where you want to spend your first two years together, and if that's not entirely in your home...get going!

2. **Emphasize "routines" over "schedules."** For example, we do this and this before going to bed, regardless of the time zone and whether or not we're sharing a room (or bed).

3. **Discourage brand loyalty.** This can help avert crises at Grandma's house as well as in restaurants and foreign markets. Even if your toddler's eating pasta seven meals a week, mix it up with different shapes and sauces (or butter or olive oil).

4. **Encourage a palate for universally available foods.** Rice, yogurt, vegetables, fruit, beans, and noodles can be had in virtually any country and don't differ too much from one home or restaurant to the next.

5. **Get a globe or put a world map on the wall and make reference to it often:** when reading a story about an Emperor in China, when watching a movie about animals in the Amazon, when mentioning cousins in Indiana, and of course, when planning your next adventure.

6. **Help your child form realistic expectations of travel.** If all he hears mentioned are the fun times you'll have when you get there, the 3-hour plane ride to get there may feel especially frustrating. If your "total trip" also includes time spent in the car, on an airplane or train, ferry or shuttle bus, or will require waiting in lines, make sure to mention it—along with an explanation of what you'll do during those times. Eventually, he may surprise you with some great suggestions of his own.

7. **Be the most enthusiastic traveler your child knows.** Share your excitement about where and how you will travel, express your gratitude for the circumstances allowing you to go, and even when you've been circling the airport for an extra hour you hadn't bargained for, never lose sight of the bigger picture of your trip and help your child to do the same.

8. **Praise your child for being a great traveler—every chance you get.** The rigors of travel can test any of us, and our kids are to be commended for every step of it they undertake with any amount of patience or grace. From infants taking their very first flights to toddlers lugging their own suitcase through a hotel lobby, little ears are listening to your affirmations.

9. **Create a travel scrapbook just for your child to record his adventures, large and small.** As he gets older, he can help choose the pictures and watch for special mementos along the way to add to his travel book. I like to print their favorite photos right from our printer (on good but not photo paper) and let them cut and paste them into their own books, along with ticket stubs from the trip. Over time, this has made it easier to get photos during the trip when they realize they want to capture a favorite moment for themselves, and they've become somewhat fanatical about hanging on to those sentimental ticket stubs (like their mother!).

Three Secrets to Stress-Free Travel with Kids

1. The belly laugh: don't leave home without it.

I was once asked what I thought was the single most important item to bring when traveling with a baby. Expecting to hear about some inventive piece of new baby gear or perhaps a travel-size pediatric first-aid kit, the man looked stunned as I answered, "Your sense of humor." It prevents nervous breakdowns, makes up for lost luggage, and magically minimizes unsightly stains—of which there can be plenty when traveling with a baby (remember, just "Grin and wear it"). And while humor probably won't help you find your way through the mazelike alleys of Venice when lost, you are far more likely to wander through this world with a pleasant look on your face and get the most out of your travels in spite of any bumps in the road. And so is your child.

2. Walk softly, and carry travel insurance.

Travel, by its very nature, brings with it a certain amount of uncertainty. Missed connections, delays, Montezuma's revenge, lost baggage, wrong turns, and train strikes can change the face of even the best-laid travel plans. All you can do is be as prepared as possible, and getting travel insurance will not only help you rest better in the nights before your trip as the first child at your preschool is sent home with flu, but it can make all the difference in case there's an unexpected change during your trip, like your suitcase starting its vacation on a nearby island (always pack your swimsuits in the carry-on, always) or your family missing its connecting flight—that only leaves Heathrow once a day. With the right travel insurance plan, your kids could be covered for free, and you may even be able to protect those frequent flier miles you've cashed in for the trip. (See recommendations of Travel Insurance for families at www.TravelswithBaby.com.)

3. Remember: Spit-up happens. Travel anyway.

I have also found it helpful to keep in mind that many of the difficulties that arose during our travels would have happened whether we'd stayed at home or not: the troublesome new tooth, the diaper blowout, even the ear infection. If you try to plan every trip around the possibility of a rough night with your child, you might never leave your home, and you'd still have your share of rough nights in the early years—but without the refreshing change of scenery during your days or the precious memories (and photos!) from your family's getaway. Just remember: spit-up happens. Wouldn't you rather it happens to *you* on the way to Waikiki?

✔ Ten Things to Do Before You Leave Home

☐ **Visit, or at least phone, your child's doctor.** Mention your travel plans and discuss any concerns you may have including: status of vaccinations, illness while traveling, sleep disturbances, food safety and allergies, and finding medical assistance for your child at your destination. If your child hasn't seen his doctor in a while, a check-up may be reassuring ("ears are clear," etc.), and it could be helpful for parents of infants and babies to have a current weigh-in.

☐ **Call your airline within 72 hours of your departure** to reconfirm your seat assignments and, if applicable, your bassinet reservation and/or children's meals (see Airplane Bassinet Checklist, pg. 264).

☐ **Check your child's travel kit** (see pg. 61) to see if any items are running low or need to be replaced. Move fingernail clippers, tweezers, and any other non-carry-on items into a checked bag.

☐ **Revisit Childproofing on the Go**, pg. 181.

☐ **Take inventory of the gear that will be traveling with you.** Is your car seat FAA approved for the flight and can you point to the label on it? Are the stroller wheels still up to snuff? Can you find the sun shields, mosquito nets, or other accessories you plan to take along?

☐ **Replace old sunscreens** (your brand and your child's) if you're heading for a sunny destination. Sunscreens lose their effectiveness with time, and small children need the best protection available.

☐ **Arrange to have your mail stopped** while you are away. You can do this quickly online at www.usps.com or by calling 1-800-ASK-USPS (1-800-275-8777).

☐ Remove anything in your refrigerator that will not outlast your trip.

☐ **Make arrangements with a neighbor or friend** to set out your garbage can and recyclables for pick up, feed pets, water plants, etc.

☐ **Empty your diaper pail!**

CHAPTER 6
Travels with Your Unique Child

Temperaments in Transit

As travel guru Rick Steves writes in his book *Europe Through the Back Door*, "Travel is intensified living—maximum thrills per minute and one of the last great sources of legal adventure." Of course, parenting a small child is no snooze either. When you combine the two, the results could either lead to a nervous breakdown or the best time off you've ever spent in your life. For the best family vacations possible, use this section to help identify and prepare for the most likely challenges that may surface during trips with your unique child.

You may have already noticed that your child thinks, behaves, and reacts to certain situations differently from his playmates, and perhaps even from how you do. Whereas one child may adapt seamlessly to changes in sleeping or eating schedules, a different child may be deeply troubled by these differences. Consider the cautious child who quietly observes at length before attempting a new activity, and then her more active counterpart who learns by simply doing—bruises, bumps, and all. These differences are not simply the consequences of good or bad behavior, nor, as parents with multiple children discover, environment or upbringing. What make children different from the get-go are their inborn temperaments.

"Temperament," as defined by *The American Heritage Dictionary*, is "The manner of thinking, behaving, or reacting characteristic of a specific person." In the late 1950s, researchers Alexander Thomas and Stella Chess identified key temperament traits that were present in individuals from birth, and influenced the way they developed and the choices they made throughout their lives. Researchers have found that often a child's dominant temperament traits can be identified as early as 4 months of age. In some children, just one temperament trait may dominate. In others, there may be multiple traits combining to create their unique worldview.

Recognizing your child's dominant temperament traits—and just as importantly, how you or your partner's may differ from your child—will give you a tremendous edge in planning your trips together as a family. As you read over the descriptions of the eight key temperament traits that follow, note where your child tends toward one extreme or the other and see the tips and suggestions that follow for traveling with children of these temperament types.

Activity Level: High Energy vs. Low Energy

High energy – Is your child highly active, needing much more physical exercise and freedom than many of his peers? Does it seem like he's constantly on the move, even when he's playing in one area?

Low energy – Is he more relaxed and content to sit still for long periods of time, playing with toys in one area of the room, or calmly watching TV?

Travel with the High-Energy Child

Try to keep this child as mentally active as possible during periods when he must remain in his car seat or at the table. Bring plenty of books or books on tape, and play soothing music to help keep him calm. Coloring books and even play-dough can be helpful. We've also found the "Doodle Pro" style of magnetic drawing boards indispensable during travel and in restaurants (no mess or loose pieces). Travel trays that attach to the car seat or stroller can provide an important space for activities and entertainment (see Travel Trays, pg. 78).

Everyday scrapes and bruises are more likely with this child at home and certainly while traveling, so keep the Band-Aids and antiseptic handy even while sightseeing. Injuries could be a real concern when visiting destinations outside the U.S. where safety standards (railings, windows, crosswalks) are not what they are at home, and where pedestrians do not have the right of way.

When flying, avoid pre-boarding the aircraft with this child, and instead let him remain physically active as long as possible. Book bulkhead row seats to help avoid battles over kicking a forward passenger's seat on aircraft. On trains, try for seating configurations with tables where he can color and keep busy, or where two rows of seats face each other so he can play on the floor in between.

If you need to make a long-haul or overseas flight with this child, try to schedule a nighttime flight when his energy level will be lowest (even if he doesn't sleep, he will hopefully be more content to sit still). Pack along some boxes of shelf-stable milk and crackers to help avoid juices and sugary foods while traveling.

Travel with the Low-Energy Child

This child not only shows a tolerance for stroller use much longer than some children, at times he may even prefer to sit and be strolled on your vacation, and that's just fine—simply taking in the new surroundings may be using much of his energy (especially if he is also Cautious or Slow-Adapting). Try to choose a travel stroller that will accommodate a higher upper weight limit and longer legs (usually 40+ lbs), and you will likely get your money's worth as you continue to use it for trips during the preschool years.

Plan vacations packed with sit-and-do activities, like building sand castles and watching sharks and jellyfish at the aquarium. For trips by car, train, or airplane, he may be quite content to pass the time in his seat so long as he has something to do (audio books, drawing boards, or movies). On very busy and active days, respect that he will need some down time to recharge his batteries, and plan breaks accordingly.

Approach to New Things: Eager vs. Cautious

Eager – Does he rush into new places, ready to explore, find the best toys, and make new friends? To see what snacks might be available? Is he happy to try a new food or wear a new jacket?

Cautious – Is he slow to warm up to new people and surroundings? Is he hesitant to talk with strangers and new acquaintances, turning away from them and in toward you? Does he prefer tried and true toys and clothes, and the same favorite books?

Florence, Oregon: My "Eager" traveler in action. No sooner can I make it up to the sleeping loft of this vacation rental behind her than she's standing on a futon, dismantling a lamp with one hand, and with the other hand? She has just discovered a latch that lets the window open—outward (this is when Mommy drops her camera).

Travel with the Eager Child

Childproofing is a top concern when arriving on a new scene, as this child may waste no time in testing every drawer, window, door, and balcony rail before you can take off your jacket. Be ready to explore *together* so you can act on any unsafe situations and explain any new safety rules or procedures. Stand guard when entering the territory of unfamiliar pets (e.g., a relative's home) as your child may get too familiar too quickly for some animals. Also be on the lookout for street dogs, strays, and wild animals so you can hopefully spot them before your child does.

Each feature of the hotel room calls to him—the hair dryer, the shampoo bottles, the minibar, the phone (unplug it if you must to avoid constant battles). For relaxing vacations, it will be important to plan trips in spaces where safety concerns are minimal and activities are abundant. To your advantage, this child will most likely be delighted to join children's activity programs and drop-off nurseries, mingling with other children, discovering new toys, and engaging in activities, allowing you to join the snorkel trip or kick back by the pool without guilt.

Travel with the Cautious Child

Whenever possible, seat yourself between your child and strangers or people she is not familiar with, even if they are relatives you yourself have known since birth. Family reunions can especially overwhelm this child, where many people may expect hugs and kisses, as well as holding privileges. Remember that you are your child's advocate, and be ready and willing to politely say no to people on her behalf. Practice saying phrases like, "Now's not a good time—maybe later," and "She's a little shy, just give her some time."

She may prefer to observe other children playing in the splash pool or on the playground from a safe distance before joining in, or need your company while she gets familiar with the new children and supervisors at a kids' camp type program at the resort or on your cruise ship. Understand that in all likelihood, you may be your child's playmate for the duration of your trip, so plan for activities you can both enjoy together. Your child is not just slow to warm up to new people, but also to other novelties including places and foods. Pack along some favorite snacks from home to help while she adjusts to new cuisine, or be prepared to do some of your own cooking. Single-destination vacations are favorable.

Physical Regularity: Very Regular vs. Unpredictable

Very regular – Does your child keep a consistent schedule with little influence from you? Does she sleep and wake at the same times each day, nap for similar lengths of time, and even have bowel movements at predictable times?

Unpredictable – Do her physiological needs and functions vary from day to day, with different waking times and varied lengths of naps? Is it hard to anticipate when the next bowel movement will strike? Or whether or not she will take an afternoon nap?

Travel with the Very Regular Child

Use her predictability to your advantage when planning your vacation days. You will have the benefit of knowing ahead of time what to expect in the way of nap times and duration, appetite, energy levels, and even bowel movements. Ideally, the itinerary will fit her existing schedule as much as possible, allowing for her regular meal and nap times, and her usual bedtime (within reason). If your child goes to bed earlier than you, consider a vacation rental apartment, condo, or suite with a separate space for her to sleep in while you enjoy the balcony, lanai, hot tub, a good book, or a long bath. It might be helpful to have a baby monitor with you (bring yours or rent one from a local baby gear rental agency).

Plan ahead to take turns with your partner staying in and resting or reading while she naps while the other goes out to do activities, whether enjoying the pool, going for a jog, visiting a museum, enjoying a spa treatment, or simply taking a break to read in a local café. If flights or drives are timed with her naps, the travel gods will likely smile upon you as long as she has what she needs to be comfortable (see Changes in

Napping Routines, pg. 92). Try to avoid red-eye flights that will interrupt her sleeping schedule. When adapting to a big change in time zones, you might want to set the alarm clock on arrival for her usual wake-up time in the new time zone and jump back into the schedule as quickly as possible.

Travel with the Unpredictable Child

This child comes with his own set of checks and balances as far as travel is concerned. What you may gain in the way of flexibility (interrupted sleeping routines), you may make up for in surprises (blow-outs and unexpected trips to the bathroom). Although there is no guarantee he will nap on the flight, there's no reason to assume the worst if he doesn't—he'll more than likely make up for lost sleep at a later time (a comfortable travel stroller will help him get the extra zzz's he needs when he needs them without slowing you down).

His unpredictable appetite means that he may not eat enough at formal mealtimes to carry him through the day's activities. In fact, in restaurants, it may be wise to offer him part of your meal rather than paying for a child's meal that may sit untouched (accept the doggie bags with grace). If his eating schedule does differ from yours, remind yourself that he may be feeling hungry at times when you are not, and always be sure to carry some snacks with you to fend off the blood sugar blues. Accommodations with kitchens, or at least refrigerators, can help meet his varying needs for food (one of our children often does well with a bowl of cereal or other snack at bedtime to help round out missed calories during the day).

Because his elimination process may "ebb and flow," always keep back-up clothing in the carry-on or diaper bag, and consider purchasing an extra car seat cover or the Piddle Pad (see more products in Pottying On the Go, pg. 98). Accidents are more likely during the potty-training era for this child, so plan and pack accordingly, and it will feel like much less of a problem if you choose accommodations where you'll have easy access to laundry.

Adaptability: Fast-Adapting vs. Slow-Adapting

Fast-adapting – Does she adjust quickly to changes in routine or scenery, go with the flow when it's time to change from the crib to the toddler bed, or wear the purple pajamas instead of the pink without complaint?

Slow-adapting – Does it take a while for her to sleep or eat normally in new settings? Is it a big problem if the usual nightlight, stuffed animal, or book isn't present at bedtime?

Travel with the Fast-Adapting Child

The stars are in your favor when you travel with this child. New scenery, new foods, and new faces are generally not a problem, and may even be met with enthusiasm. Although this trait may be a great strength when it comes to traveling, be aware that it may also bring other traits closer to the surface that shouldn't be taken for granted during travel. Remember the expression, "I'm easy to get along with…when things go my way."

Consider, for example, a Fast-adapting child with Low Energy. She may move from one activity and destination to the next seamlessly, until suddenly her energy reserve is depleted. Without warning, she seems to melt or has a tantrum from out of the blue, and you find yourself thinking, "This isn't like her." Yet once she gets the rest or down time she needs, she is back to her usual self.

If she is Fast-adapting and Eager, you may need to plan a vacation with plenty of different activities and/or other children to play with to help keep her happily engaged and, if you yourself are *not* Fast-adapting and Eager, from driving you up a tree. She may be ready for kids' clubs earlier than most, so look for resorts and cruise lines with programs that accommodate younger travelers, especially those who are not fully potty trained (see Best All-Inclusive Resorts with Children Under 5, pg. 54, and the Cruise Lines comparison table, pg. 391).

Travel with the Slow-Adapting Child

As a general rule, the fewer transitions necessary the better the vacation with this child, so you may lean toward vacations centered on one location, with similar sights and activities each day. Start preparing this child for the trip well in advance, creating a picture in her mind of what she can expect. If you are Fast-adapting, retrain your brain to think in her terms and realize that details you might not even consider worth mentioning in advance, like where you will be seated in the airplane and how everyone will need to wear seatbelts, are very important to her process.

Your transitions during travel will be much easier when you walk her through each step of your vacation beforehand, including how you will get to and through the airport, where you will be staying, and what you will do each day. Read a book about a trip on an airplane or the destination you will visit together. If she's old enough, let her help you pack for the trip, discussing in detail the things you will see and do and how you will use the items in the suitcase or carry-on. Discuss where she will sleep and in what kind of bed (bringing a familiar travel bed or bedding can be helpful).

As you travel, give her as much advance warning as possible when you will be changing activities or locations, whether it's leaving the hotel swimming pool, getting back into the car, or going to a restaurant. When flying, choose seats toward the rear of aircraft where she can better observe the goings-on during your flight, including the drink or meal service and passengers using the lavatory.

Try to time arrivals at new destinations early in the day so that she has time to adjust to her new surroundings before dinner and bedtime. Familiar bedtime routines will be extremely important on vacation with this child, as her supply of adaptability may well be depleted by day's end.

Intensity: Intense vs. Mellow

Intense – Does he express his likes and dislikes on a grand scale? Does he use his body to help express his feelings, tensing muscles or emphasizing with his hands?

Mellow – Do you need to watch closely or ask to know if he is enjoying something or not? Do you need to remind him to take off his jacket when he gets too warm?

Travel with the Intense Child

Watch vigilantly for your child's cues, especially if he's beginning to show signs of overstimulation, fatigue, or discomfort. You'll want to address any of his needs or concerns before they escalate. If he acts out in a public space (of which there are so many during travel!), remember that yelling will only throw more fuel on his fire. And if he throws a tantrum in the car, stop when it is safe and get to the bottom of the real problem.

Although it's important not to give in to unrealistic requests or misbehavior, it will be wise to try to uncover and address the deeper need (e.g., low blood sugar, fatigue, a frustration from not being heard, boredom, anxiety about what's coming next) so that everyone can proceed happily with the vacation—or flight. Although you may need to stay on your toes much of the time traveling with this child, you will also be rewarded for your efforts with outstanding displays of his joy and delight when things go right.

Travel with the Mellow Child

Similar to the Low-sensitivity child, you will need to check in regularly to make sure she's getting what she needs in the way of food, drinks, and temperature control—enough clothing or too much? Illness can creep up on her quietly as you likely won't hear much complaint until it surfaces full-blown, so don't overlook the possibility of an ear infection or other illness developing as you travel if other clues are presenting themselves.

Also, watch for signs of discomfort in new social settings, such as the family reunion, the kiddie pool at the resort, or the dining room on the cruise ship, and help her give voice to those feelings. You may head off some potential crises by coaxing out her concerns early on and addressing them. If you miss her subtle cues, she may not express her feelings until much later, sometimes by acting out. Otherwise, she's an easygoing traveler in most respects—enjoy!

Mood: Positive vs. Negative

Positive – Does your child usually look at the world through rose-colored glasses? Does she most often walk into the room with a smile? Does she assume unknown children will be friends?

Negative – Does she frequently anticipate trouble or disappointment, view new children or toys with suspicion, or first see others as a potential threat? Does it take a little time for her to be convinced and the clouds to clear?

Travel with the Positive Child

Most destinations and activities are perfectly fine with this child, especially since it probably wouldn't occur to him that he might *not* like taking a trip somewhere (unless a Negative sibling tries to plant the seed!). He goes along happily with most activities, expecting the best of your vacation plans, and trusting a good time will be had by all.

But while travel with the Positive child may sound like a piece of cake, you probably already know better than to put your parenting skills on autopilot with him. Be very careful not to overlook his other dominant traits that may be obscured by his overly rosy outlook until reaching a crisis state. For example, a Positive and Highly Sensitive (see pg. 121) child might be having too much fun at the arcade to realize he's maxed-out his sensory threshold—until he suddenly reaches the breaking point. A very Positive child who is also Low-energy may run himself ragged before realizing he needs to slow down or stop and rest, which could mean you spend the rest of the afternoon resting in your room rather than hiking to the waterfall (unless you have a child carrier or backpack that can accommodate him; see recommendations beginning on pg. 72).

Travel with the Negative Child

"Uncertainty of the unknown" can bring out her lower expectations for your trip, so help her keep her eyes on the prize by sharing pictures of the beaches or city you'll visit, showing her vacation brochures, and visiting relevant websites ahead of time. Help assure her she'll have some control over things, but don't put her in charge of the vacation.

Encourage her to try new things, but help assure her she'll have some options if she doesn't like them. For example, if she tries the kids' camp program for an afternoon but doesn't like it, she won't have to go back, or if she tries a bite of your salmon pasta and doesn't like it, she can have a hot dog. Agree that you'll go to the museum and see X, Y, Z important things at the top of your list (Mona Lisa, Etruscans…), and let her check them off your guide map as you go. Afterward, you'll break for lunch, and then do something at the top of her list, which you can keep in your purse to revisit as appropriate.

When her other dominant temperament traits are challenged, it can especially trigger negative feelings, so be sure to honor her other temperament traits and watch for signs. For example, the Negative and Highly Sensitive child may suddenly "hate everything" at the zoo when she is simply overheating and needs to take a shade break with a cold drink.   When your Negative child reaches preschool age, it can be helpful to get her in the habit of using alternative phrases like:

I don't like it! → I'd prefer something else.
I don't want to! → I'd rather do something else.

Not only does it sound more polite, but it replaces the "all or nothing" kind of thought pattern with a new emphasis on finding a solution. Not only will that be valuable in life, but it's essential to having a family vacation that everyone can enjoy, big and small.

Attention Span: Distractible vs. Focused

Very distractible – Is your child easily distracted from the activity at hand, jumping up from story time to investigate a toy across the room? Is it easy to move from an outburst to a new activity by simply suggesting it?

Very focused – Does she focus well on one activity or toy at a time, regardless of changes around her? Is it a challenge to change activities when she's engaged in a drawing or playing with a certain toy?

Vancouver, British Columbia: What a "Very Focused" child looks like. My daughter could have spent the entire afternoon enjoying this one exhibit at the Vancouver Aquarium—seriously. We had to agree to a cut-off time.

Travel with the Very Distractible Child

You may need to pack a little extra patience when traveling with this child, as a crack in the ground on the path to the beach may be every bit as interesting to him as the beach itself. You never know when something will catch his fancy, or what it will be next.

This child may have trouble eating enough at meal times while you are out at restaurants, in a ship's dining room, or on an airplane or a train. Help him stay focused on his food—and seated at the table—by bringing a familiar dining booster from home and seating him as far from the busiest distractions as possible, like away from the kitchen, the entrance, or windows, if possible. You may even want to feed him something in your room first to be sure he gets enough to eat.

Be very careful in airports, and especially at train stations where something may catch his attention before you realize he's off and exploring. Use your stroller to keep your child safely strapped in while you check in at the airport or use a public restroom. Child safety harnesses (a.k.a. "leashes") could be a very wise idea for toddlers and early preschoolers that are prone to bolting or wandering wherever there's just too much exciting new stuff to see, observe, and explore—especially if yours is also a Highly Active child. Be prepared that your child may not sleep a wink on the airplane or train (see Changes in Sleeping Routines and Changes in Napping Routines, beginning on pg. 88). On the bright side, with your positive and enthusiastic prompting, this child will usually move from one site or activity to the next without much hesitation, allowing you to enjoy many experiences in a shorter vacation.

Travel with the Very Focused Child

One of the great perks of travel with a Very Focused child is that long car rides or flights are not too much trouble as long as she has an activity to work at or travel toy she enjoys (art and creative projects are ideal). Not every aspect of travel with this child is going to be so easy.

Where the Very Distractible child may wander into harm's way in pursuit of a distraction while out and about, the Very Focused child may fixate on some particular hazard in hotel room—an air-conditioning wall unit, an outlet or accessible power strip, the hair dryer with the curly cord—and be very difficult to distract from it without rearranging the furniture or leaving the room (read Childproofing on the Go, pg. 181, and address what you can on arrival, before she zeros in on something unsafe).

Taking in too many differing sights and activities in a day can be frustrating for this child, when just as she becomes fully engaged with one place or one toy, she has to let go and turn her attention to something new. While you might expect that giving her plenty of notice when, in ten minutes…and in five minutes…and in two minutes…you'll all be switching gears, it may not do much to "break the trance" of a very focused child. It may be more helpful to simply join her at her level when it's time, putting a gentle hand on her shoulder, and making eye contact when you first explain what needs to happen next.

It may also be helpful to bring along a special travel toy, activity book, or puzzle that she can return to throughout your trip as a reprieve from many changes around her. To your advantage, she may be entertained at length by the same fountain in the park, exhibit at the aquarium, or bucket of toys at the beach, giving you a chance to relax and enjoy the moment as well.

Sensitivity: High Sensitivity vs. Low Sensitivity

Highly sensitive – Is he easily upset by loud noises, bright lights, and stimulating environments? Does he wake up easily from unexpected noises?

Low sensitivity – Could he happily go about his business in the middle of a tornado? Do you need to remind him to adjust his volume in some social settings, or not to play with other children's toys without asking?

Travel with the Highly Sensitive Child

In the restaurant or along the boardwalk, the food options, noises, or odors may make it difficult to feed this child at the same time and place as others in the family, so when possible, plan a vacation that will take the pressure off at meal times rather than put it on. Having flexible dining options and the ability to create custom meals at your accommodations could be especially important ingredients for a happy family vacation with the Highly Sensitive child.

In addition to experiencing her own frustrations, this child picks up on other people's frustrations as well, so also take care with how you express yourself when the trip doesn't go as planned (flight or train delays, traffic jams, lost luggage, etc.). If she is sensitive to noise, request a room away from the elevator or ice machine, and prepare for takeoff and landing by saying "We'll hear the engines start in a minute, they'll sound like a loud hum...can you hear them now?" to help assure her unfamiliar noises and sensations, including those in her ears, are as they should be.

Accept that Disneyland-type experiences may simply be overwhelming for this child in her early years—three rides may be enough for her, regardless of how long you planned to visit. Be careful not to plan too tight of itineraries as what feels like a full, fun day to you may get to be too much pressure to arrive too many places on time, and too many different experiences to process in her own special way. If you're thinking travel with a highly sensitive child sounds like too much trouble, just wait until you hear her recounting memories from your vacation of things you'd barely noticed at the time, all making you realize how deeply she experiences travel and appreciate what a keen mind she has for details (look forward to some great travel journals as she grows!).

Travel with the Low-Sensitivity Child

This child has few inhibitions, and usually few complaints, which makes him an easy travel companion in many respects. However, you may want to avoid red-eye and overnight long-haul flights and train rides where he might not sense or appreciate that other passengers are trying to sleep before he is ready to.

When visiting holy places, be sure to explain to toddlers and preschoolers ahead of time what makes the place extra special and what you will and won't do while visiting it. Remember to check in with your child frequently to make sure he is comfortable as he might not notice his discomfort until it becomes a real problem, like carsickness, low blood sugar, or dehydration.

Also, be aware that low-sensitivity can sometimes amplify other traits. For example, an eager child with low sensitivity may talk the ear off a stranger during your train ride—which can be great, so long as the stranger doesn't mind. And an active child with low sensitivity may literally climb the walls, which won't be a problem if you vacation somewhere with a playground and plenty of suitable structures for him to climb!

More Tools for Temperament

In the words of Sir Francis Bacon, "Knowledge is power," and knowledge about your child's temperament can be a powerful tool for parenting—while on vacation and at home. If you'd like to learn more about temperament, here are some helpful resources for parents and caregivers.

Online Assessment and Information

The Preventive Ounce is a nonprofit organization and research project created to better help parents understand their children's temperaments. Visit their website to create a custom temperament forecast for your infant, toddler, or preschooler and use it to help navigate upcoming issues for your unique child in the months ahead. Find out more at www.preventiveoz.org.

Helpful Books on Temperament

Raising Your Spirited Child: A Guide for Parents Whose Child Is More Intense, Perceptive, Persistent, and Energetic, by Mary Sheedy Kurcinka, 2006, Harper Paperbacks (revised edition).

The Temperament Perspective: Working with Children's Behavioral Styles, by Jan Kristal (Foreword by Stella Chess), 2005, Paul H. Brookes Publishing Co., Inc.

Temperament Tools: Working with Your Child's Inborn Traits, by Helen Neville and Diane Clark Johnson, 1998, Parenting Press, Inc. (Foreword by James Cameron, Ph.D.).

Understanding Temperament: Strategies for Creating Family Harmony, by Lyndall Shick, 1998, Parenting Press, Inc.

Part III:
Special Considerations

CHAPTER 7

The Baby Abroad

When Does Your Child Need a Passport?

For virtually all international travel, your child, even as an infant, will need a valid passport. At time of writing, there are two situations where your child under 16 years old may still travel internationally without a passport, though doing so could prove very complicated in the event of an emergency.

In either of these situations, your child and any member of your family traveling that is traveling without a passport would not be able to board an international flight home if needed, so I strongly advise you get passports for everyone traveling internationally in your family in spite of these allowances:

- **Kids by land or by sea:** U.S. and Canadian children 15 years and younger may still travel to and from contiguous territory (including Mexico for U.S. children) by land or by sea with an original or certified copy of a birth certificate, a Consular Report of Birth Abroad, a Naturalization Certificate, or a Canadian Citizenship Card.

- **Closed-loop cruises:** U.S. adults and children may be allowed to embark on certain "closed loop" cruises, where they depart from and return to the same U.S. port on the same ship, with a WHTI-compliant (Western Hemisphere Travel Initiative) document that provides proof of citizenship such as an original or certified copy of a birth certificate. Adults must also have a government-issued photo ID.

Again, if there is any unexpected event—one of your family members requires hospitalization, there is a sudden problem at home, a weather event dictates a sudden change of plans, or there is a problem with your ship—any members of your family without valid passports will not be able to take an international flight back into the U.S. without a valid passport.

Your Child's First U.S. Passport

When passports are required for air travel, they are required of *everyone*, even newborns and infants. Be prepared to present passports for each family member, any required visas, and other required travel documents whenever you cross international borders with your child, including when you travel between the U.S. and the Caribbean, Bermuda, Panama, Mexico, and Canada.

As with any first-time passport application, your child will have to apply for his passport in person. A few things differ when applying for passports for minors under the age of 14, however. In addition to proof of citizenship, you must also:

- Provide proof of relationship to the applying parents or guardians.

- Provide parental identification, and appear together, both parents in person, or submit a notarized statement of consent from the absent parent (form DS-3053, available online at www.travel.state.gov).

- To save time, you can print your child's passport application from the U.S. Department of State website at www.travel.state.gov/passport and complete it at home. Sure, you might feel a little silly stating the color of eyes that may still be changing—or the color of hair that has yet to sprout. Just do the best you can and remember that you'll get a second chance in another 5 years when your child's first passport expires. Following are the step-by-step instructions on getting your child's first passport.

First passport: This could be the start of something good...

Steps to Getting Your Child's First Passport:

1. **Fill out an application form.** You can download a passport application form (DS-11) online from www.travel.state.gov/passport or pick one up from any passport agency to fill out in advance. Do NOT sign it until you are standing before the Passport Acceptance Agent and are told to do so.

2. **Submit proof of U.S. citizenship for your child.** Most commonly, this is a certified U.S. birth certificate with a raised registrar's seal.

3. **Present evidence of child's relationship to parents or guardians.** A certified U.S. birth certificate that names both parents will suffice. Also acceptable: an adoption decree with adopting parents' names, certification of birth abroad with parents' names, or a court order establishing custody or guardianship.

4. **Provide identification for parents.** Your own valid U.S. or foreign passport, driver's license, military or government ID, or alien resident card from BCIS.

5. **Appear and sign in person—BOTH parents.** Yes, BOTH parents must be present at the time of application, or one parent may appear and sign if there is a notarized statement of consent authorizing passport issuance signed by the second parent (form DS-3053, also downloadable at www.travel.state.gov/passport). If there is no other parent to apply, you must submit proof of "sole authority to apply," such as a certified birth certificate or court order listing only one parent as guardian, or death certificate of the non-applying parent.

6. **Provide two passport photos.** Photos must be identical to each other, measure 2" x 2" in size, and have been taken in the past 6 months, showing "current appearance"! More details on photos and how you can take your own follow in the next section.

7. **Provide a social security number.** You will need to provide your child's social security number.

8. **Pay the fees.** Passport fees include an application fee and an execution fee. For children under age 16, the current fee for a passport book is $80, and the execution fee is $25, for a grand total of $105 (fees may change).

9. **Wait for the passport.** With increased demand for U.S. passports, 10 weeks is not an unusual amount of time to wait for processing. If you are in a hurry, you may pay an additional $60 to expedite processing, and pay for faster shipping methods each way (overnight or priority).

Getting a Passport Photo for Your Child

Getting an acceptable passport photo for someone who can't even sit up—let alone support his own head—can be a bit challenging. Be warned that some passport paparazzi simply refuse to photograph infants, and even toddlers, but a few have come up with creative methods to get the shot. Call prospective passport photographers first to make sure they will accommodate your needs (and timing), or better yet, take your own photos at home.

If you have a basic digital camera, you can easily save yourself the sitting fee, time, and potential chaos of having a stranger snap the shot. You can use your computer or the equipment at your local drug store to crop the picture as needed and print your copies. Here are the guidelines and some tips for taking your child's passport photo yourself.

Guidelines for Taking Your Child's Passport Photo:

- Your child should appear against a plain white background—a simple bed sheet, blanket, or white wall will suffice.

- Your child's face should appear in full view, looking directly at the camera (think "nose level"). If your child is still an infant, enlist a helper to prop him up against one hand, or simply photograph him lying down and looking straight up at the camera. Just be sure your photo is not taken at a strange angle and doesn't obscure part of his face.

- The final photos should be 2" x 2", with your child's face (from chin to top of head, including any hair) appearing at least 1" and not more than 1 3/8".

Passports for Canadian Children

For citizens of Canada, applying for your child's first passport is a similar process to that in the U.S., though you may not have to apply in person. While Canadian children who had received passports while younger than 3 years old used to receive passports valid for no more than 3 years (with a free one-time replacement), this has been phased out in favor of the new 5-year ePassport for all children 15 years and younger.

- **Children 0 to 15 years of age** – Passports issued to children in this age range are valid for 5 years. Current fee: $57 Canadian.

- **Proof of parentage (revised in 2012)** – A passport application for a child under 16 years must include one of the following to prove the child-parent relationship: a long-form birth certificate issued by the Canadian provincial or territorial vital statistics office that includes the name of the parents (also accepted as proof of Canadian citizenship), a court-issued adoption order indicating the name of the adoptive parent(s), or a foreign birth certificate that indicates the name of the parent(s).

- **Passport photos** – Dimensions of Canadian passport photos should be 2" wide by 2 ¾" long. Canadians residing in the U.S. may submit U.S.-size passport photos, however.

- **You need not apply in person** – You may send your child's application by mail, but you must have the Declaration of Guarantor section of the form completed by an eligible guarantor who has known you for at least 2 years. The guarantor must also sign a statement on the back of one of your child's passport photos to certify that it is a true likeness of the child. (See more requirements of the Guarantor at www.pptc.gc.ca).

Printable forms and instructions are online at Passport Canada: www.pptc.gc.ca/forms or you can call 1-800-567-6868 from within Canada or 1-819-997-8338 from the U.S. and other countries.

Canadian children traveling across borders with one parent or other caregivers should also carry with them a notarized letter of consent, similar to the sample shown on pg. 133.

Travels with One Parent, Grandparents, or Others

If you will be traveling with your child across international borders without her other birth parent—whether by airplane, automobile, train, or cruise ship—you must have a notarized letter of consent from the other parent which includes the names of all children traveling, name of adult(s) accompanying children, dates of travel, method of travel (e.g., cruise line, airline), countries to be visited, and the consenting parent's contact information. The same situation applies when a child will be traveling abroad with his grandparents or other adults that are not his parents, and a similar letter will need to be written and signed by both parents, and notarized.

Following is a sample letter of consent you may customize for your trip. Also included in the sample letter is a clause giving permission to the "trip custodian" to authorize any necessary routine or emergency medical treatment during the trip—which is especially recommended when a child will be traveling without either parent.

If you are legally the sole guardian of the traveling child, you may instead provide the legal documentation that names you as such, be it a court order of sole custodianship, a death certificate, a birth certificate that names only you as parent to the child, or an adoption decree.

Parents and Children with Different Names

Parents should be prepared to provide proof of their relationship to their child in spite of the difference in names appearing on passports, e.g., a mother that has chosen to keep her maiden name, which is different from her child's surname. Most commonly, a notarized copy of a birth certificate that lists both parents can be used to provide this information. When traveling abroad, even hyphenated last names may cause confusion at some borders, so any extra documentation that may help explain your naming convention and expedite your crossing could be of help.

Sample Letter of Consent for One Parent Traveler or Other Guardians:

Date: [DATE OF WRITING]

I/we [YOUR NAME] give consent for my/our minor child(ren) [CHILD OR CHILDREN'S FULL NAMES] to travel to [NAMES OF ALL COUNTRIES TO BE VISITED] with [FULL NAME(S) OF ADULT TRAVEL COMPANION(S)] from [DATE OF DEPARTURE] to [DATE OF RETURN] aboard:

[LIST ALL AIRLINES AND FLIGHT NUMBERS, CRUISE LINES, TRAIN NUMBERS, OR STATE "BY AUTOMOBILE"].

In addition, I/we give permission to [NAMED ADULT TRAVEL COMPANION(S)] to authorize any necessary routine or emergency medical treatment for our child(ren) during this trip.

If needed, I/we may be contacted at:
[YOUR PHONE NUMBER(S)]
[YOUR ADDRESS]

[YOUR PRINTED NAME(S)]
[YOUR SIGNED NAME(S)]

Notary's printed name:
Notary's signature and seal:

Convenient Conversions

Renting car seats, buying diapers, determining which over-the-counter remedy is right for your child as you travel…there will likely be times on your trip that you'll need to know weights and measures in the local system. Before you leave, at least be sure to jot down your child's current weight and height in metric, or in the U.S. Customary System, in case you need it. These quick-reference conversions are also included in the *Take-Along Travels with Baby* guidebook (where you can also record your child's current measures with your Trip Notes) in case you need them as you travel.

Children's Weights in Pounds and Kilograms:

7 lbs = 3 kgs
10 lbs = 4.5 kgs
13 lbs = 6 kgs
18 lbs = 8 kgs
22 lbs = 10 kgs
33 lbs = 15 kgs
44 lbs = 20 kgs
55 lbs = 25 kgs
67 lbs = 30 kgs
80 lbs = 36 kgs
88 lbs = 40 kgs

Children's Heights in Inches and Centimeters:

18.5" = 47 cm
22" = 56 cm
25" = 63.5 cm
28" = 71 cm
30" = 76.2 cm
32" = 81 cm
35" = 89 cm
38" = 96.5 cm
41" = 104 cm
45" = 114 cm
48" = 122 cm

Temperatures in Celsius and Fahrenheit (Rounded)

0°C	32°F	30°C	85°F
7° C	45°F	35°C	95°F
15°C	60°F	40°C	104°F
24°C	75°	Normal body temperature: 37°C or 98.6°F	

At Least They'll Speak "English"

When choosing a destination abroad, your little family may find it somewhat comforting to choose one that frees you from carrying a traveler's phrase book in your already crowded diaper bag. But that would be too easy, and hardly worthy of the stamp in your passport. So as your little Ambassador of Goodwill launches you into conversations with the Queen's locals or other members of the ex-Commonwealth, you may find it helpful to commit to memory a little of the baby-speak. If it begins to sound a bit silly to you, just remember that *they* are the ones speaking English.

American	British
Stroller	Pushchair
Travel stroller	Buggy
Baby buggy	Perambulator (or pram)
Pacifier	Dummy
Diapers	Nappies
Crib	Cot
Portacrib	Travel cot
Airplane bassinet	Sky cot

Preparing for Cultural Differences

Your guidebook warns you to cover your shoulders when visiting the sacred places, to remove your shoes when entering a home, and to never place your chopsticks on your bowl in "prayer" position. But there are some cultural differences that only the traveler with a baby may appreciate.

Hands Off My Baby!

Throughout much of the world, and in Asian cultures especially, it is considered quite normal and even polite to touch a stranger's baby when expressing admiration and affection for the child. The stroking of your infant's cheeks, tickling of her feet, and squeezing of her hands (that almost immediately go back into the mouth) may happen at any turn.

As we traveled to the Far East with our firstborn, we were shocked as everyone from flight attendants, rifle-toting security guards, cigarette-smoking taxi drivers, and a broom-wielding street sweeper (while holding the trash collection bag) had their hands on our baby before we could blink. We soon came to appreciate the times when strangers only briefly pinched her cheeks or held her hands before allowing us to go on our way.

Be warned: A quick clap of the hands and extension of the arms is code for, "Give me the baby." Although holding a stranger's baby is considered a perfectly normal expectation to many people in the world, it can be extremely alarming to the average American parent, who would never dream of passing her child off to a stranger—especially while visiting a foreign land. However, if your child is secured in a frontpack carrier or stroller, you have one immediate layer of defense, making it much easier to smile in acknowledgment of a compliment, but continue on your way.

In restaurants and on airplanes, you may have a more difficult time politely escaping the requests of your child's admirers. But if you aren't comfortable letting strangers hold your child, don't. Just remember, your obligation is first and foremost to your child, not random strangers you meet on your journey. If you still feel awkward, or cornered, just say your child is shy, or explain that it's naptime and you don't want to excite the little one.

The Real "Tourist Attraction"

In some cultures, children are so revered that you may find your family surrounded by a small crowd of locals at times, especially if yours is the first child of its kind that they've seen in real life (with light hair and light eyes, in particular). It can, at times, border on frustrating as you try to make your way to the dock on time, compete for a taxi cab, or breastfeed your baby without a flock of strangers snapping photos with cellular phones. Or as you enter a much-anticipated holy site in respectful barefooted silence, only to find an enthusiastic group of worshippers facing not the Golden Buddha before you, but the golden child in your arms. Hands are no longer pressed together in prayer, but are clapping along to sing-song rhymes as they compete for the biggest smiles from your child. If it should happen to you, embrace the moment. It may well become one of your fondest memories of traveling as a parent.

Temple of the Emerald Buddha at the Grand Palace, Bangkok: Just try and stop the waving and giggles.

Attracting Older Women

In places like Korea, India, and Italy, where grandmothers play a key role in the upbringing of children, older women may especially show an interest in your child—every time you turn around. Get ready. Grandma knows why your baby is crying. Grandma knows what your baby needs. And rest assured, Grandma is here to help. She will tell you what you need to know to be a better mother, even if you can't understand a word she's saying.

One American mother living in Italy quickly came to accept that any time she left her house with the baby, she'd better bring a sweater—even on a hot summer's day. Every twenty paces along the city street, a different grandma would stop her to admire the baby and quickly convey the shock and horror that the baby was too cold and she needed to put on its sweater right away. Twenty paces later, another grandma would insist that the baby was too hot and the sweater must come off at once. Twenty more paces, and the child would die of exposure if the sweater wasn't put on at once.

Trips to the market became exhausting for mother and child alike, but she quickly discovered it was much easier to bring the sweater along than to have a grandma follow her all the way home, to make sure she got more clothing for the baby.

Yet, as annoying as it may be at times, you have to appreciate how lucky the communities watched over by grandmas are to have them. Try not to take offense if you are offered suggestions or unsolicited advice. Remember that, as a traveler, you are a guest in someone else's country, and you wouldn't be there if you didn't have some interest in experiencing the culture. So, smile. Nod. Say, "Thank you, Grandma," when you've had enough and hightail it on to your next destination.

Breastfeeding and Other Cultures

Although breastfeeding is "back in fashion" in much of North America, as in much of Western society, there are still pockets where you'll find people unaccustomed to seeing babies nurse, especially in public and social situations—which is where you'll often find yourself as a traveler.

Some mothers have found they are actually more comfortable nursing their children abroad than they are doing so at home in North

America. Of course, this can depend on which part of the continent you call home. Berkeley, California, held the first Guinness World Record for simultaneous breastfeeding, and with good reason; breastfeeding is so commonplace in the San Francisco Bay Area that a new mother may actually feel more conspicuous bottle-feeding in public than she would breastfeeding a child.

Many Latin and Asian cultures in particular hold fast to the notion that breastfeeding is only done out of necessity by those who cannot afford to bottle-feed their children. I have seen mothers become stunned when they realize that I, an American woman who can afford to travel the world, have chosen to breastfeed my babies. But clearly, awareness of the benefits to both mother and child is growing worldwide. In 2007, the Guinness World Record for the most women simultaneously breastfeeding their children was broken in, of all places, Manila, the Philippines, with more than 15,000 moms participating.

When it comes down to it, I think you'll find that regardless of race, class, or nationality, most people would much prefer to see a happy, breastfed baby than listen to a crying, hungry one. What is most important is that you are as comfortable nursing as you can be, regardless of where you roam. If you find your comfort level is affected by the comfort levels of the people around you, there may be times when *you* would be more comfortable nursing in private. Likewise, there may be times when your child may also feed much better in a quiet setting where there are few distractions. If you need to, don't hesitate to ask waiters, museum guards, or tour guides where you might find a quiet spot to sit down with your baby.

Sightseeing with Private Guides and Escorts

As experienced do-it-ourselves adventurers, my husband and I explored many a foreign city entirely by public transportation and by foot—in our pre-parent lives. We were "low-to-the ground" and loving it, catching glimpses of local life and seeing cities block-by-block-by-block (whether the blocks held any particular interest or not).

At some destinations abroad, this may still be the best way to explore with your child as well, pushing the stroller along, wearing the backpack carrier, or letting your child stretch his own legs, all the while discovering any hidden city parks or points of interest along the way. In others, it may be well worth joining a small group on an organized tour for a half or full day.

Consider a small group tour with your child in locations where:

- The heat or air pollution may be oppressive, and especially hard on your child.

- Public transportation is not reliable or is nonexistent.

- The sites you wish to visit are far from one another, or from your accommodations.

- A language barrier may make it difficult to get the most from your visit to the sites on your own.

- You would prefer to leave the driving to the locals.

- Your family's safety may otherwise be at risk.

Chichen Itza, Mexico: Our private driver not only took us to the ruins of Ek Balam and for a swim at Ik Kil Cenote, he connected us with a Mayan archeologist who gave us an amazing tour of Chichen Itza (see pg. 142).

While visiting Bangkok with our daughter, one of the best decisions we made was to take a half-day escorted tour of the temples with a local,

English-speaking guide. With just six of us along for the ride (plus our daughter) in an air-conditioned minivan, we had no trouble hearing our enthusiastic guide or getting answers to our questions. And after spending his entire life in the city, our guide taught us far more about Bangkok and Thai culture than our guidebooks offered us (www.diethelmtravel.com). At the same time, we befriended a handful of folks from the farthest English-speaking corners of the globe. Before we left Thailand, we'd opted to join a couple of similar groups in other regions, and we still have a hard time imagining how we could have seen, done, and learned half as much on our own—especially while attending to the needs of our daughter.

These day trips and half-day trips can be more affordable than you might expect, especially when you consider the alternative cost of a car rental, insurance, gas, entrance fees, and any fees for an audio or a human guide. However, if your baby or toddler is riding along for free, she will probably be expected to ride in your lap—with no space allotted for a car seat. Depending on the size of the vehicle (a typical city bus, mini bus or motor coach doesn't typically offer seatbelts anyway), the destinations and route, and your comfort level with the entire picture of the specific outing, you may wish to reconsider—or inquire if you can buy an extra ticket for your child's seat. If you are visiting a destination where taxis and private vehicles do not typically have seatbelts for rear passengers (India, Thailand, etc.), traveling in a larger vehicle like a minibus may actually be your safest option on the road.

If you decide to join a group, it is always a good idea to contact the tour operator before booking and fill them in about your situation (e.g., an infant in a sling travels easily through ruins or past priceless frescoes, while a walking 2-year-old is another situation), and ask them plenty of questions about the tour.

Questions to ask the tour operator:

- Are there restrooms available at each stop—and time to use them?
- Are children welcome at all the tour stops?
- What is the child rate, and from which age?
- Are there safety belts in the vehicle (and is a car seat allowed)?
- How much time is spent driving? (It may be more than you think.)

Your hotel can probably put you in touch with some local travel agencies offering excursions, or visit the city or region's website to see if they have recommended local excursions and guides. You can also visit the websites listed at the end of this section to get an idea of what tours are available at your destination.

Another option may be to hire your own private car and driver—an especially great alternative when you have two children or more, or would simply like more flexibility. For example, in Cancún and the Riviera Maya, you can hire a van that seats up to 12 people for one flat day rate (10 hours) with a driver and cooler included, and choose your own start time and destination (Tulum, Chichen Itza, etc.). You can make as many stops for swimming, refreshments, photos, and diaper changes as you like along the way. Or pay an hourly rate (around $35 per hour) for open service to do your local sightseeing and shopping (www.cancunvalet.com).

ON THE WEB:

In addition to web searches for your destination and the attractions you would like to visit, you can find private and group sightseeing excursions for your family with these sites, sometimes with package or combination deals.

Gray Line – www.grayline.com

Viator – www.viator.com

CHAPTER 8

Health "Ensurance"

Ten Pre-Trip Tips for Healthy Travels

The best way to deal with illness or injury during your vacation is to avoid it in the first place. As Ben Franklin liked to say, "An ounce of prevention is worth a pound of cure," and that's certainly the case when traveling, especially with young children. While that's not always possible, here are ten things you can do to help improve the odds that your crew stays as healthy as possible during your travels.

1. **Take probiotic supplements before and during your travels.** Approximately 80% of the body's immune system functions in the intestines, where billions of live and active cultures help keep it working at its best. Look for shelf-stable capsules for grown-ups and chewables for kids. Powders are available to mix for babies.

2. **Have your child visit the pediatrician** for a check-up before your trip. It's a good opportunity to update any vaccinations, discuss any potential health risks for your destination, check the ears one last time (especially if they are prone to infection), and weigh in so the proper dosage of remedies or medicines may be given if needed during the trip.

3. **Make sure everyone's routine vaccinations are up-to-date**, including the adults'. Schedules are available for both at www.CDC.gov. An accelerated vaccination schedule may be advisable for babies and young children traveling abroad. (For more

information, see Travel Shots and Vaccinations, beginning on pg. 163.)

4. **Consider getting flu shots**, and remember flu seasons vary around the world. (See more on flu and flu shots on pg. 164.)

5. **For travel abroad, visit the Centers for Disease Control's website at www.CDC.gov** to read up on any traveler's health advisories, risks, or advice for your destination, and ask your physician or consult a travel clinic for advice about any health issues or recommended travel shots for the area you'll be visiting.

6. **Make sure mom and dad have supportive, practical shoes** that are well broken-in before the trip begins. Travelers tend to spend a lot of time on their feet as it is, and traveling parents often have the added weight of their children on their feet as well. Nothing slows down a traveler like blisters or, worse, a twisted ankle.

7. **Stash travel packs of antibacterial "Redi-Wipes" or "Wet Ones"** (premoistened hand wipes) in the sides of purses, diaper bags, day packs, etc., and use often to fend off mischievous microbes that may otherwise thwart your travel plans. As you pack for your trip, be sure to include them in your carry-on.

8. **Make sure everyone will have appropriate clothing that fits** to handle the full range of weather conditions you may encounter, including surprises. Lack of warm clothing or adequate sun protection, for example, can create extra stress for the body and make you vulnerable.

9. **Drink plenty of water** the days leading up to your trip, as well as during your trip. It will help keep your body functioning at optimal levels and make you less vulnerable to illness.

10. **Keep a healthy attitude!** As Deepak Chopra writes in *Ageless Body, Timeless Mind*, "Our cells are constantly eavesdropping on our thoughts and being changed by them. A bout of depression can wreak havoc with the immune system; falling in love can boost it." So if you haven't already, fall in love with your trip and the idea of traveling with your child!

Koh Phi Phi, Thailand: Our pop-up sun tent has traveled the world, providing shade where needed, privacy for both nursing and changing clothes, and serving as a mobile clubhouse for the kids.

Having Fun in (Spite of) the Sun

It's no secret that little ones have more sensitive skin than adults, and that includes a sensitivity to the sun's harmful rays—and the products created to help absorb them. Most of this sensitivity is due to the baby's developing skin still being relatively thin, and even naturally darker-skinned babies can sunburn far more easily than older children. For these reasons, it's best to avoid sun exposure as much as possible for all children less than one year of age.

Fortunately, there are many ways to minimize baby's sun exposure without passing his entire first summer indoors with the shades drawn. Although an adult's first precaution is often to slather on a powerful sunscreen, such products should only be considered backup to other methods of sun protection where babies and young children are concerned. Be aware that the American Academy of Pediatrics does not recommend the use of sunscreens—even those formulated for babies and small children—on babies younger than six months.

Even older babies can be sensitive to the active ingredients in sunscreen, so be sure to use only a product made for children, and to first test on a small area of your child's skin. As with an adult's sunscreen, be sure it provides protection from both UVA and UVB rays, and reapply at least as often as the label advises, even if the lotion is "waterproof." (Avoid using sunscreens that contain the insect repellent DEET. See next section on Managing Mosquitoes, beginning on pg. 148, for more information.) If a child under the age of one develops a sunburn, you should contact your pediatrician right away.

Here are some tips to help minimize sun exposure on your vacation. For more ideas, see Great Products for Healthy Travels, pg. 157.

- **Bring portable shade** – Pop-up sun tents and sun canopy extensions or UV shields for strollers can all help your child stay cool and protected, and fold compactly for travel. Consider the RayShade for strollers and other recommendations at www.TravelswithBaby.com.

- **Wear UV-protective clothing** – Available now in everything from swimwear to casual corporate attire, it blocks far more harmful UV rays than clothing alone. Many garments are also designed for maximum coverage with clever ventilation and/or moisture-wicking capabilities.

- **Rent the umbrella** – Beaches often leave babies exposed without escape from the sun. If sun umbrellas are available for rent, waste no time in renting one (they may run out as the crowd thickens). If deciding between a public beach or paying admission to a private one, the extra facilities—including shade umbrellas—at the private beach may be well worth it, and may enable you to enjoy more time at the beach as well.

- **The indispensable sun hat** – Your best bets will brim over on all sides and have some form of strap to help keep the hat on in a breeze or when the child inspects it. An extended back flap will help guard the gap that sometimes forms between shirt and hair (good designs at www.flaphappy.com). Keep an extra in the day bag in case the primary blows overboard or otherwise disappears.

- **Wide-brimmed hat for parent carrying a baby** – We call it "the sombrero effect." Don't forget to shade thyself—and you may sometimes help shade your child in the process.

- **Pop-up shade tents** – Great for creating a shady retreat on sunny beaches and in campsites where shade is scarce and sun is plentiful. Many models include sand pockets on the sides to help keep them in place, plus windows that can tie up for increased ventilation, or tie down for increased UV protection when desired.

- **Rear and side car window shades** – They not only shield your child from the sun, but also help keep the car's internal temperature down. Available in roll-up styles, with suction cups, and static clings—including a photochromic (light sensing) shade for improved visibility from One Step Ahead. The First Years makes a fabric shade for the rear window of sedans that can be especially helpful for backseat passengers.

- **UPF-rated clothing and swimwear** – Hi-tech fabrics can now offer little ones UPF 50+ protection (up to 98% of the sun's rays). A wide variety of hats and clothing are available for infants through preschoolers, including ultra lightweight jogging-style suits complete with built-in vents and sun protection hoods, and sporty-looking swim attire styled after wetsuits. Another plus for travel: Many of these fabrics clean up easily and dry overnight (if not sooner). The following companies offer a good selection of UPF-protective clothing for babies, toddlers, and young children: One Step Ahead (www.onestepahead.com), Solartex (www.solartex.com), and Coolibar (www.coolibar.com).

- **Light, white, cotton clothing (long sleeves and pants)** – It's hard to beat the basics. Cotton breathes well and feels good against the skin. In its lightest colors, it also helps to keep temperatures down and mosquitoes at bay.

- **Infant, toddler, and children's sunglasses** – A small selection is available, though the most popular continue to be Baby Banz and Kidz Banz sunglasses with soft straps that go behind the head to help keep them in place. For the picky baby, SoftShades offer the comfort of wrap-around foam.

Managing Mosquitoes

When traveling with infants and young children—whether for a simple weekend camping trip in Calgary or an eight-month sojourn in Southeast Asia, you'll need to be especially aware of the risks of mosquito-borne illness and prepared to protect your family.

Here are just a few reasons you might need to rethink the importance of insect protection for your trip, and possibly at home:

- Cases of West Nile Virus have now been reported in the western hemisphere from Canada to Venezuela. According to the World Health Organization, Cases continue to be reported in parts of Africa, Europe, Asia, Russia, and the Middle East.

- Even when staying in resort areas where there is not thought to be a risk of malaria, your sightseeing trip to visit Mayan ruins, for example, might actually take you into an area where malaria is still considered a risk.

- Planning a passport-free long weekend in Puerto Rico? Don't overlook that a record 21,000 cases of dengue fever were reported there in 2010.

However, traditional insect repellents used to deter mosquitoes and prevent their bites contain the active ingredient DEET, which studies have indicated may be especially harmful to young children. If you'll be traveling with a baby or toddler you need to protect from mosquitoes, this section could be especially important for you.

We'll look at proven DEET-free alternatives that are considered safe for the whole family, the guidelines for using DEET-containing products on small children, and other ways you can help prevent mosquito bites as you travel with your family.

But first, if you're traveling abroad, remember to check for health concerns in all of the areas you'll visit within the country in the Travel Health section at www.CDC.gov, which will include mosquito-borne illnesses. In some cases, you may be glad to discover anti-malarial drugs are recommended for visitors to one part of the country, for example, but not others—and adjust your travel plans accordingly to avoid the need for these (more on specifics on malaria, pg. 168).

Using DEET-Free Insect Repellents

You may have heard of various bath and plant-based oils that can be used to help repel insects. Soybean oil, for example, has been found to effectively repel mosquitoes from humans, and it has been added to Canada's list of registered insect repellents, though it has not yet been added to the EPA's list of registered repellents because items chosen for that list, so far, have required registration because of their potential risks. At time of writing, the EPA states on its website:

> *EPA is considering whether repellent products should be removed from the exemption because effectiveness is critical to disease prevention. In addition, EPA is considering whether to re-evaluate the initial safety determinations for the ingredients considered to be minimal risk. Examples of ingredients used in unregistered insect repellents are citronella oil, cedar oil, geranium oil, peppermint and peppermint oil, and soybean oil.*

Here's what we do know: Soybean oil may provide protection from mosquitoes from one to 3½ hours, depending on the product. According to a study published in *The New England Journal of Medicine* comparing DEET and non-DEET products, "Only the soybean-oil-based repellent was able to provide protection for a period similar to that of the lowest-concentration DEET product we tested" ("Comparative Efficacy of Insect Repellents Against Mosquito Bites," N Engl J Med, Vol. 347, No. 1; July 4, 2002).

The "lowest-concentration DEET product" they refer to in this study was a product formulated for children: OFF! Skintastic for Kids (SC Johnson). The soybean oil–based product they tested was also formulated for children: Bite Blocker for Kids (HOMS). Since then, HOMS has created an even longer-lasting formulation that is also safe for use on babies and children—meaning the new, DEET-free Bite Blocker product may actually outlast many DEET-containing products formulated for children. We first tried Bite Blocker on our family's trip to Thailand, with good results. It was also nice having the option of a lotion repellent to apply to our baby, rather than a spray (it's available in both formulations).

Since then, I have tried a number of other plant-based repellents as well included here, and depending on availability in your area and your specific needs, you might also look for these:

- California Baby Bug Repellent Spray – Repels fleas, mosquitoes, ticks, and biting flies. Active ingredients: citronella, lemongrass, cedar. Not waterproof.

- Bite Blocker Xtreme – Repels mosquitoes, blackflies, and ticks. Active ingredients: Soybean oil, geranium oil, castor oil. Sweatproof and waterproof.

- Buzz Away Extreme – Repels mosquitoes, gnats, blackflies, and ticks. Active ingredients: soybean oil, geranium oil, castor oil, cedarwood oil, citronella oil, peppermint oil, and lemongrass oil. (Also available in individually sealed towelettes, which I keep in my day pack for "surprises" and reapplications on the go.) Sweatproof and waterproof.

The key to using any of the naturally derived insect repellents is application—and reapplication. Since they work through scent only, rather than going into the bloodstream, you should reapply most of these products every 2 to 3 hours for mosquito protection, and every 2 hours for protection against ticks (read product directions for specifics). Also, you can apply the sprays to clothing, hats, shoes, diaper bag, stroller…for increased protection during your outings. If you'll be in a particularly hot or humid area, or in and out of water, be sure to look for a waterproof and/or sweatproof formulation.

Lavender oil and bath oils like Avon's Skin So Soft may also be used, but their effectiveness is limited to less than an hour, and lavender oil itself is considered effective for only 30 minutes or less. Also, citronella-containing products are not recommended for children under the age of 2.

Please note: In studies, tests of wristbands and electronic sound deterrents have proven ineffective in repelling mosquitoes.

Using DEET-Containing Products on Children

The American Academy of Pediatrics (AAP) advises against using DEET-containing products on babies under 2 months of age, and the Canadian Pediatric Society advises against using DEET on babies under 6 months of age. Both organizations agree that young children should receive no more than one application per day, and in a low concentration not to exceed 10% (most products for children are 4.5%). The AAP also discourages parents from using products that combine repellents with a sunscreen as DEET is not water-soluble and the amount of DEET on a child increases each time the sunscreen must be reapplied.

If you feel the risk of mosquito-borne disease at your destination warrants the use DEET on your child (risks of dengue fever and malaria are not to be taken lightly), take care not to apply it to their hands, nor over scrapes or irritated skin, nor underneath clothing. Also be sure to keep sprays from getting into children's eyes, and wash off with soap after the risk of mosquito bites is past.

Here are some general guidelines to play it safe when using DEET with small children.

- Never use DEET-containing products on a child under 2 months old.

- Only use DEET-containing products as a last resort, when other measures will not sufficiently protect children against the risk of mosquito-borne or tick-borne illnesses.

- Do not apply DEET to children under 2 years more than once per 24 hours.

- Only use a product that is created specifically for children.

DEET-Free Ways to Help Prevent Mosquito Bites

Before giving up on the family camping trip or the eco-tour, consider these simple DEET-free ways you can help prevent mosquito bites.

- **Avoid using scented shampoos or lotions** on your child—or yourself, as sweet fragrances attract mosquitoes.

- **Dress yourself and your child in light, plain-colored attire** as bright colors attract mosquitoes—and some wasps including yellowjackets. (Also keep this in mind as you choose toys and gear to bring along.)

- **Use mosquito nets designed to fit around strollers and infant car seats.** Some framed backpack carriers may also be used with bug nets.

- **Find out which time of year, or season, mosquitoes are least problematic at your destination** and try to visit at that time (e.g., is late summer best because the creek has dried up, or is it worse, because the creek has partially dried, leaving standing pools of water?).

- **When camping, try to choose a site as far away from still or slow-moving bodies of water** as possible. You'll have far fewer mosquitoes in your camp, making it much more pleasant to enjoy that campfire.

- **In severe mosquito zones, look for air-conditioned lodgings** where mosquitoes are less likely to penetrate your sleeping quarters.

- **Where air conditioning is not available but mosquitoes are abundant,** ask and confirm with hotels whether there are bed nets for guests.

- **Have the entire family take cool showers or baths after a hot afternoon.** Since mosquitoes can be drawn to skin's heat, scent, and perspiration, you'll be much less enticing when they come out at dusk.

- **Use a soybean oil–based or other naturally derived mosquito repellant,** such as Bite Blocker and those listed on pg. 150.

- **Buy clothing with built-in insect repellent** that is safe to skin and can survive a lifetime of trips through the washing machine (or create your own—see next tip). You can find Insect Shield clothing available in baby-sized leggings, parent-sized shirts, sun hats, and more from several outdoor brands. Most Insect Shield clothing will remain effective through 70 washings.

Arenal Hanging Bridges, Costa Rica: Before our trip to Costa Rica, I treated some key items with permethrin—which also stops ticks in their tracks (always follow instructions carefully).

- **Treat exteriors of gear, tent, jackets, hats, and more with permethrin,** which can provide additional insect repellent from items near you and your family. Permethrin repels mosquitoes, ticks, and other insects, is the active ingredient used in Insect Shield clothing, and is used to treat bed nets in malaria-risk zones (it is also used in lice shampoos for kids and flea dips for dogs). Unlike repellents used on skin, it will remain effective through your entire trip provided you don't send treated garments on more than six trips through the washing machine (if so, consider Insect Shield clothing). Always apply permethrin in advance of your trip, outdoors, with great care in accordance with the instructions.

The Top Things You Should Know About Ticks

Ticks are found throughout the world, but only a few species can bite and infect humans. Those few species, however, are also found throughout the world, so chances are that wherever your travels take you, you should take basic precautions to help protect the whole family from tick bites during time spent outdoors in brushy or wooded areas.

Here are some helpful things to understand about ticks and do to prevent tick bites and the spread of tick-borne illnesses.

- **Ticks generally pose the greatest risk to humans after they have turned one year old** (usually late spring in most regions) and begin looking for the *second* host in their life cycle. For example, on Martha's Vineyard, where there are an estimated 50 deer per square mile and Lyme disease is now endemic, the months of April through June are the most concerning for ticks and tick bites, while mid-summer—after most surviving ticks have moved on to the next host in their life cycles—is not. A second season occurs in the early fall, as adult ticks move on to their next hosts.

- **Insect repellents need to be reapplied more frequently to repel ticks (arachnids) than they do to repel mosquitoes (insects).** Even if the front label of your repellent boasts 4 to 8 hours of effectiveness, for example, the directions on the back are likely to recommend reapplication every 2 hours to prevent tick bites.

- **Ticks cannot jump or fly, but rather climb aboard a host as it passes by them and makes direct contact.** Staying in the middle of walking and hiking paths, steering clear of tall grasses and brushy areas, and making sure children wandering on their own two feet do the same can be especially important in avoiding contact with ticks.

- **Once a tick finds its host, it usually takes from 10 minutes to 2 hours to find its feeding site**. If your family is dressed in light-colored clothing, with blocked access (e.g., pants tucked into socks during hikes), it will improve your chances of seeing a tick and removing it before it bites.

- **Clothing treated with permethrin is extremely helpful in preventing tick bites and the spread of tick-borne illnesses,** whether done commercially with the Insect Shield process or at home with a spray. Ticks that land on treated clothing are immediately affected, and will die within a few hours. Even if they continue to crawl from treated clothing onto the skin, they are less likely to bite, and if they do bite, it is unlikely that they will live long enough for transmission of most tick-borne illnesses to be passed.

- **Also be aware that Lyme disease is not the only tick-borne illness of concern, and is not the most damaging.** There are ten known tick-borne illnesses in the U.S., and tick-borne encephalitis (TBE) is endemic throughout most countries in Europe and some eastern portions of the Russian Federation.

- **A vaccine to prevent tick-borne encephalitis (TBE) is available and may be recommended to travelers** planning to visit certain areas in Europe and parts of Russia. If you plan to spend time in wooded areas in these regions, you may want to ask your doctor or travel health clinic about the vaccine.

- **Remove a tick as quickly and cleanly as possible.** Ideally, you will use fine-tipped tweezers held perpendicular to the tick's body, gripping the tick as closely to the skin as you can. If parts of its mouth break off, try to remove them with the tweezers as well. Clean the site of the bite with rubbing alcohol, an iodine rub, or soap and water.

- **In some areas, ticks removed from a person's skin can be placed in a secure container and submitted for identification** and possible testing, especially where tick-borne illnesses are endemic. You may also want to take a photo of the tick for identification if you have a camera with you.

- **The three main signs to watch for in the days and weeks after a tick bite are 1) Fever and chills,** which might develop soon after the bite up to a few weeks afterward; **2) Rash,** which could be either a bulls-eye radiating out from the site of the bite or a spotted rash, depending on the illness; and **3) Aches and pains** either in the muscles or possibly joints. If anyone in the family experiences these symptoms after a tick bite, contact a doctor right away.

Four Big Reasons to Breastfeed for Healthy Travels

If you are breastfeeding, there are plenty of reasons why you may want to continue doing so through your upcoming travels. Most obvious is the convenience of having nourishment on-demand, with nothing to pack, wash, refrigerate, or warm up along the way. But there are other advantages to breastfeeding while traveling, particularly where your child's health is concerned.

1. **Boosted immunity for your baby.** According to the United States Breastfeeding Committee, breastfed children "are less likely to suffer from infectious illnesses and their symptoms (e.g., diarrhea, ear infections, respiratory tract infections, and meningitis)." As you travel the world—or your neighborhood—your body creates antibodies to counteract the illness-causing germs that you encounter (ahh-choo!). These antibodies can be passed along to your child through your breast milk to help boost her immunity to the same bugs she has likely encountered. In their widely acclaimed resource *The Breastfeeding Book*, Martha and William Sears report that a drop of breast milk contains around one million white blood cells, which can help a baby resist infection. That's powerful medicine—without medicine.
2. **A sterile source of nourishment.** Having to sterilize bottles and find suitable water for drinking and mixing formula can complicate travel with infants and small children and increase the risk of illness, especially when travel takes you to destinations where the tap water is not to be trusted. But with breast milk on tap, you can nourish and hydrate your child anytime and anywhere in your

journey—and without the worry of water safety issues concerning other travelers.

3. **Ease of water absorption for child.** Because breast milk is absorbed so perfectly in an infant's digestive system, there is no need to supplement with water in addition to breastfeeding, even when a baby is traveling in extreme heat or suffering from diarrhea.

4. **Supply and demand** – You needn't worry over how much to have prepared for the flight or day of sightseeing, how many bottles or nipples or sippy cups you'll need to have clean and ready, or how to handle the surprise growth spurt during your vacation. Your traveling child has perfect nutrition, regardless of flight or train delays, or heightened airport security regulations.

To help ease your travels while breastfeeding, see Nine Tips for Nursing on the Go, pg. 97, and Breastfeeding and Other Cultures, pg. 138.

ON THE WEB:

If you need breastfeeding information or support during your travels, **La Leche League International** www.lalecheleague.org (1-800-LALECHE) has many online resources and can help you find a local chapter with on-the-ground support and referrals at destinations worldwide.

The International Lactation Consultant Association, online at www.ilca.org (1-919-861-5577), can help you find a board-certified lactation consultant in destinations across the U.S. and around the world.

CHAPTER 9
Going Farther Afield

Food and Water Safety

Hepatitis, giardia, and salmonella are not words that often headline travel brochures, but they are among just a few of the harmful microbes a tourist may experience first-hand if he doesn't exercise some caution when eating and drinking far from home. As the CDC and countless travelers advise, "Boil it, cook it, peel it, or forget it!" especially when it comes to foods for your children during travel in developing countries.

Babies and children, given their inexperienced digestive systems and immature immune systems, are far more susceptible to food- and waterborne illnesses than their parents. But the temptation of icy fruit drinks and treats can be a real and regular temptation that you may have to confront, particularly when offered directly to your child by well-meaning strangers (of which there may be many when you travel with small children). Trying to assuage a picky eater may make it even more tempting to okay the ring of pineapple or mango lassi that piques her interest. Yet, for small children, this can be a dire mistake.

Guidelines for Safe Dining and Drinking

If you are traveling to an area where food and water safety is a real concern, be prepared to:

- **Avoid foods from street vendors.** As friendly and generous as they may be, they often have little or no refrigeration available for the foods they prepare, and likely do not have a place to wash their hands with clean water and soap.

- **Dine in restaurants frequented by many western travelers.** They are more accustomed to satisfying western stomachs and standards, and if they don't, you would probably have heard about it. Restaurants in larger chain hotels are generally a safe bet, and ask for recommendations from other travelers, and/or hotel staff. You can also check online ahead of time for traveler recommendations on sites like www.tripadvisor.com.

- **Prepare some of your own meals.** Even if you are staying in a room without a kitchen, your family can still enjoy some of the local produce brought home and washed and peeled carefully. If you will be staying somewhere with cooking facilities, you may have better luck satisfying your child's tastes and save money by cooking your own meals—not to mention, you can make sure your foods are thoroughly washed and cooked. A trip to a local market and experimenting with local foods can also be a fun way to experience your destination.

- **Bring along plenty of snacks.** Nonperishable snacks in the daypack can be critical in staving off hunger between the sights when other options, like street food and small restaurants, may pose a risk. Dried fruit, energy bars, granola bars, packaged cheese and cracker "kits," sealed packages of applesauce, and crackers are quite portable and can be brought from home. (And there's nothing like peanut butter on crackers to help with the midnight munchies of a jetlagged traveler.) You can also pick up sealed and safe packaged foods in local markets.

- **Drink bottled water and beverages only from sealed containers.** A general rule of thumb is to not accept any bottled water you haven't broken the seal of yourself, and the same is true for other beverages when visiting questionable establishments (where your soda may be watered down, but the profits are not).

- **Look for labels with "IBWA" or "NSF" certification.** If the bottled water isn't a brand you recognize, check the label for the

"IBWA" (International Bottled Water Association) or "NSF" (National Sanitation Foundation) certification.

- **Avoid fresh-squeezed and prepared juices during outings**. These should be thought of as the triple threat: as delicious and refreshing as they may be, they can harbor hazardous germs from either the fruit, the water, or the ice (not to mention the hands preparing them), so it is generally best to avoid them except where you can be sure they are prepared safely, and to stick to packaged and bottled juices while out and about during sightseeing and travel.

- **Pass on the ice.** Even if you've made sure your drinks are safe, the ice could still be a big gamble. Few establishments actually make ice from bottled water, and those that do will likely include a mention on the menu. Freezing water does not kill the harmful microbes that may be in it.

- **Bring prepared formula** – If you are using formula for your child, it may be safest and easiest to pack a cardboard box (or extra suitcase) of pre-mixed formula that is ready to serve and requires no water to be added. If refrigeration isn't available for the leftover portions, or you will be gone too long for this to be practical, you may need to make do with bottled water, in which case you may be glad if you packed a few starter bottles of water from home (again, a checked cardboard box may be helpful) until you can purchase more from a trustworthy source at your destination. Distilled water is preferable to "spring water" or "mineral water" as it won't interfere with the balance of minerals already present in the formula.

- **Bring it to a boil.** If you need to boil water for safe consumption, the rule of thumb is to let it boil for one full minute, or for three minutes at high elevations (over 6,562 feet or 2,000 meters). Boiling drinking water for extended periods of time is not recommended as it can increase the concentration of lead in the water.

- **Don't count on a filter.** The kinds of water filters commonly used by backpackers do not filter out many worrisome microbes, including giardia, so travelers who use water filters are still advised to boil or purify their water after filtering.

- **Purify in a pinch.** If all else fails, be prepared to purify some water yourself with purification tablets available at most outdoor stores and pharmacies. Bring your own water bottle(s) from home and head out each day with your own safe supply (a 1-liter water bottle will simplify things since it is usually 1 tablet to 1 liter of water). Since purification does little to improve the flavor of drinking water, you may also want to pack along a little powdered Gatorade or Kool-Aid to mix in for good measure—you will all need to drink plenty of water, so make it as enticing as possible!

- **Wash and sterilize baby bottles, sippy cups, and your own water bottle with care.** Although the tap water in U.S. cities is now considered safe enough for washing infants' bottles, it would be prudent to raise your standards when you travel. Especially if the water from the tap is not considered drinkable where you stay, do not use it untreated for washing bottles and nipples, nor sippy cups, reusable water bottles, and the like (air-drying does not necessarily kill the critters). The same care should be taken with any teething toys, pacifiers, or other items that go into your child's mouth.

- **Wash the hand that feeds you!** All of these precautions will do little good if, in the end, you don't wash your hands and those of your children before eating. Keep antibacterial "Redi-Wipes" or "Wet Ones" in your daypack and use them often—especially for children whose hands frequently find their way into their mouths (mealtime or not).

ON THE WEB:

To find out if your destination is considered to have a high risk for food- or waterborne diseases, visit **the CDC's website** at www.CDC.gov/travel, where you can select the country or countries your family will visit, and be sure to select the options that will help you get specialized information for travel with children, pregnant travelers, and visitors staying in homes of friends and family, among other options. You can also find out about the safety of tap water and food in 1440 cities on **the IAMAT site** at www.iamat.org.

Small Children Swimming Abroad

Nobody likes the thought of it, but the truth is some amount of sewage may be present in the water we swim in at beaches, in lakes, in streams, and even in swimming pools—even in our own hometowns. Human and animal feces can carry with it any number of diseases, many of which can survive for long periods of time in salt water and in chlorinated pools and spas. And since babies and small children are the most likely candidates to swallow some of the water they are swimming in, parents should exercise extreme caution when deciding where to let their children swim, especially when visiting destinations where standards for sanitation and sewage treatment are not as high as those at home.

Waterborne illnesses are especially common:

- Where the diseases already thrive (illness begets illness).

- Where the waste water is not treated or strictly regulated.

- Where spas or hot tub temperatures help the chlorine evaporate quickly.

- Where swimming pools receive inadequate or insufficient maintenance.

- Where babies and very young children play in the water, diapered or not.

Although a host of skin, ear, and upper respiratory illnesses can be contracted through swimming, diarrheal illnesses are by far the most common ailments contracted by swimming, and it should be noted that an infected person who has been suffering from diarrhea, including resort guests suffering traveler's diarrhea, can spread the disease in water even without having an accident. (If you are sick, kindly stay out of the water!)

Wherever you vacation, remember that babies and small children, even in swim diapers, contribute to the communal pool of germs when their stool comes in contact with the water. So if your child does go swimming or wading, please do your part as a parent to keep your child diapered in the water and change those swim diapers frequently.

Vaccinations and Travel Shots

Updated and Accelerated Vaccinations for the Family

While many of the diseases routine vaccinations protect against may now be rare or nonexistent in the U.S. and most of the Western world—such as polio, measles, whooping cough—they are still present and even common in other parts of the world. Even crossing paths with many travelers at major international hubs could potentially put you and your family at risk if not adequately protected from these preventable diseases.

Before traveling abroad, it's wise to make sure all members of the family have their routine vaccinations up to date. What's more, since the recommended immunization schedule for infants and children in the U.S. does not account for international travel at very young ages, your child's physician may advise an accelerated schedule for certain immunizations. For example, the Hepatitis A vaccine is not routinely given in the U.S. until age 2, but younger children traveling abroad who will be eating table foods may need this protection sooner.

Be sure to discuss your travel plans and timeline with your child's physician as well as your own, and address any upcoming immunizations that may need to be adjusted for your travels. Since most vaccinations require four to six weeks to become fully effective, do not delay any vaccinations needed for your trip. You will also need to find out whether additional travel shots are recommended or required for travel to your destination.

Travel Shots for Babies and Young Children

To better understand what travel shots may be recommended—or even required—for your travels abroad, visit the Centers for Disease Control and Prevention online and look up any countries you'll be visiting (www.cdc.gov or call 1-877-FYI-TRIP). Any decisions about vaccinations for your child should be made with the help of a qualified healthcare provider who will consider the specifics of your trip, your child's age, and any medical history of importance.

For example, a family planning travel to a resort in Thailand may have very different needs from a family planning to visit more rural parts of the country. As soon as you have a good idea of where and when you will travel, plan a talk with your child's physician and/or a professional at a travel health clinic.

Here is a little more background on the most common travel shots that may be discussed and any considerations for child travelers (for information on travel shots and breastfeeding, see pg. 165).

Common Travel Shots and Child Travelers

Hepatitis A – Destinations worldwide

Throughout much of the world, including Mexico, Central and South America, the Middle East, Africa, the Indian subcontinent, and parts of the Far East, the disease is quite common, so it is a good idea to keep the whole family current with this vaccination. However, in North America, children do not commonly receive their first Hepatitis A vaccination until 2 years of age. If your child will be eating table foods where food and water safety is a concern, consult with your pediatrician to find out whether an earlier vaccination or immune globulin (IG) shot is advisable.

Rabies – Destinations worldwide
In some situations, the rabies vaccine may be recommended for young children traveling to areas where the disease is found in animals, particularly dogs. Since children are more likely to try and play with unfamiliar animals, and are more likely to get bitten by them, this may be an especially wise precaution for children who are old enough to be adventuring on their own two feet, but are still too young to understand the potential dangers of animals on the loose. Ask your pediatrician for more information and advice about the rabies vaccine if it is included among the recommended travel shots for your destination.

Typhoid – Destinations worldwide
Typhoid fever is transmitted from person to person, usually through contaminated food and water. Therefore, practicing food and beverage safety smarts should be your first line of defense against this disease. Children 2 years and older may also receive a vaccination to help prevent typhoid, but it is not recommended for children younger than 2 years.

Yellow Fever Vaccine – Africa and South America
Because yellow fever, a disease transmitted by mosquitoes, is very common in some parts of Africa and South America, proof of yellow fever vaccination is required for entry into some countries (visit www.cdc.gov to see if your destination is among them). However, the CDC reports that infants are at a high risk for developing encephalitis from the vaccine (which contains a live virus). The vaccine is not given to children under 6 months of age. The CDC advises that the vaccination be postponed until the child is at least 9-12 months old if possible, and to avoid travel to yellow fever regions before a child is 9 months of age. Yellow fever vaccinations can only be given at designated clinics; locations by state are available at www.cdc.gov or by calling 1-877-FYI-TRIP. Be sure you receive your certificate of proof of this vaccination, and keep it with your travel documents to avoid any hassles.

Vaccinations for Breastfeeding Mothers

According to the Centers for Disease Control and Prevention, many travel vaccinations and routine immunizations have been shown to pose no danger to a breastfed child when given to the nursing mother. In some cases, vaccinations are not recommended for breastfeeding women because a live virus used in the vaccine may pose a risk to the child or because not enough data has been collected with regards to breastfeeding and a particular vaccination (as noted below).

If you are breastfeeding and need to be vaccinated for your trip, you may want to discuss the vaccinations with your doctor (and which, if any, are covered by your insurance). And be sure to mention you are breastfeeding when visiting a travel health clinic to receive your vaccinations.

Vaccinations considered safe for nursing mothers:

- Immune globulins (IG)
- Diptheria-Tetanus
- Hepatitis B
- Influenza (inactivated)
- Measles
- Meningococcal meningitis
- Mumps
- Polio (inactivated)
- Rubella
- Varicella

Vaccinations with precautions for nursing mothers:

- Hepatitis A (Immune globulin recommended instead)
- Influenza (flu) (Inactivated virus "flu shot" encouraged instead of live virus)
- Japanese encephalitis
- Pneumococcal

- Rabies (Data not available, but it is commonly given to nursing mothers without observed effects in infants)

- Smallpox

- Tuberculosis

- Typhoid (Data not available, but may be used when risk of exposure is high)

- Yellow fever (Theoretical risk of transferring to breastfed infant, but unavoidable if traveling to endemic areas)

ON THE WEB:

To check for recommended travel shots for the areas you'll be visiting, go to www.CDC.gov/travel. More information about recommended vaccinations for travelers, including helpful explanations and discussions of travel shots for child travelers, pregnant travelers, and breastfeeding travelers, can be found at the following websites:

Web MD – www.webmd.com

Government of Canada – www.travel.gc.ca

Medline Plus – www.nlm.nih.gov/medlineplus

Also, you can find more information about travel shots and breastfeeding at

www.cdc.gov/breastfeeding.

Flu and Flu Shots

If you will be traveling during flu season, discuss your plans with your pediatrician and find out when the flu vaccination may be available for your child. Children under the age of 5 receive the inactivated influenza vaccine that is given as a shot; children age 5 and older may be given the nasal mist flu vaccine. Since the flu virus itself is a moving target, the vaccination must be updated annually to remain effective against the latest strain.

If you would like your child to receive a flu shot, do so as soon as possible to avoid untimely infection and the possibility of a vaccination shortage. As fellow travelers and the primary caregivers for your child, it may be wise for you and your partner to get vaccinated, too. And remember, the official "flu season" can vary by destination.

Flu seasons around the world:

- Northern Hemisphere: November – February
- Southern Hemisphere: April – September
- The Tropics: All year long…

Malaria Prevention for Young Children

Traveling to a malaria-affected region with small children should be considered with the utmost seriousness. According to the World Health Organization, malaria kills an African child every 30 seconds. It spreads as easily as mosquitoes bite people in the night, and the CDC declares malaria to be "one of the most serious, life-threatening diseases affecting pediatric international travelers."

Malaria is presently considered a risk in parts of Asia, Africa, Central and South America, Eastern Europe, the South Pacific, and certain Caribbean Islands. For travel to some countries, such as Costa Rica and Thailand, you may be able to avoid the risk of malaria by simply avoiding certain regions during your visit. In others, such as India, malaria may be considered a risk anywhere you go.

While anti-malarial drugs are available and are recommended for travelers who will be visiting affected regions, none of these ensures 100% immunity, and not all medications are suitable for all travelers.

Who can and cannot take anti-malarial drugs?

A few anti-malarial drugs can be given to infants and small children, though it can be difficult to get the complete doses into very young children because of the unpleasant taste, which is one more reason why it's wise to wait until children are older (old enough to understand the importance of getting the medicine down) to travel to malaria-risk areas.

At an elephant farm, Thailand: You may be able to simply steer clear of malarial areas in the countries you want to visit by checking the interactive map at http://cdc-malaria.ncsa.uiuc.edu as you plan your travels.

Also, be aware that which anti-malarial drug is recommended can vary by destination and the strain(s) of malaria present there, and not all anti-malarial drugs are suitable for young children. For example, doxycycline is not suitable for children under 8 years, and atovaquone/proguanil is not suitable for children under 25 lbs. As well, some anti-malarial medications should not be taken by breastfeeding women, and anti-malarial medications are generally not recommended for pregnant women.

If you must take your infant or child to a malaria-affected area, consult with your pediatrician immediately to figure out your child's best course of prevention, and be sure to talk with your own physician and/or consult a travel clinic for advice about anti-malarial prophylaxis for other members of the family as well.

Tips for travel to malarial areas with young children:

- **Know the signs of possible infection and seek medical help immediately** if any are seen, including a simple fever. Malaria can harm small children much more rapidly than adults, and they suffer complications from the disease at a much higher rate.

- **Know where to get help before you go.** You can check with your pediatrician for possible referrals and the embassy abroad to find out where you would need to go in case of a medical emergency (many U.S. Embassy websites, for example, include listings of local health resources). Joining IAMAT (more details pg. 173) will also give you access to local healthcare provider listings in the region you will visit.

- **Consider medical evacuation coverage** for your whole family. Whether you are traveling in a remote or developing nation, or you are staying in a cosmopolitan capital abroad, you might be very glad to have emergency medical transportation to the hospital of your choice in your own country.

- **Bring permethrin-treated mosquito nets** (for the crib, stroller, infant car seat, beds) with you to ensure you'll be protected by these simple but effective barriers when possible.

- **Wear permethrin-treated or Insect Shield clothing,** available for adults and even infants. More information on pg. 153.

- Read the tips and advice in Managing Mosquitoes, pg. 148.

ON THE WEB:

For more information about malaria risks and recommendations in the areas you might visit, and help planning travel outside of these risk zones when possible, use the Malaria Map Application at http://cdc-malaria.ncsa.uiuc.edu.

CHAPTER 10
In Case of Illness...

Medical Help Where You Need It

The bad news is, sometimes babies and children get sick. The good news is, it's a universal phenomenon and virtually anywhere you go in the world, you can find the help and resources you need for dealing with it. Following are some recommendations for how you can best prepare to nip illness in the bud should it strike during travel, whether for you, your child, or any member of your family.

- **Create an electronic health record**. Having your health records in one secure place that may be accessed by a medical professional if and when needed can be especially helpful when traveling, should someone in your family need unexpected medical care. Your insurance information, vaccinations, allergies, prescriptions, and even emergency contact information can be instantly accessed. If you don't already have an electronic health record in place, ask your physician and pediatrician about creating one before your next trip.

- **Ask about online consultations or email**. Your child's physician (and your own) may offer online consultations or help via email, which can be a great help if you have unexpected health concerns or questions far from home. (How great is it to be able to send a photo of your child's mysterious rash from your phone to your pediatrician back home?) Check with the doctor's office to see if this is an option.

- **Ask the advice nurse.** Your doctor's office and/or your medical insurance provider may offer an advice line staffed by registered nurses. Many medical insurance companies offer this service to subscribers, though it is not always widely publicized. Contact your insurance provider and your doctor's office if you aren't sure if this service is available to you, or if there is a different phone number to use while traveling abroad.

- **Ask your pediatrician.** Your pediatrician may be able to give you a direct referral in the city where you will visit. If there will be a big difference in time zones, you might ask for this information before your departure to help save time should you suddenly need it.

- **Ask the front desk.** Many hotels often have local doctors they can recommend, or addresses of nearby urgent care clinics and hospitals, in case their guests need medical care.

- **Find a local doctor online.** You can use the American Academy of Pediatrics' website to search by location for doctors, pediatricians, or pediatric dentists in the U.S. and Canada, all of whom are members of the American Academy of Pediatrics (www.aap.org/referral).

- **Join IAMAT.** If your family will be traveling to a region where English-speaking or Western-trained doctors may be difficult to find, the International Association for Medical Assistance to Travellers (IAMAT) can help you find a doctor if needed, and at pre-set prices. Membership is free, but a donation to the organization is encouraged. More information at www.iamat.org.

A Traveler's Guide to Ear Infections

Just the thought of a possible ear infection during travel is enough to keep some parents from ever leaving home. It is hard to see a child in pain, it is hard to soothe a child in pain, it is hard to sleep with a child in pain, and in the case of babies and young children: it is sometimes impossible to tell what the pain is even from.

With more than three out of four children experiencing at least one ear infection before the age of three, odds are yours will, too. So what do you do if you suspect that your child may have an ear infection and you're nowhere near your pediatrician's office?

First, stay calm. Monitor your child's symptoms. If she is not old enough to tell you, "I have acute pain in my middle ear," or something to that effect, consider the following:

It's less likely to be an ear infection if your child...

- Has not recently had a cold. Ear infections generally begin when "germs" from the illness travel up the Eustachian tube.

- Has no fever or a low fever of less than 101° F (could be teething).

- Meets the above criteria and becomes more like herself after a dose of acetaminophen or ibuprofen.

It's more likely to be an ear infection if your child...

- Has been fighting a cold that has produced yellow or greenish mucus.

- Has a fever of 101° F or more.

- Cries or fusses more in a reclined position than when sitting up.

- Has pus or bloody discharge coming from the ear (pus without fever could indicate swimmer's ear).

If your child's symptoms point toward an ear infection, and no discharge or pus has been seen, you can begin treating the pain immediately with Similasan Earache Relief drops, which are available over the counter at most pharmacies (good to have in your suitcase or child's travel kit, especially if your child is prone to ear infections). You may also give the correct dosage of either ibuprofen or acetaminophen (Dr. Sears advises that you can safely use both medications together if one alone is not enough), and apply a warm compress to her ears (or warm washcloth, or water bottle filled with warm water, whatever you've got on hand).

Continue to monitor and alleviate your child's symptoms, as you are able. If they persist, you can proceed to find a local doctor in the morning. And it may be helpful, possibly even reassuring, to understand a little more about ear infections and their treatment. Here are some of a traveling parent's biggest fears about ear infections:

Palermo, Italy: When she hadn't smiled in a photo for days, we knew something wasn't right. Surprise! A double ear infection, so far from home.

What if we can't see a doctor—or get antibiotics right away?

Many parents' first assumption about an ear infection is that antibiotics must be acquired and begun immediately. Ear infections may be the result of either bacteria or a virus reaching the inner ear—and since antibiotics cannot treat viruses, they simply will have no effect on some ear infections, though they are often prescribed regardless. Recent studies have also shown that 80% of ear infections will clear up on their own in less than a week without antibiotics. In fact, the American Academy of Family Physicians and the American Academy of Pediatrics now recommend a treatment approach that emphasizes observation and pain relief before using antibiotics. However, on occasion, complications can occur, and if antibiotics can help your child begin to feel better and recover more quickly (which they most likely will if it's a bacterial infection), that is worth a lot—especially when traveling! So the bottom line is, don't panic if you can't get to a doctor immediately when you suspect an ear infection, but by all means do what you can to help your child feel better until you can get there.

Does the drainage from the ear mean the eardrum has ruptured?
Pus or bloody drainage from the ear can be alarming and, in the case of an ear infection, usually means the eardrum has ruptured. This is not as devastating as it sounds, however, and it usually results in an immediate feeling of relief for the child. The ruptured eardrum is usually treated with antibiotic eardrops prescribed by your child's physician.

Should we delay the flight?
If your child is indeed diagnosed with an ear infection, it could be a good idea to delay flying until the infection has passed—if possible. Extra fluids built up in the ears can make it even more difficult for the pressure to equalize in a child's already narrow Eustachian tubes. Discuss the type of ear infection and stage that it's at with the doctor and tell her when your flight is currently scheduled. If possible, bring some pain reliever (e.g., Infant's or Children's Tylenol) and Similasan Earache Relief drops onboard when you do fly, just in case there is any lingering discomfort.

Common Travel Ailments and Remedies

Babies and children can be even more susceptible to common ailments than adults while traveling. Their inexperienced immune systems and indiscriminant hand-to-mouth contact combines with the usual stresses we may all encounter while traveling—less sleep, strange foods, greater exposure to the elements, etc.—to make our tiny travelers more vulnerable. Following are some common ailments to creep up on kids during travel, along with practical info and tips for dealing with them when away from home.

Dehydration

Approximately 50% of an adult's body weight is water, but a baby's body weight is more than 75% water. For this reason babies and young children can become dehydrated far more quickly than adults, so it is especially important to keep the fluids flowing to them and through them as you travel. Heat, sun, high altitudes, and wind exposure can all increase the risk of dehydration, as can illness accompanied by vomiting and diarrhea. Breastfeeding mothers must be extra careful to stay hydrated enough for themselves and their babies who depend on their milk. If you think your child may be at risk for dehydration, watch out for the following warning signs.

Common signs of dehydration in infants and young children:

- Fewer than six wet diapers in a day
- No tears when baby or child cries
- Dark urine
- Sunken eyes
- Wrinkled-looking skin

If increasing your child's fluid intake doesn't seem to be helping, or illness is causing dehydration to worsen, be sure to contact a doctor right away. If you will be traveling to a remote location, discuss treatment options with your child's doctor before you leave. If children's pre-mixed oral electrolyte solutions like Pedialyte or Ricelyte will not be easily available at your destination (including on cruise ships in exotic regions), it may be wise to pack along some just in case you need it. Your child's doctor can advise you on the proper portion and strength for your child before you go. Note: Gatorade and adult sports drinks are not recommended for babies or young children.

Diarrhea

Diarrhea is one of the most common ailments a child may suffer from during travel, primarily because their inexperienced immune systems are more likely to succumb to food- and waterborne illnesses encountered through eating or merely from their frequent and indiscriminant hand-to-mouth contact (or even toys or pacifiers touching the floor). Watch closely for symptoms of dehydration (described earlier) as it is the greatest risk associated with diarrhea in babies and small children. The CDC advises immediate medical attention for infants and small children with the following symptoms.

Seek immediate medical help when diarrhea is accompanied by:

- Signs of moderate to severe dehydration
- Blood in the stool
- A fever greater than 101.5 F
- Persistent vomiting

Milder cases of diarrhea or unpleasantly loose stools may be improved by eating these popular toddler foods we affectionately call "hinder binders," or you might remember them best as "The Firm Five":

The Firm Five

- Cheerios
- Bananas
- Applesauce
- Cheese
- Yogurt

Constipation

Constipation can affect children for many reasons while traveling, including a refusal to eat new and unfamiliar foods that may be necessary to maintain a balanced diet or, for potty-trained or potty-training children, a fear of using new facilities (see tips and advice to help with this in Changes in Potty Training Routines, beginning on pg.

98). If you suspect diet is the cause of the constipation, try to reduce the constipating foods in the diet, including The Firm Five mentioned in the previous point, and replace them with more high-fiber options. If fruits and vegetables are refused, remember these alternatives can also work wonders. Note: high fiber foods should always be consumed with plenty of fluids.

High-fiber foods for picky eaters:

- Beans (baked beans, kidney, pinto, etc.)
- Sweet potatoes
- Peas
- Popcorn
- Graham crackers
- Whole wheat bread

Cough and Congestion

FACT: The average cool-air humidifier stands a good chance of getting broken traveling through the airport baggage system, not to mention it takes up a heck of a lot of space in the suitcase. While it's not always practical to travel with a humidifier, here are some ways you can help ease cough and congestion while away from home.

- If the air is particularly dry where you're staying, run a hot steamy shower to help humidify the air.

- A "vapor plug" that plugs into standard electrical outlets (like the air fresheners) can also be used to release aromatic oils of menthol, eucalyptus, etc., into the air to ease congestion. Brands include SudaCare and Pediacare.

- Vicks BabyRub and other baby-friendly chest rubs can also be massaged onto the chest and neck to help clear congestion and sooth dry passages for babies. Most are recommended for children 3 months and older.

- Use the saline nasal drops from your child's travel kit to help loosen crusty debris and moisten nasal passages.

CHAPTER 11

Safety Concerns

Childproofing On the Go

Never expect that hotel architects, decorators, or housekeeping have small children in mind as they do their work. In our stays at various hotels, we have barricaded minibars with our luggage, brazenly rearranged what furniture wasn't bolted down, and modified window coverings with various hair accessories all in the name of child safety.

We once entered a thoroughly modern hotel room to find someone had indeed brought us a portacrib as requested, though he had set it up directly beneath an enormous light sconce protruding from the wall that would have served well on a whaling ship. If it didn't brain our daughter as she stood up in the crib, it surely would have harpooned one of us after laying her down beneath it.

It was a good example of why you can't take anything for granted on arrival at a new destination. While that particular safety snafu was obvious to us on arrival, there have been other close calls of things that were not: At a vacation rental, we found a pretty stained glass window in the sleeping loft that was within my daughter's reach and appeared to be shut. Remarkably, it was not latched and opened outward at two stories above the ground. At a mountain resort, our tired wooden deck rail moved when pressed against, and my son quickly discovered a pair of balusters that were no longer secured to the deck. At a popular resort in Hawaii, my toddler daughter ran to the railing of the balcony to see how far up we were as I quickly saw she was small enough to fit through the metal railing (since replaced).

How you spend your first moments at your new accommodations can be critical to your child's safety. If your child is mobile, I strongly recommend you inspect your lodgings before you let him loose to explore them himself. In some situations, you may be able to simply leave him buckled in the stroller or placed in the portacrib while you do a quick safety check. In others, you might want to let your partner keep him entertained outside or in the lobby until you've completed your Checking-in Safety Checklist.

✔ Checking-In Safety Checklist:

- ☐ **Door locks** – Can you latch the main door to ensure your child won't go sightseeing without you? Does the bathroom or any other room have locks within your child's reach?

- ☐ **Low/large windows** – Are the windows low enough for the child to run into, or climb out of, or access by climbing on other furniture in the room? Do they open wide enough that toys—or a child—might fall through (remember, screens will not stop children from falling)? Can they be locked shut so your child cannot open it? Is there a "protective" rail or grillwork outside the window that might tempt the child?

- ☐ **Patio doors** – Can your child unlatch or operate the door unassisted? Is the glass so wide it is a walk-through risk? Is the glass so thin or old it might break if bumped by a toy or gallivanting child?

- ☐ **Balconies or decks** – Are the railings close enough to keep curious children and babies from slipping under or through? Even more-modern hotel buildings may still have railings spaced too widely for small children and babies (remember they're much narrower turned sideways), so be sure to inspect for yourself before your child comes exploring. Are there steps to the deck or down from the balcony? Any outdoor furniture that could give your child "a lift" too close to danger?

- ☐ **Curtains, blinds, and window treatments** – Give draperies a friendly tug before your child does to ensure they're securely anchored. Get loose operating cords, delicate drapes, and unsafe window treatments up and out of the way, bundled with a rubber band if needed.

☐ **Heating/AC** – Is the heating or AC unit accessible to your child? Could it be dangerously hot or pose a risk from the operating fan? Are the controls within his reach?

☐ **Electrical appliances, outlets, and cords** – Watch out for coffeemakers, alarm clocks, and hairdryers that may be pulled off of surfaces by curious toddlers, either by their cords or the objects themselves. Lamp, TV, and Internet cables and cords may also need attention. Outlets may appear where not expected, such as at the base of lamps on desks or bedside tables.

☐ **Kitchens or kitchenettes** – Check cupboards and drawers for knives, coffee makers with glass carafes, and other hazards that may be within reach, including matches if the stove is gas. Dishwashing detergent and/or cleaning supplies may be kept in an accessible cupboard. Be aware that ovens, refrigerators, or dishwashers may be more easily opened than yours at home.

☐ **Bathrooms** – Soaps, shampoos, and lotions may need to be moved from within reach. In vacation rentals and personal homes, check for cleaning supplies, medicines, matches, and other hazardous products that may be stored in the bathroom. Be sure to store your own toiletries and travel kits out of reach of your child (those with built-in hooks or loops that can be hung from robe hooks or from shower or closet rods can be helpful).

☐ **Minibars** – Can your child open the minibar by herself? Are there items inside that could be of danger (glass bottles, peanuts or other allergens in snacks, etc.) or could set you back more than you had planned for this vacation? You may need to set a suitcase in front of it or rearrange furniture.

New York City: Taking the subway with two kids in strollers? Watch your pockets. And no, I didn't just hand my camera to a complete stranger (thanks, Mom!).

City Smarts for the New Parent

After traveling across the country, across the Atlantic, and across the Pacific with my family, I've become more convinced than ever that people are essentially good. You may be pleasantly surprised, and at times overwhelmed, by the kindness and generosity strangers may show you as you travel with your baby or small child.

But don't take it for granted. The truth is the world has its fair share of pickpockets and others who regularly prey on out-of-towners, and the preoccupied parent whose arms seem always burdened with gadgetry or gear if not a child can be an easy target. And remember, pickpockets come in all shapes and sizes, and fashion statements. Parents, on the other hand, stand out in any crowd.

As my husband and I exited the busy metro in Barcelona, pressing on through the morning commuters with our stroller toward the elevator promised on signs overhead, only to get pushed onto an escalator instead, we acted confidently as ever that we knew what we were doing and where we were going—in spite of the daypack that surely gave us away, but we couldn't seem to do without. He balanced the loaded stroller with our daughter strapped in it onto the materializing steps in front of him as I stood behind him, thus guarding the daypack.

During our ascent, a few people passed beside us, including a blond woman in a business suit who, with all manner of importance, inserted herself in between us as if she had no idea that we were together. In a matter of seconds her fingers had found the heavy-duty Velcro securing my husband's front pocket, the one in which he happened to be carrying his wallet. Would you let go of your child's stroller in the middle of an escalator to fend off a pickpocket? Fortunately he held on, and the Velcro held on, too, just long enough to thwart her attempt.

Before I could fully appreciate the fact that an attempted robbery was in progress on the steps in front of me, we were at the top of the escalator and off she went with a wallet-size box of cigarettes in her hand, among a dozen downtown professionals. I have never heard my husband speak so harshly of a beautiful stranger, but oh, how he praises the many virtues of heavy-duty Velcro.

As you get ready for your Urban Adventure (more tips, pg. 42), here are some tips to keep in mind on how to look like less of a target for the unscrupulous, starting with ways you might actually look *more* like one than you might realize. Be safe out there!

How to look like a target for pickpockets:

- **Wear a daypack** – Yes, that handy contraption that helps parents keep their hands free and is worn by travelers everywhere. Not only do they scream, "I'm a tourist! Hit me!" but their zippers can easily be transgressed without your even knowing it, especially in crowds.

- **Wear impractical shoes** – Flip-flops, high heels, huaraches, and the like can make you extra awkward as you negotiate street curbs and subway steps with your stroller or child in hand. One little push can send you fumbling while a better-shod stranger makes off with your wallet or purse.

- **Carry a child in your arms** – Terrible as it sounds, most unsavory characters know that a person holding their life's most precious possession in their hands will be able to do little else with them— even if they feel a hand in their pocket.

- **Push a stroller** – Would you abandon your stroller on a busy street corner to chase down a purse-snatcher? Would you let go of your stroller on an escalator to push away a pickpocket? There are people in this world who have thought through these answers and look forward to spending your cash.

- **Take lots of pictures** – That fancy camera you bought for Junior's birth is itself an attractive target, but so are other items of interest as you gaze through the view finder, focusing on your child's every facial expression, trying to capture that perfect photograph for the next Christmas card.

- **Show off your smartphone.** If you decide to keep things simple by using your smartphone to take photos in your travels, remember this: they are a wildly popular item for theft, even on the friendly streets and street cars of San Francisco. If you do show off your camera to everyone in a public space while snapping priceless photos of your child, be very thoughtful as to where you put it away when you are finished and know that someone else might be as well.

How NOT to look like a target for pickpockets:

- **Use a cross-body messenger bag or purse** instead of a daypack to keep your hands free and essentials close to you during outings. One with a zippered top and an outer flap that buckles over the zipper is especially good.

- **Invest in some pickpocket-proof pants** for mom and dad when traveling in warm climates.

- **Take a jacket with inner pockets** that can fit wallets, phones, and what's needed when traveling in cold weather. Wear it zipped in crowds and on public transportation.

- **Always take a test drive with your luggage and gear** before your trip if you'll be managing multiple suitcases, people, and other items without a Sherpa or personal butler. The time to find out it's more than you can handle is before you're dropped off on a street corner in Rome at 11 p.m.

- **Arrange for private car hire instead of taxis.** Depending on your destination, private car hire for your family may cost roughly the same as or little more than taking a taxi. When arriving in an unfamiliar destination, especially at odd hours, you can be sure your ride will be there to greet you, avoid a potentially long taxi queue, and hopefully avoid any unpleasant surprise routes or charges. Not to mention, it makes you look official.

- **Let your purse be your decoy.** At some point I realized it was much better to have a credit card–size wallet with my cash and credit card I could zip into a secure pocket, while continuing to carry a cross-body purse with all the other things I needed during outings (a few diapers, sun glasses, etc.). In case of a purse snatcher, I may be out my favorite pair of sunglasses, but I'd still be able to buy a new pair to replace them.

- **Familiarize yourself with public transportation before you arrive.** Many websites can help you navigate the main routes you'll need and understand your ticketing options before you arrive, which can help you enter the public transportation system with more confidence, less fumbling, and better attention to your surroundings.

Great Products for On the Go Safety

Portable safety gates – These pressure-mounted gates can be installed in minutes without any hardware or alteration to existing door frames. KidCo has a "Gateway to Go" that folds compactly enough to fit in the suitcase in its own travel case (but not in the carry-on). Evenflo and Safety 1st each offer an extra-wide soft travel gate or that expands up to 5 feet wide and rolls up for travel at. Neither is designed for use at the top of stairs, however.

Door finger guards – They keep children from locking themselves in bathrooms and other rooms, while also preventing doors from shutting on little fingers. A dense foam "clamp" slips onto the door itself up where little hands can't reach it, and slips off easily for when you are ready to shut the door (or check out). These can also be helpful when sharing connecting rooms in a hotel or cruise ship, where you want to be sure doors aren't completely shut. Brands available include KidCo, KidKusion, Safety 1st, and The Door Mouse finger guards.

Sliding cabinet locks – These handy gadgets work with all manner of cabinet knobs and pulls that are positioned side by side (generally up to 6" apart). Adjustable for a custom fit. Sliding cabinet locks are available from DreamBaby, KidCo, and Safety 1st.

Rubber bands – Helpful when bundling long blind cords or electrical cords, or temporarily shortening draperies. Be sure to keep out of your child's reach.

Nerja, Spain: I have faced many interesting childproofing dilemmas in our travels. Toddler-proofing a bidet was a particularly interesting one.

Garden training wire – This coated wire (usually green) works wonders wending its way through and around cabinet drawer pulls and knobs of all shapes and sizes, regardless of the distance between them. Helpful in blocking access to Grandma's curio cabinet, among other things.

Child safety harness – Especially helpful with early walkers and energetic 1-year-olds who need to walk off energy during travel, but have no sense of danger. Some, like the Baby Buddy Deluxe safety harness, can also be used to help keep climbers in shopping carts and high chairs. We liked the "wee backpack" variety (see Brica's By My Side) our kids were very proud to wear through the airport and we could stash a couple of diapers, a travel size pack of wipes, and one or two board books inside for convenience. Use a carabiner clip to attach to your belt—especially helpful when you'll have a younger child in a stroller and one at your side.

Inflatable bath tub inserts – Like a little inflatable raft for your baby or toddler, but with the water on the inside for bathing. Not only do these help provide bruise-free bathing for babies on the go, but they also fill a critical niche for most families on cruises who don't have the benefit of a bathtub in their cabin (most only have a shower stall). And in warm weather, yours may even serve as an impromptu splash pool for your child. Some brands include Kel-Gar's Safe Tub, The Secure Transitions Tub by One Step Ahead, and the Safety Duck Tub by Munchkin (complete with squeaking beak).

Mommy I'm Here Child Locator – It looks like a little teddy bear and attaches to shoe laces, belt, or overall strap. The parent carries a corresponding transmitter in his pocket or on his keychain, and activates it if needed, sounding a high-decibel beep to help locate the child. Works at a range of up to 150 feet apart.

Safety Tat child ID tattoos – Waterproof, hypoallergenic, and latex-free, these write-on tattoos can last for weeks, keeping your contact info safely on your child in case it's needed.

Ten Important Steps for Safer Family Travels

When planning travel with kids, it's easy to get caught up in every *other* possible angle of your trip—tourist visas, flight details, transportation, operating hours of main attractions, food—besides your family's safety and security. But any time you travel, especially with children, safety should be a top concern. After all, being prepared for possible complications will help you rule out some before you even leave home, can help you travel with more confidence once you get out the door, and can help you swiftly manage any unpleasant surprises along the way. Here are ten steps I recommend you take for safer travels.

1. **Share trip details with friends or family.** It's important that the folks at home be able to contact you if needed, but it is also a wise idea to regularly check in with someone as you travel so that they know right away if you aren't in the right place at the right time, and can act quickly in case your family needs help or assistance.

2. **Make copies of important documents.** Passports, airline tickets, birth certificates, driver's licenses, itineraries, and the like—where would you be on your trip without them? It's a good idea to keep copies of your important travel documents in your suitcase as you travel, along with the phone numbers for your credit and ATM cards in case they become lost or stolen.

3. **Register your trip.** If you are a U.S. citizen and will be traveling abroad, you may want to register your trip with the U.S. Department of State. It's a free service that helps ensure the Department of State can assist you quickly in case of an emergency at your destination, including a natural disaster, terrorism, or civil unrest. U.S. residents living abroad can also use this service to get routine updates for their area. More information at https://travelregistration.state.gov.

4. **Insure your trip.** As I mention throughout this book, you can purchase trip insurance to protect against a wide range of unforeseeable problems and related expenses, including trip cancellation, interruption, and delay; emergency medical treatment or evacuation; lost, stolen, or damaged baggage; financial default of an airline, cruise line, or tour operator; hurricanes; and terrorism. Your credit card company may automatically include some level of travel insurance if you use it to purchase travel (including car rental insurance), so be sure to ask for details. See recommendations of travel insurance for families at www.TravelswithBaby.com.

5. **Take extra precautions for your child.** Remember it only takes a moment to lose sight of each other in crowded settings, or for a small child to step into harm's way—especially in unfamiliar territory. Keep your child close to you at all times, and make good use of your child carrier or stroller while you're out and about.

When this isn't possible, consider using the products for out-and-about safety recommended at www.TravelswithBaby.com). Also, complete a child safety kit or card complete with an updated photo of your child to carry with you during your trip. At www.yoursafechild.com, you can order child safety kits, shoe labels, and self-laminating child ID cards the size of a credit card—handy for your wallet. The Polly Klaas Foundation offers free child safety kits and includes a booklet for parents on "How to teach abduction prevention without scaring your child (or yourself)," which can be ordered online at www.pollyklaas.org.

6. **Flock together.** Rarely do travelers expect to lose track of each other at the market, the train station, the amusement park, or even the beach. By resisting the urge to split up, even for just a few minutes, you could save yourselves much anxiety and many vacation hours lost to looking for one another. If you do need to separate briefly, to use the restrooms for example, always agree on exactly where you will wait for each other afterward.

7. **Bring the ugly diaper bag**. Many diaper bags are tastefully designed to "blend in" with grown up attire, and on your trip to the Culture Capital, especially, you may prefer a sleek diaper tote to the one covered in Winnie the Pooh. To the untrained eye, however, one may look a lot more like a purse or even a laptop case. If you travel with it anyway, keep in mind how enticing it may appear set on the park bench, slung over the back of your stroller, or left on the seat of your rental car. There are times you may prefer to leave it gaping open wide with a clear view of the treasures that it holds.

8. **Keep it under wraps**. Where tourists wander, pickpockets follow. When traveling with your child, you will find yourself in even more compromising positions, keeping your attention on getting your child safely through a crowd, taking pictures, struggling with gear, changing diapers in public restrooms, and so on. This is no time to take chances with your cash, credit cards, or other important travel documents. Get a good travel wallet that you like and use it.

9. **Take and tuck a business card**. If your hotel has business cards at the front desk or in your room, pick one up—or two if possible. Tuck one in your child's pocket each day, and keep a second in your travel wallet. In the unfortunate event that your child wanders

or gets separated from you, it could help you get reunited much more quickly. Or if you are out sightseeing and have trouble finding your way back by car, bus, taxi, or train, having the hotel address handy could help, not to mention having the name and address as translated in the local language when you're abroad (e.g., you'd be surprised how many Hiltons and Holiday Inns there can be in a given city, and most of them are not the one you are staying at).

10. **Always consider your exit strategy**. When venturing out to some sights, it may be easiest for your family to take a taxi. But will it be as easy to take a taxi back? And how might you return otherwise? Make sure you bring along phone numbers for local taxi companies just in case there aren't any in sight. But more importantly, be wary of situations where unscrupulous drivers may charge you an astronomical return fare knowing you (and your precious little family) have no other options. In some situations, it may actually be safest to take public transportation, or hire a local guide to escort you and your family, or join an escorted group tour for visits to outlying destinations.

ON THE WEB:
U.S. citizens can register their trips abroad with the State Department at https://travelregistration.state.gov.
Get free child safety kits at www.pollyklaas.org and www.yoursafechild.com.
Find helpful product recommendations for out-and-about safety during travel with kids and temporary childproofing at www.TravelswithBaby.com.

Part IV:
Travels by Automobile

CHAPTER 12

Before You Go by Car

Car Seat Laws Across State Lines

If you're traveling to the U.S. or its territories, you should know that car seats or "child safety seats" are now legally required for all children less than 4 years old riding in private passenger vehicles in all 50 states, as well as the District of Columbia, Guam, the Northern Mariana Islands, Puerto Rico, and the Virgin Islands. Where it gets confusing is what happens next in each of these locations.

For example, Florida and South Dakota are the only states in the U.S. that have not yet enacted booster seat laws at time of writing, and children are only required to use an age- and size-appropriate restraint until their fourth birthdays. Beyond that, an adult safety belt is accepted from 4 to 5 years in Florida, while a safety belt is required through 17 years in South Dakota (although the state strongly recommends using boosters for children up to 80 lbs or 4 feet 9 inches tall, or 144.78 cm).

In other states, children may be required to use boosters until their 5th birthdays in South Carolina, until their 6th birthdays or standing 55" tall in New Hampshire, until their 7th birthdays in Pennsylvania, and until 8 years or weighing 80 lbs in New Jersey. Many states also specify that children should be in the back seat only if space allows.

How can you make sure you'll be compliant in every state you visit? The simplest way is to follow the NHTSA recommendations for using belt positioning safety boosters for children up to 4' 9" tall (57" or 145 cm).

How to Play It Safe in Every State:

- Children under 1 year old ride in a rear-facing safety seat, regardless of their weight.

- Children at least 1 year old, weighing 20 to 40 lbs, ride in a forward-facing safety seat (rear-facing may still be safest; see details in next section).

- Children who have exceeded the height or weight limit for their forward-facing safety seat, are nine years old or younger, and are less than 4'9" tall should ride in a safety booster seat.

- All children under the age of 12 ride in the back seat.

ON THE WEB:

To check the latest car seat laws and safety booster requirements for the state or U.S. territory you'll visit, go to the Governors Highway Safety Association website at www.ghsa.gov, where a state-by-state list of requirements includes links to each individual state's website and traffic safety information (note: always check the state's site for the most current information).

Car Seat Laws and Other Countries

International standards for child safety and car seat use vary widely, so it's a good idea to find out what you can before you arrive on the scene with your child—and possibly a car seat that is not technically "legal" (grrrrr).

For most world travelers, following the NHTSA's recommended guidelines for child safety seat through belt-positioning booster use (pg. 197) will far exceed local safety standards for child passengers in some regions. However, in countries with stringent car seat safety standards—e.g., the U.S., European Union, Australia—the car seat laws may only address those seats that have been tested to their own country's standards and bear their own standards mark.

In other words, just because an Australian car seat may be tested to the most rigorous standards in the world does not mean it is accepted by local law enforcement in the European Union or the U.S. In fact, it is not. And just because a Swedish car seat may boast superior protection because it can be used rear-facing through four years of age does not mean it is legally accepted for use in the U.S. or Australia. Without the current standards mark of the local country (or the European Union), car seats brought in from abroad are not accepted for use under local laws in Europe, Canada, the U.S., Australia, or New Zealand.

What's more, how each country, state, or province arrives at the age when children no longer need child safety seats or boosters in order to be safe with only the seat belt is somewhat of a mystery. While in the U.S. and Canada, most booster laws (where they exist for the state or province) stipulate that children should use boosters until achieving a minimum age of somewhere between 6 years and 10 years of age—or reaching 57 inches (145 cm.) in height, the U.K. requires that children ride in safety boosters until 12 years of age—or reaching 53 inches (135 cm.) in height. Yes, two years older than the maximum in Canada, *or* 4 inches shorter than that in height.

Here are some key examples to help you understand how requirements can vary as you make your travel plans (and remember all are subject to possible change):

- **In Canada,** all forward-facing car seats are required to be installed with an upper tether in addition to the seatbelt or LATCH. Beyond that, the nation's car seat and booster laws are set by each province and vary from some provinces having no booster seat requirement for children weighing over 40 lbs/18 kg (currently Alberta, Saskatchewan, Yukon Territory, Northwest Territory, and Nunavut), to the strictest provinces requiring booster seat use until 9 years of age (currently British Columbia, New Brunswick, and Nova Scotia) or even 10 years (Prince Edward Island). However, each province enforcing a booster seat law dismisses the requirement if and when the child reaches 57 in. or 145 cm. in height, except in Quebec, were they specify that children may forego their boosters once they reach a minimum seated height (from seat to top of head) of 25 in. or 63 cm. For details of car seat requirements in each province and links to the most current provincial child safety laws, visit www.parachutecanada.org.

- **In the U.K.,** all children under 12 years old or less than 135 cm. tall (53 inches, specified as 1.35 meters) must have an appropriate car seat or booster seat when traveling in an automobile, with the exception of taxis or for-hire shuttles, which are not required to provide a car seat. Children who are more than 135 cm. may ride without a car seat or booster, but they must ride in a rear seat using the safety belt. More information at www.childcarsafety.org.uk.

- **In Germany,** all children under 12 years or less than 150 cm (59 inches) are also required to be in an appropriate car seat or booster, and you can be fined 30 Euros just for allowing a child under 12 years old to ride in the front seat of a car.

- **In Sweden,** children ride rear-facing in their car seats until they are at least three years old—and many safety experts feel that's why Sweden boasts the lowest traffic fatality rate for children in the world. In fact, The American Academy of Pediatrics and many other sources advise that small children use their rear-facing car seats up until the maximum height or weight limit allowed for the car seat. While many U.S. convertible car seats accommodate rear-facing riders up to 30-35 lbs and around 36" tall, Sweden now manufactures car seats for rear-facing riders up to 4 and 5 years old. (See more at www.carseat.se.)

- **In Australia,** you will need to rent a car seat there that meets Australia's safety standards—some of the most stringent in the world—that works with the special tether anchors found in Australian automobiles. Car seats manufactured for the USA and U.K. markets are not accepted. Car seats that are will be stamped with the Australia Standards mark "AS."

- **In New Zealand,** some U.S. and European safety certified car seats are accepted IF they also bear the New Zealand Standard "S" mark to show it is certified for use in the country (most U.S. car seats don't include this mark, so check carefully). Children here are now required to ride in an appropriate restraint until their 7th birthdays, and from 7 years to 8 years "if" an appropriate restraint is available. More information at http://www.nzta.govt.nz.

- **In Japan,** car seats are currently required for children riding in private passenger vehicles until their sixth birthdays.

- **In Southeast Asia, including Thailand and Vietnam,** it can cost the average factory worker more than 100 hours of wages to purchase a car seat. As you might expect, you won't see many people using them, and renting one for your visit may be virtually impossible. Your best bet in these regions will be to rent a car from a large international agency (Avis, Hertz, etc.) and to verify ahead of time that your rental car will have suitable seatbelts or LATCH in the backseat for your car seat. If the rental agency can't guarantee a car seat will be available to rent, plan to bring your own car seat to use on vacation. Also be aware that taxis, shuttle vans, and other cars for hire in this part of the world may not have any seatbelts in the rear seats at all.

Finding current car seat and booster laws abroad

Unfortunately, most countries around the world do not publish these legally binding requirements for visitors in easy-to-find English Web pages, and what information you are more likely to find in online searches—forums with outdated or "best guess" information about car seat laws in other countries—may be misleading. To find out the most current laws concerning car seat and safety booster usage at your travel destination, I recommend:

If you'll be renting a car, contact the local office of the rental car agency (not the corporate toll-free phone number or email) and ask for the current local requirements, and whether they vary by state or province within the country. Also, be aware that if you'll drive through additional countries on your trip, laws may differ as you travel.

Contact a local baby gear rental agency, which provides child car seats at the destination as well as other baby gear. They are most often owned and operated by parents themselves, and also must be experts on the local requirements (and are the most likely to guarantee the type of seat you will want and need for your child, whereas rental car agencies often do not—details in Renting a Car Seat, pg. 225).

Malaga, Spain: If you aren't yet familiar with rigid LATCH or ISOFIX—now a requirement in some countries, but only recently approved in Australia—this is what it looks like. To the left you can see the black ISOFIX anchor points in the Spanish rental car, and behind the car seat at its base are the metal LATCH attachments, extended for easy installation. Once connected on both sides, the car seat simply slides backward for a snug fit against the seat back and locks into place. Easy!

ON THE WEB:

To find a local baby gear rental agency providing car seats and safety boosters at your travel destination, visit **The Worldwide Directory of Baby Gear Rental Agencies** at <u>www.TravelswithBaby.com</u>.

Nicoya Peninsula, Costa Rica: Sure, the cattle and watermelon trucks can slow you down, but it's all worth it once you get to drive your children through that first river!

Advice for Driving with Children Abroad

Driving abroad can be exciting enough without a diaper-clad copilot. After climbing confidently behind the wheel, you may find yourself confronted by road signs that appear to be related to driving, or possibly to parking, or—at third glance you realize they are actually illustrating the picking up of dog poop (Spain). Elsewhere, you may quickly discover that red traffic lights actually mean a rolling stop to local residents, who for some strange reason are getting out of their car to help move yours on its way (Italy). Or you might discover that the painted street lanes are merely for decoration in the few places you encounter them (India). Or after finally relaxing during the windy drive down the "wrong" side of country roads, a flock of sheep suddenly appears on the highway before you (New Zealand).

Driving in other countries can give you plenty to think about besides following a map or minding your speed—which may be gauged by numbers that make no more sense to you than the gearshift pattern of the car that you have rented. Not to mention that, yes, you need to shift gears again—with your left hand—and for a moment you can't remember which side of the road you should be driving on.

If I had only one bit of advice to give on driving abroad with small children in the car, it would be: "Don't." Yet once you add children to your equation, you're more likely than ever to consider renting a car when you travel. If your trip abroad will require driving at some point, you will want to learn all you can about driving in the country before you get behind the wheel. Here are some pointers to help you be as prepared as possible.

- **Rules of the Road** – A simple Google search for "driving in…" and the country you're planning to visit may connect you with plenty of information on the subject. You can also visit the country's tourism site(s) and search for driving information (find it at the Tourism Offices Worldwide directory www.towd.com), or contact that country's embassy in your own country to see if they can provide you with driving rules and regulations. To find contact information for the embassies in Washington, D.C., visit www.embassy.org.

- **Driving Culture** – It is also a good idea to spend some time observing the driving "culture" and traffic patterns in the area before you join in. While the printed literature may tell you that you're required to have a security vest in your vehicle at all times (Austria), it may not mention anything about motorcycles having the right of way on sidewalks (Taiwan). Now add to that a potentially crying baby or shouting child, low blood sugar, and a complete lack of legal (for all you can tell) parking spaces, and you will quickly see why public transportation is preferred by parents in many cities.

- **International Driver's Licenses and Permits** – In addition to your valid driver's license from home, you should bring along an International Driver's Permit (IDP). This additional form of ID is recognized in more than 150 countries and translates your information into eleven different languages (including English). The simplest, fastest way to obtain your IDP will most likely be to visit the American Automobile Association's website, www.aaa.com, and print the online form to complete at home. You will also need two passport-size photos with your signature on the back of each and a photocopy of your valid U.S. driver's license. If you bring this to your local AAA office (member or not), they can issue your IDP immediately.

- **International Road Signs** – At www.aaa.com, you will also find a helpful collection of international regulatory, warning, and prohibitory road signs that you might encounter when traveling abroad. You needn't be a member to take a look (or take advantage of any of their other AAA Travel Agency features), and it can certainly help prepare you for the abundance of less-than-intuitive signage that awaits you out in the world.

- **Maps and Directions** – Any language barriers could make it especially challenging to ask for, and particularly to follow, directions in an unknown land. So before you leave home, get all the maps and directions you can to help plan your drive—and do not count on your GPS navigation helping you every step of the way. Would you be able to find your way without it? You may need to at some point in your journey.

Installing Car Seats with Confidence

The first time you installed a car seat, you may have spent hours wrestling the seatbelt or fishing for LATCH attachments, checking the angle, jiggling the seat, tugging on the tether, only to swear at long last that the seat would stay put until you sold the car (even if your child had outgrown the seat and left home long before).

If you plan to travel far and wide, you will need to become fluent in "Carseatese." You will want to be able to remove and install your child's car seat in any manner of rental car, relative's car, shuttle van, or taxi—quickly and with confidence. The good news is that, like most things, practice and a few good pointers make it all possible. As you prepare for travels with your car seat, remember these installation basics:

Installing Your Car Seat

- **Route the vehicle safety belt or LATCH belt** through the appropriate path and buckle.

- **Apply your weight** to help press the car seat into the vehicle seat, with your knee if possible, and tighten the belt.

- **Make sure the car seat doesn't move** more than 1 inch in any direction.

Installing Your Child

- **Rear-facing seat straps** should be at or below the shoulders.

- **Forward-facing seat straps** should be at or just above the shoulders.

- **Chest clip** should be at armpit level.

- **Straps should be snug** so that only one finger fits between it and child's collar bone.

Seatbelt Specifics

If you have grown accustomed to the simplicity of LATCH at home (standard in U.S. vehicles model year 2003 and newer), it may be daunting to face the prospect of myriad seatbelt configurations awaiting you and your car seat as you travel. Shoulder belt? Lap belt? Locking clip? Here's what you need to know when seat-belting your car seat into unfamiliar vehicles.

Types of Seatbelts You May Encounter...

Manually adjusting lap-only belt – Similar to seatbelts found on airplanes, you can pull the free end of the seatbelt to shorten it, and the latch plate locks to hold the seatbelt in place once adjusted.

Automatic locking retractor (ALR) – This belt pulls out from the retractor, then locks in place at the specified length. It cannot be lengthened from this point until it has been completely retracted again.

Emergency locking retractor (ELR) – This seatbelt moves freely in and out of the retractor and only locks in place when the vehicle comes to a sudden stop. These belts are not recommended for use with car seats unless a vehicle manufacturer's belt-shortening clip is provided. ELRs were discontinued after 1995.

Switchable ELR/ALR combination retractor – Most of these belts will move freely for normal adult use, like an ELR. But they can switch to ALR mode by pulling the belt all of the way out of the retractor (after you have buckled the seatbelt through the car seat), then allowing the belt to retract to fit the car seat. There may be a label with instructions on switching modes affixed to the seatbelt.

Continuous loop lap/shoulder belt – One belt passes through the latch plate of this belt, forming both the lap and shoulder segments. If the latch plate locks in place once buckled, holding the car seat in place with the lap belt portion, no locking clip is needed. If the latch plate slides freely along the belt, you will need to use your locking clip.

Automatic seatbelts – These should never be used with car seats. If the lap belt portion is not automated, and you can unhook the automatic shoulder belt, that may be wisest—but check to see if the lap belt is an ELR, in which case a manufacturer's belt shortening clip should be used. Most automatic seatbelts are in the front seats and can be avoided by simply using the back seat.

The Lowdown on Locking Clips

Vehicles manufactured for the U.S. market after September 1, 1995 (model year 1996 and beyond), have all been required to feature safety belts that can secure child safety seats without the need for locking clips or additional hardware. If you might be riding in vehicles from earlier years, and/or will be using a car seat abroad, you may need to use a locking clip.

Locking clips are the H-shaped metal clips that still come packaged with most child safety seats, and are usually stored under the base. The clip is used to fasten together the lap and shoulder portions of a shoulder seatbelt where the strap slides freely through the latch plate. The clip should be used just above the latch plate to prevent the seatbelt from sliding through it. See your car seat manual for specifics on using a locking clip with your model.

A freely sliding latch plate on a continuous loop safety belt, which requires a locking clip for safe car seat installation.

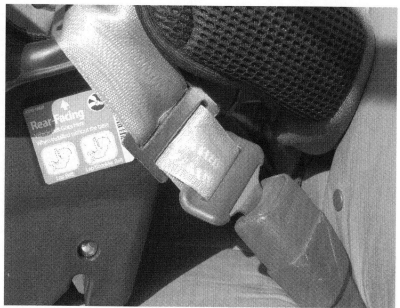

The same safety belt with a properly used locking clip.

Seven Ways to Smooth Your Travels with the Car Seat

1. **Improve your manual dexterity** – First, take another look at your car seat manual, where you'll find instructions for use with all the various seatbelt configurations and safety features you might encounter on your trip. If you've misplaced your manual, you may be able to find the instructions online (www.TravelswithBaby.com also has links to manufacturer websites with instructions and manuals online). Most new car seats include a place to store the manual in them or allow you to tuck them in under the car seat cover so you will always have it with you—a great help when you find yourself scratching your head in the back of a rental car. Fold over the corners of the most relevant pages for installation for easy reference.

2. **Get clipped** – If it isn't already in use in your car, check to make sure a seatbelt locking clip is stored under your seat. If you don't have a locking clip, it is a good idea to travel with one just in case you come across a seatbelt that slides freely through the buckle (see your manual for details on when and how to use a locking clip with your model of car seat). You can pick one up for around $2 or $3 at most stores selling car seats and baby gear.

3. **Move it** – While experts generally agree the center of the back seat is the safest place for your child's car seat, it may not always be practical (or possible if you have two children in car seats). Differently shaped back seats may force you to use a side seat or remove head rests to get a secure fit. You may also need extra space in the backseat for diaper changes. If you can, practice installation in a friend's car if you can, and in the various possible seating positions.

4. **Recline 'er** – Back seats of cars can vary widely in shape, slope, and size, so make sure your infant is reclined a full 45 degrees to prevent her head from drooping forward, even if this means inserting a rolled up baby blanket or shortened foam swimming noodle at the crack in the car seat. If her head still droops forward, chances are the seat is not reclined enough and an adjustment should be made.

5. **Be so inclined** – Let toddlers and older babies that can support their heads well and have gained good control of their neck muscles ride rear-facing with less recline, in the range of 15 to 30 degrees from vertical. This helps them see out the window, look around the car more easily, and generally ride more happily. This may also help you better fit that rear-facing convertible car seat into the back of a cramped rental car.

6. **Consult the experts** – If you'd like a second opinion on your installation or help working out any kinks, a quick trip to www.seatcheck.org or a toll-free call to 1-866-SEAT-CHECK will help you find the nationally certified safety seat inspectors located in and around your zip code.

7. **Look before you buy** – The next time you are in the market for any kind of car seat or safety booster, be sure to take a look at the NHTSA's latest Ease of Use Ratings available online at www.NHTSA.dot.gov. The annual report provides usability ratings for nearly one hundred child restraint systems, including ratings for installation instructions and execution.

CHAPTER 13

On the Road

Pacing Your Journey

Making good time doesn't always make for a good time, especially with children. Instead of pulling over for a quick refueling or a quick diaper change on an as-needed basis, try to lump as many things together as you can in a single stop, including some sort of physical activity and a change of scenery from that of the car's interior. Plan ahead to take scheduled, meaningful breaks, and address the major issues before they become a crisis.

The mother of an active toddler explained to me that she used to find the long drive to her in-laws' unbearable—until she began planning the trip with strategically timed breaks at certain fast food restaurants along the way. To qualify, each restaurant features indoor (climate-controlled) playgrounds. Their son gets an adequate break from his car seat, burns off some energy in a suitable (and safe) environment, often meets other playmates, and has more stops to look forward to throughout the long day of driving to Grandma and Grandpa's house. What's more, Mom and Dad don't have to worry about finding food he will like, and they can relax knowing there will be a restroom.

If "the McDrive" isn't for you, look for state parks and points of interest along your route that may combine a rest area with a nature trail, beach access, or picnic area. Even interstate rest areas often include lawns, picnic tables, and short paths of some kind (pack a ball to toss or roll, plenty of snacks, and drinks). If you will be traveling in inclement weather, it may work best to take a break at a shopping mall where your family can stretch its legs indoors, find sustenance, and perhaps a play area (if only a toy store). By taking time for activities during your drive, you will also improve your odds of having a more restful night when you arrive at your destination.

For more on-the-go tips and ideas for fair-weather road stops and best-bet rainy day road stops, as well as recommended ways to help keep small kids entertained in the car, be sure to pack along the travel companion to this guide, *Take-Along Travels with Baby: Hundreds of Tips to Help During Travel with Your Baby, Toddler, and Preschooler.*

Weed, California: On the first of our annual road trips to Oregon with a toddler in tow, a gas station attendant recommended a nearby park to us. Today, it continues to be a picnic and play stop we all look forward to— including the yearly photo op with the purple dinosaur.

Dealing with Diapers, Dining, and Such

The Quick Car Change

One of the most daunting details for many new parents is how to change all those messy diapers on the go. Sure, SOME restrooms are equipped with changing tables, but can you expect them to be at all (or any) roadside rest areas as you travel? State parks? Historic sites?

Restaurants and delis? Unfortunately, these conveniences are still few and far between.

The "Quick Car Change" is much easier with a firm bed pillow (and waterproof mat on top) to help even out sloping or bucket seats.

I once purchased a milkshake at a national fast food franchise just for the privilege of using its diaper changing station in the restroom—only to discover there wasn't a changing station, nor was there room by the sink or anywhere else to change a diaper, aside from the dirty floor. I was obliged to return to the parking lot and change my daughter on the passenger seat of our car as burger-munching patrons watched from the restaurant windows in disapproval. Oddly enough, I have had more luck finding baby changing stations in Starbucks cafés than in the national fast food franchises that target families.

As far as vehicles are concerned, minivans, SUVs, and station wagons are the most accommodating for roadside changes as you can simply open the rear gate and utilize the level surface there—assuming it isn't loaded with gear. But if you're on the go in a sedan, try this formula:

Equipment Needed for the Quick Car Change:

- One firm bed pillow (also handy for breastfeeding)
- Flannel-backed vinyl (you can trim for a custom fit)
- Clean diapers
- Diaper wipes
- Plastic bag for disposal, slide-lock or other
- Antibacterial wipes or a liquid hand sanitizer

Step 1: Wedge the bed pillow against the passenger seat or backseat so that it creates as level a surface as possible (and overlaps the emergency brake, if applicable).

Step 2: Lay flannel-backed vinyl over the pillow to create a waterproof, but soft barrier. You can purchase it by the yard at a fabric store or in crib size at most baby stores.

Step 3: Be sure to place the fresh diaper beneath the baby before removing the dirty diaper—just in case.

Step 4: If there isn't a trash receptacle handy, use your plastic bag to store the dirty diaper until you find one. (A slide-lock bag is especially helpful in sealing away odors.)

Step 5: Since most diaper wipes do not contain germ-killing agents (namely alcohol), antibacterial "Redi-Wipes" or "Wet Ones" are an easy way to ensure clean hands on the go. You can also use liquid hand sanitizer (e.g., Purell), though it can be nice to have the disposable cloth for wiping off assorted "stickies and ickies" on hands and other surfaces.

Travel-size antibacterial wipes and baby wipes fit easily into the glove box (or console in larger vehicles), plus a couple of diapers. With your glove box loaded, you have your diaper changing essentials ready to go at a moment's notice, all within easy reach when you use the passenger seat.

You may have also seen some "car changing mats" or "stations" that provide a built-in wedge on one side to help even out the slope of the car seats and may even have some pockets for organization. One of these could save you some space in the car, but they're not nearly as comfy for grown-up naptime as a good old-fashioned pillow.

Cloth Diapering on the Go—Are You Crazy?

To our newest generation of moms, even those who opt to use cloth diapers at home, taking cloth diapers for a weekend outing may sound ridiculous and completely unnecessary. But as parents who traveled with babies just a generation or two ago know, it is plausible. And for parents interested in keeping up cloth, a weekend of cloth diapering on the road needn't be any more trouble than a weekend of cloth diapering at home.

First of all, if you aren't already using flushable diaper liners, I strongly recommend adding them to your diapering routine (made by Imse Vimse, Kooshies, and Diaperaps). They greatly simplify poop patrol (the solids stick to the sheet, not the diaper), and help shield your child's skin from a wet diaper—especially helpful while traveling. In fact, they can also be helpful while traveling with disposable diapers as well.

Using the dry-pail method, which is most popular now and how it's commonly done with diaper services, we found that a large plastic pail we had originally purchased filled with kitty litter (since emptied) made the perfect diaper pail for weekend trips by car. The lid divides so that two-thirds can be flipped up to add soiled diapers, and then it snaps closed airtight. It even had a nice carrying handle for transporting it to and from the car.

If you are using disposable wipes while traveling, simply keep an extra plastic slide-lock bag handy for stashing the used wipes until you next encounter a trashcan. For the bigger jobs, consider using flushable toddler wipes that can go into the potty with your flushable diaper liners.

Eating and Feeding on the Road

Even if you are solely breastfeeding at the time of your trip, it could be very helpful to have a couple of bottles of your milk ready to go in case baby's hunger pangs are not timed with a safe place to pull over. The same is true for bottles of formula or "moo juice" for older children. If your little one is picky about temperature, you might consider some of the warming methods recommended on pg. 81, some of which may warm jars of baby food as well.

Drinks and snacks can be conveniently stowed in a small ice chest or insulated pack that will fit on the floor of your car's back seat (in most cases, it will be accessible to the passenger riding in the front seat) or between the front seats in minivans or SUVs with space. A waterproof chest is especially helpful if you'll be relying on hotel ice to keep things cool—there aren't any zippers to leak water as the ice melts, as there might be in some soft-pack coolers.

While restaurants may be convenient en route and give shelter from inclement weather, they don't often do much for the imagination or help burn off energy (the "McDrive" may be an exception). A happier alternative can be a good old-fashioned picnic, which can save you money while providing a healthy dose of fresh air—not to mention room to throw a Frisbee or fly a kite while the sandwiches are made.

Carsickness Survival Guide

Carsickness can sneak up on any member of the family, but children— trapped in the back seats and oftentimes seated lower than the car windows—can be especially prone to the condition. Before you hit the highway, be sure you're as prepared as possible in case the condition arises, and do what you can to avoid it altogether.

US I-70 between Bryce Canyon National Park and Moab, Utah: You can't always predict when carsickness will be a problem. You can, however, do your best to try and prevent it—and to be prepared in case it becomes a problem in spite of your best efforts.

Tips to Avoid Carsickness:

- **Decrease the recline** of rear-facing car seats for babies once they can support their heads well. The American Academy of Pediatrics suggests a 33 to 15 degree recline for older babies and toddlers riding in rear-facing seats.

- **Position forward-facing toddler car seats in the center position** when possible to give a full view of the road ahead, rather than the back of your seat.

- **Avoid the blood sugar blues** by keeping meals balanced and as timely as possible. Back-up snacks should be low in sugar (beware of fruit juice) to avoid sugar spikes and the woes that follow.

- **Stay hydrated.** If your child has been in higher temperatures than usual and/or overly active, remember that babies, toddlers, and young children become dehydrated more quickly than adults and older children. Consider giving some sportsdrink (like Gatorade) or Pedialyte to help restore the balance of electrolytes.

- **Keep fresh air circulating** through the car either through open windows or vent settings and remember that air conditioning may be your new best friend.

- **Use motion sickness wristbands.** Many adults and children alike swear by special medicine-free wristbands that use acupressure to relieve motion sickness. Some are available now sized specially for children.

- **Avoid entertainment through toys, books, and electronics that are held down** on your child's lap. Instead, help encourage your child to look up and out the windows by playing games like "Red car! Blue car!" and singing songs, or listening to audiobooks. And don't forget to pack along your *Take-Along Travels with Baby*, with lyrics to several "Easy Songs to Sing in the Car" and suggestions for several other ways to keep kids happy on the go.

Tips to Help Manage Carsickness:

- **Pack along ginger snaps and cold soda** (e.g. ginger ale or 7up) for those prone to carsickness who are old enough to enjoy them.

- **Keep some sizable slide-lock bags handy** (or airsickness bags should you have them on hand...) in case an episode arrives before the next turnout.

- **Invest in a second car seat cover** if your child gets carsick often or easily so you'll have a fresh one ready to go in times of need (the whole family may thank you). Extra covers are usually available through the manufacturer or baby gear retailers (or see www.TravelswithBaby.com for help finding yours).

- **Install an under-the-car-seat seat protector.** Most create a waterproof barrier and allow for easy cleanup of the various spills and thrills associated with driving with children, including carsickness.

- **Keep a plastic trash bag (or a few) in the glove box to** contain soiled items and their odors until they can be cleaned (large slide-lock storage bags may work, too).

- **Have sanitizing wet wipes ready to go** (like antibacterial "Redi-Wipes" or "Wet Ones") to help clean surfaces, seat straps, hands, and more.

- **Pack along a bottle of Folex brand upholstery cleaner,** which requires no rinsing, and is non-toxic and odor-free.

- **Discuss carsickness with your child's doctor** if it is a frequent problem, and ask about any suitable medications that may be of help on your next driving vacation. .

Packing for a Comfortable Road Trip

When planning a trip by car, it is tempting to "just bring everything." But as you load your car, you may quickly discover that's not possible—nor is it practical if you hope to access some items during your journey without unloading the entire vehicle. On the other hand, less is not necessarily more when you pack for a trip with children. Missing key child-size items (winter coats, life jackets) can seriously complicate matters depending on your travels, and some items can be difficult to replace when far from home.

As you strive to simplify your road trip packing list, here are some pointers to keep in mind:

- **If your child is still in diapers,** it will be very helpful to have seat or floor space reserved where diapers can be changed.

- **If your child is potty training,** it may prove invaluable to have a training potty in the car for unexpected stops.

- **If your child is a sensitive sleeper**, accustomed to sleeping in her own space, it might be well worth the space needed to accommodate her portacrib or bassinet. These will also provide safe, clean spaces for your child to sprawl and play while you do any childproofing or other setting up at your destination. Travel beds are another space-saving option for traveling infants through preschoolers (see travel beds and sleeping solutions, pg. 76).

Our 3-gallon water dispenser with tap. Fill with water and ice at the hotel each morning and you're ready to refill water bottles (and icy lemonade cups) as needed throughout the day's drive.

- **Pack a 3-gallon water dispenser with a tap.** It's easy to use for refilling personal water bottles and cups on the go, and is convenient at your destination—plus, you won't have empty water bottles of the disposable type cluttering the car.

- **Keep a flashlight handy** for double-checking maps and finding snacks without waking up your child. It can also be helpful when searching through an overstuffed trunk at night and staying in hotel rooms or at other unfamiliar lodgings.

- **Bring extra receiving blankets** and keep them accessible for roadside stops and picnics. Roll up the end of one blanket in the window of your car for a little shade and privacy. Spread it out on the lawn at a grassy park to give your baby a place to stretch and sprawl.

- **Bring a small ice chest that will fit on the floor** of your automobile's back seat. It's a convenient place to store water and drinks, bottles, teething toys, and snacks, and in most cars it will be accessible to the person in the passenger seat.

- **Bring a firm bed pillow** along for the ride. It helps even out bucket seats for a diaper change, provides support while breast- or bottle-feeding, and provides extra insulation from heat for your back-seat cooler.

- **Pack a small suitcase for each family member** instead of sharing larger luggage. This will help you find things more quickly (e.g., that unexpected change of clothes) and stay better organized throughout the trip.

✔ Roadside Emergency Checklist

Even if you are an AAA member or have roadside assistance coverage included in your insurance, and even if you have a cellular phone with you when you drive, you may need to make do for some time until help arrives—or need to make do on your own if you find yourself without cell phone coverage or an exhausted battery where you need it most. Extreme temperatures or foul weather can complicate roadside surprises with babies and small children as well, so before you leave home on your next family road trip, be sure you have the following items in your car.

☐ Fix-a-flat emergency tire repair (in a can)

- [ ] Spare tire & jack
- [ ] Jumper cables
- [ ] Replacement wiper blades
- [ ] Replacement headlight bulb
- [ ] Umbrella
- [ ] Rain poncho
- [ ] Quarters for unanticipated parking meters or turnpikes
- [ ] First-aid kit, complete with infant and child medications
- [ ] Flares or emergency lights/reflectors
- [ ] Emergency blanket (mylar "space blanket" recommended)
- [ ] Emergency water reserve for both car and passengers
- [ ] Emergency snack reserve
- [ ] Emergency cash reserve (perhaps stored in your wallet)
- [ ] Pen and paper for emergency note-taking or note-leaving

Taxis, Kids, and Car Seats

While taxis can be a major convenience for travelers near and far, the traveler with a baby or small child in tow may find them especially helpful—except, perhaps, for the need of a car seat. You may find yourself wondering if you really need to bring along the car seat for your next urban adventure if the only times you'll be in a car are on quick jaunts around the city by taxi. If you've spent any time in large cities, you may have already noticed parents popping in and out of taxis with their children on their laps. To answer a very frequent question, it is done and, outside of perhaps Scandinavia, it is in most cases legal. Whether or not it is safe, or preferable, is another matter.

In most states, cities, and countries around the world, drivers of taxis and other for-hire vehicles (shuttles, minibuses, town cars) are not legally responsible for providing child safety seats. In turn, this means that parents and caregivers hiring the driver are not legally responsible for having their child in a car seat because one does not exist in the driver's vehicle. Privately-owned passenger vehicles, however, are subject to different laws (which can vary by state, province, and country, as discussed in Car Seat Laws Across State Lines and in Other Countries, beginning on pg. 196).

But while you may not be thrilled at the prospect of bringing along your car seat during your day's outings to Central Park, the Statue of Liberty, and the Metropolitan Museum of Art, you will hopefully think twice before leaping into unfamiliar cars driven by complete strangers with your child on your lap.

Here are some travel-friendly alternatives to children riding unrestrained in taxis:

- **Get a travel-friendly car seat for infants and toddlers.** For infants, rear-facing carrier car seats that can be used without their bases are simple to install and remove using basic seatbelts (read your manual for details) and can be paired with a basic stroller frame during sightseeing. For babies and toddlers, the Sit 'n' Stroll car seat that projects stroller wheels and handle when needed can be very helpful for travel and sightseeing by taxi. See more travel-friendly car seat recommendations in Great Products and Gear for Travel, beginning on pg. 66, and at www.TravelswithBaby.com.

- **Get a RideSafer travel vest for children 3 years (and 30 lbs) and older.** This car seat alternative meets or exceeds FMVSS 213 for use in motor vehicles. More details about the RideSafer travel vest in Car Seat Alternatives begin on pg. 66, and a detailed review of the RideSafer is available online at www.TravelswithBaby.com.

- **Use public transportation.** In major cities, you may be able to use public transportation during most of your visit, and in many locations this will be preferable to sitting in traffic and far more affordable than relying on taxis. Many major airports also have train service from the airport to the city center (or other destinations), so if you can manage your group and your luggage without an airport cart, you may be able to skip the taxi ride or at least shorten it significantly (possibly avoiding interstate or highway driving).

- **Use a shuttle or car service that provides car seats or boosters.** If you are planning on taking a taxi just between an airport and your hotel, you may be able to book a shuttle service, taxi, or town car ahead of time that can provide a car seat for your child (call local services to inquire about car seats and make reservations).

Recommendations for services providing car seats and boosters in New York and Paris are online at www.TravelswithBaby.com.

The RideSafer travel vest, for children 3 years and older, uses guides to put the safety belt where it belongs on the child. An optional top tether also makes it compatible with lap-only safety belts where a tether anchor is available. See more photos and the complete review at www.TravelswithBaby.com.

CHAPTER 14

Renting a Vehicle for the Drive

Choosing a Rental Car and Agency

Branches of the major international rental agencies, like Budget, Hertz, and Avis, have sprouted up everywhere from Austria to Zimbabwe. Their omnipresence makes these megabrands seem especially convenient if you need a one-way rental for your trip (from Austria to Zimbabwe, however, is not recommended). They are also the most likely agencies to be able to offer you the options you seek, such as an extra-roomy vehicle or a child's safety seat. And naturally, they might also charge you the most for these conveniences.

To help determine which agency will really provide the best value for your trip, contact the companies directly with all of the specifics of your driving itinerary, and be sure to find out what "a standard midsize" or any other model of car means at their office—car models and brands can vary widely from office to office, even within the same corporation. Hopefully this will reassure you that you are getting the best value possible.

If you are planning to rent in a small town, be especially sure to call ahead and make contact. You might be surprised to learn that just because there is an office of said agency in a certain village on the Spanish border, it isn't open on the day of the week, or on the certain holiday you've never heard of, when you need to pick up the car. Or that, even though the agency's location is listed as being at a train station in Pennsylvania, you must call a local number when you arrive and wait 40 minutes for the manager's nephew to pick you up in his pizza delivery car and drive you to the office on the other side of town.

Renting from major airport locations and offices in large cities is usually a fairly straightforward procedure, but again, be sure you know the hours of operation for the days you'll be renting and returning. If you are deciding between two or more agencies located at an airport, make sure you know if either or both require a shuttle to an off-site location. If you have a choice, the cost savings may not be worth the time spent waiting with your child (possibly in rain, snow, wind, or cigarette smoke) for the next shuttle to arrive, or riding in a crowded minibus stacked precariously with other people's luggage.

Also, be sure your rental car will have enough room for your family and its gear. The economy or "subcompact" models are generally described as holding 4 people, 1 large suitcase, and 1 small suitcase, and though you may only be 3 people, chances are your luggage and gear will exceed these standards. Also, be forewarned that if your child uses a rear-facing car seat, some rental cars—especially in Europe—may not have backseats large enough to accommodate your car seat. Unfortunately, as rental car sizes go up so do rental car prices. Try to do your homework ahead of time to make sure you're getting the best deal on the car you'll need, so you don't get stuck with an overpriced last-minute substitution.

Renting Car Seats

If you are arriving at your destination by train or by plane with a lap child, or if the driving is just a small portion of your adventure, it may be a great convenience to rent a car seat along with the car. Most car rental agencies now offer to rent child safety seats for somewhere around $10 to $15 per day, or sometimes for a flat fee of around $35 to $50 for your trip. But be aware that car seats—particularly the size or type needed for your child's age—may not be guaranteed at all locations. I once hashed out all the details of a one-way rental between small towns in Europe with a car seat included, and in finalizing my reservation, I was then told to call back (at no specific time or date) to confirm whether or not the car seat would be available at my pickup location. Since that "minor detail" had everything to do with whether or not the car rental would work for us and our planned itinerary that trip, I elected to cancel the rental car reservation and make other arrangements, as you might too.

Generally, if you are renting from an office in a major airport or city, this shouldn't be a problem. The agency should ask you for details about your child's age, weight, and height to ensure the proper car seat or booster seat will be provided (and if they don't, you tell them). When you arrive at the rental office, your car seat may already be installed for you, or it may be handed to you along with the car keys. So be prepared to install it yourself, or at least perform a thorough inspection to make sure it has been installed properly for you (also see photo and caption, pg.201).

You may also be able to rent a vehicle with an integrated (built-in) car seat, though you should call the rental agency directly to confirm availability and make your reservation. Integrated car seats are available in some newer Chrysler, GM, and Volvo cars, but are generally only forward-facing (for children at least 1 year and weighing 20 lbs or more) and offer little or no recline, with minimal side support, all of which makes them less than ideal for napping during travel. Those that can also be used as belt-positioning boosters for older children, however, may prove a great convenience to some families.

ON THE WEB:

If you'd like to rent a car seat or safety booster with your car, here are some of your best bets for rental agencies to try:

Alamo	www.alamo.com	1-800-462-5266
Avis	www.avis.com	1-800-331-1212
Budget	www.budget.com	1-800-527-0700
Hertz	www.hertz.com	1-800-654-3131
Thrifty	www.thrifty.com	1-800-847-4389

If the agency cannot guarantee the seat you need will be available when you pick up your car, you may prefer to rent the car seat or booster from a local baby gear rental agency instead. For help finding an agency where you're bound, visit the Worldwide Directory of Baby Gear Rental Agencies at www.TravelswithBaby.com.

Renting an RV

The Case For and Against RVs

Having a complete kitchen, restroom, and beds at every stop of the way can be a major convenience for a parent with babies and children along for the ride. If inclement weather strikes, you are well sheltered and well equipped to pass the time with lights, a stereo, and possibly a TV. You can cook virtually every meal during the road trip, refrigerate and easily reheat leftovers, and enjoy the sense of security that comes with locking your door every night.

But for all the conveniences an RV affords while stopped along the way, it will not help you escape certain realities of the road trip. For one, your family may still be spending hours on the road, belted into seats, the car seat included (perhaps even more hours as you watch traffic pass you on the hills and at highway turn-outs). You may still get lost, you may still get stuck in traffic, you may still need to stop for gas—and lots of it.

What's more, traveling with your "house on your back" presents certain burdens you may never face when driving your passenger car. Let's not kid ourselves, RVs are BIG and, for many people, they can be stressful to drive (even as a back-seat driver)—especially through mountains or cities or even parking lots. And for all of the space RVs require on the road (almost the entire width of the lane), they offer little play space inside for children.

Even that convenient toilet will have to relieve itself at some point. And unless you plan to spend your nights at roadside rest areas or will be traveling where free camping still exists, you will still have an additional expense of paying for a place to park it (an extra $10–$50 per night, or more in some cases).

Speaking of expenses, you will want to carefully consider the total cost of your RV rental before committing. When I considered an RV rental for one week in the mid-season, with pickup and return from the same location in Los Angeles, my total quote came out to $1334. It would have been an additional $35 per person, but we opted to bring our own linens and blankets. The costs broke down as follows:

Sample Standard Mid-Season RV Rental for 2-5 Passengers

$945   7 Nights (includes comprehensive insurance)

$203   700 Miles (additional miles: 29 cents/mile)

$70   Supplemental Liability

-$70   Promotional Discount

$85   Kitchen Kit (plates, bowls, cookware, utensils, can opener, broom, etc.)

$102   State Tax

Total Charge $1335

Additional damage deposit (refundable after trip) $300

Additional RV Vacation Expenses (not factored in to quote above)

- Mileage fees (if you pay by the mile or go beyond your flat-rate package, in this case 29 cents/mile)
- Campground fees ($10–$50 per night)
- Reservation fees ($5 and up, in addition to campground fees)
- Generator fees (about $3/hour of use where applicable, and/or cost of gasoline)
- Campground hook-up fees if applicable (electric, water, sewage, estimate $20–$30/day for full hook-up)
- Dump fees when not using hook-ups (around $5 for sewage)
- Fuel fees for driving (expect between 6 and 13 mpg of unleaded gasoline)
- Propane (usually needed for refrigerator, heater, water heater, stove, and range)
- Groceries for trip
- Budget for any additional restaurants, entertainment, and attractions
- Pet deposit, if applicable ($50–$150, usually non-refundable)
- One-way rental fee, if applicable ($200 and up)
- Return airfare or train tickets from one-way rental, if applicable

As I pondered how much our week's vacation could total, all costs considered, I quickly realized there were a lot of other ways we could spend that same money—and time. For one thing, just putting the same $1300 toward a luxury tent, new sleeping bags, and other outdoor gear could have us camping in Fat City—and at the end of the vacation, we'd still own all of the equipment for many future vacations to come.

Or we could take advantage of any number of 3-day vacation packages that could include airfare and hotel for the three of us with little to no time spent driving. Even renting a cabin, a beach house, or condo might prove far more cost-effective—and comfortable for your family—so do consider your options carefully.

Still, there may be situations where an RV rental is ideal. Particularly if you want to visit a remote setting where other lodgings and facilities are not available and tent camping is problematic (security issues, hostile fauna, inhospitable climate, etc.). If you will be traveling with extended family, and perhaps an elderly relative or a pregnant traveler, an RV rental can be a marvelous way to go. Or if you simply need additional accommodations while visiting someone's home, an RV can be the guest cottage escape you need.

Yet in other situations, renting a conversion or campervan may provide much of what you're looking for while saving you some money—and quite possibly time.

If you are still considering an RV rental, be sure to read the next section on car seat usage in RVs. A list of RV rental agencies follows on pg. 231.

The RV/Car Seat Conundrum

When I spoke with one of the largest RV rental agencies in the U.S., I was assured that, while they do not rent car seats, lots of people who rent their RVs use them with their own car seats. I asked for more details and was told that I might need to rent a larger RV than I'd planned on in order to accommodate a car seat (belted positions in the smaller RV were reportedly restricted by a table). As we discussed more details, I learned that not one of the seats in any of their RVs provided a forward-facing belted seat that could fit a car seat other than the driver's and front passenger's seats.

As I explained that car seats are supposed to be installed either forward- or rear-facing, I was once again assured that plenty of parents rent their RVs and use car seats—generally installed on the sideways-facing sofas found in most models. At this point, the agent suggested that (since I was such a stickler) I could just install our car seat on the front passenger's seat, and we grown-ups could take turns riding in the back. When I asked if their RVs have front passenger airbags, he confessed he didn't know.

Two other major U.S. RV rental agencies also assured me that plenty of parents use their RVs with car seats—usually facing sideways on sofa areas. One of these RV rental agencies also assured me that it is not illegal to use a car seat sideways in their RVs on road trips in the U.S.—and that their insurance provider would not cover them if it wasn't legal (cover *them* vs. cover *the renter who installed the car seat*? I had to wonder). While there is a vast gray area surrounding the legalities of this issue, it seems that by and large rented RVs, as for-hire vehicles, are exempt from the same child safety seat requirements of standard passenger vehicles. Of course, it's legal to carry your child in your arms in the back seat of most city cabs as well, or on your lap in an airplane, but it doesn't mean your child will be protected in the event of a collision.

In Canada, there is already some legislation addressing this very issue. For example, the Alberta Traffic Safety Act specifically requires child safety seats to be used in RVs just as they are in other motor vehicles, and states: "CR (child restraint) can only be installed on forward-facing vehicle seats. Rear- or side-facing vehicle seats in RVs cannot be used for a CR."

To that point, Cruise America's rental FAQ on their website currently states: "Child safety seats should be used where applicable. The installation and use of these seats should follow the recommendation of the child seat manufacturer." I'm still looking for a child safety seat manufacturer that recommends installing their forward- or rear-facing car seats sideways.

Most likely your car seat manual will feature a warning like this found in the Britax Roundabout convertible car seat manual: "Forward-facing vehicle seats MUST be used with this child restraint. Side-facing or rear-facing seats in vans, station wagons, or trucks MUST NOT be used." The Graco SnugRide manual reads, "The VEHICLE seat must face forward" (their caps) above diagrams of rear- and side-facing seats shown with lines through them. And the Combi Yorktown Booster Car Seat manual states, "DO NOT use this Booster Car Seat on the following types of vehicle seats: Seats which face sides of vehicle. Seats which face rear of vehicle."

The bottom line? Before hitting the highways, freeways, and scenic bi-ways with your family in a rented RV, be sure the model you are renting will properly accommodate your car seat(s). If possible, stop by the rental agency ahead of time to take a look at the model you have in mind and see if your car seat will indeed work. Also, consider renting a conversion van or a campervan as an alternative—in addition to some other advantages, most feature rear passenger seats that face forward while driving. Information on renting campervans follows this list of agencies.

ON THE WEB:

Here are some popular RV rental agencies with locations throughout the U.S. and around the world.

Adventure Touring, U.S., www.adventuretouring.com / 1-877-778-9569. RV rentals in Los Angeles, San Francisco, Las Vegas, New York, Boston, Chicago, Miami/Fort Lauderdale, and Denver.

All Star Coaches, U.S., www.allstarcoaches.com / 1-866-838-4465. Luxury RV rentals in California, Florida, Ohio, and Pennsylvania.

Cruise America, U.S. and Canada, www.cruiseamerica.com / 1-800-671-8042. RV rentals throughout the U.S. and Canada.

El Monte, U.S., www.elmonte.com / 1-888-337-2214. RV rentals across the United States.

Auto Europe, Europe, www.autoeurope.com / 1-888-223-5555. Campervan and RV rentals in Australia, France, Germany, New Zealand, and Spain.

(Continued next page.)

(RV rental agencies, cont.)

Calcamper, Spain, www.calcamper.com / +34 938731242. Small RVs for rent from Barcelona.

Motorhome Rent, France, www.motorhomerent.fr. Small RV rentals throughout France.

Motorhomes Worldwide, International, www.motorhomesworldwide.com. Helps you locate RV and campervan rentals in far-flung destinations around the world, including Cuba, Namibia, Thailand, Argentina, South Africa, and dozens of other countries.

Renting a Conversion Van or Campervan

If you shuddered as you read the gas mileage range for RVs (yes, that was an average 6 to 13 mpg), you should be pleased to know Volkswagen's Westfalia campervan gets between 18 and 21 miles per gallon—good news if you're crossing the continent! Most conversion vans and campervans, even at 12 to 16 mpg, will save you on gasoline expenses over an RV rental while providing many—nearly all—of the conveniences you will find in an RV (some even have flat-screen TVs, mood lighting, and more).

You can even get a flushing toilet if you like, in addition to a refrigerator with freezer, cook-top range, etc., and even the kitchen sink. However, you will most likely need to do without an oven and use the campground or resort showers, though there are a handful of conversion vans out there with ovens, microwaves, and showers (with extra perks, expect prices to go up and gas mileage to go down).

As a comparison with the standard RV rental outlined on pg. 227, I priced out a Westfalia campervan for the same dates in the mid-season. Heading off the car seat installation problem, I confirmed that this model has four belted seating positions that each face forward during the drive, and two double beds during the night. Again, we opted to provide our own bedding, and also dishes, cups, and silverware this time to save the $35 per person to rent these as a "camping kit" (some other items were included this time as a "kitchen kit" as listed below). The costs broke down as follow:

Sample Mid-Season Westfalia Campervan Rental for 4 People

$750   7 nights

$105   Insurance (no charge if your auto insurance covers rental cars)

Included at no extra charge:

700 Miles (extra miles 25 cents ea.)

Kitchen Kit (cookware, utensils, propane, first-aid kit)

State Tax

Total Charge $855

Additional security/damage deposit (fully refundable after trip) $1,000

Optional extras for this rental include a porta-potty at $25 per trip, an electrical heater $15, child safety car seat $15, or a lawn chair $5. This and most other campervans may be used with electrical and water hook-ups where they are provided.

Additional campervan expenses may be similar to those outlined for RV vacations (listed on pg. 228), except for the reduced gas mileage, gasoline-powered generator, and in most cases the sewage hook-up fees or dumps (unless your conversion van has a bathroom with hook-up).

One final note: A campervan or conversion van is not only likely to be less expensive and less stressful to drive than an RV, it will also be vastly easier to park along the way (campsites included). Consider that the next time you need to pull over to change a diaper, check your map, or park near the wharf. Here are some campervan rental companies you might consider.

ON THE WEB:

Here are some campervan rental companies offering online quotes and promotions.

California / San Francisco Bay Area – California Campers
VW Westfalia campervan rentals. www.californiacampers.com / 1-650-216-0000.

California / SoCal Area – Vintage Surfari Wagons Restored vintage 1970s and 1980s VW buses for rent (and surfboards, if you like). www.vwsurfari.com / 1-714-585-7565.

Hawaii / Big Island – Imua Camper Company VW campervan rentals. www.imua-tour.com / 1-808-896-3158.

Hawaii / Maui – Aloha Campers VW Westfalia campervan rentals. www.alohacampers.com / 1-808-268-9810.

Maine / Portsmouth – Maine Campers – VW Westfalia campervan rentals. www.mainecampers.com / 1-207-240-6146.

Scotland / Edinburgh – Scooby Campers Restored 1960s VW campervans and microbuses for rent. www.scoobycampers.com / 0131-467-1312.

International – Auto Europe Campervan and RV rentals in Australia, France, Germany, New Zealand, and Spain. www.autoeurope.com / 1-888-223-5555.

International – Jucy Rentals Campervan rentals in New Zealand, Australia, San Francisco, Los Angeles, and Las Vegas. www.jucyrentals.com.

Part V:
Travels by
Airplane

CHAPTER 15

Before You Book Your Flight

Ticket Pricing and Options

How much you pay for your child to fly with you will depend on three main factors: 1) The age of your child at the time of your flight, 2) Whether your flight is domestic or international, and 3) Which airline you fly. Before you purchase tickets, be sure you understand which options are available and the advantages of each.

Lap Child or Infant Fare

If your child will be flying before her second birthday, she has the option of flying as a "lap child," defined by the airlines as a child under the age of 2 years (or less than 24 months) who rides on an adult's lap and has no assigned seat to herself. A lap child generally flies free on domestic flights (meaning flights that begin and end within the same country), and in most cases for 10% of the adult fare on international flights, though there are exceptions as noted in the Airlines Table, beginning on pg. 244.

For international flights, be forewarned that the same tourist taxes, exit fees, and all of the various fees added onto your adult ticket fare will most likely be charged for your infant as well, even when flying without her own seat. A lap child is not generally given a luggage allowance other than a diaper bag that may be carried onboard, but in most cases her collapsible stroller and car seat may be checked at the gate for no additional fee. A handful of airlines, however, will also allow you to check an extra small suitcase for your child for no additional fee (compare these perks by airline in the Airlines Table.

In some cases, you may be able to reserve a bassinet for your lap child to use during the cruise portion of your flight. If you're considering this option, be sure to read the section on airplane bassinets, beginning on pg. 264.

If you decide to travel with your child on your lap, be sure to read about Lap Child Safety, beginning on pg. 305. Also, if your child will turn 2 years old *during* your trip, you will be required to purchase a seat for her return flight. Call the airline to negotiate a split fare for your child's journey rather than paying for a pricier one-way ticket.

Infant's Seat Fare

Sadly, most airlines have done away with reduced infant seat fares that once encouraged parents to purchase seats for their under 2's, where they could fly more safely in their car seats through all phases of the flight. A handful of airlines still offer infant seat fares, including—for the moment—Southwest Airlines, which doesn't advertise this widely and only provides the discount by phone (you must call reservations). If you have a choice of airlines, be sure to compare any available discounts using the Airlines Table (pg. 244).

Be aware, however, there are also a handful of airlines that will not allow your child under 2 years to fly in his own seat, or have very strict (and sometimes surprising) policies about using car seats onboard. For details, see Exceptional Airlines on pg. 241.

Child's Fare

Since children 2 years and older are required by all airlines to have purchased seats of their own, it is helpful to know which airlines offer child discounts and at what rates before you book your next flight (compare your possible air carriers in the Airlines Table, pg. 244).

While some airlines provide a child discount based on a fixed percentage of the adult fare (75% for example), other airlines vary their pricing for children by season, country of origin, or destination. Alaska Airlines, for example, doesn't offer a standard discount for child passengers, but periodically allows children to fly free to select destinations (check for current family vacation offers at www.alaskaair.com). Air Tahiti Nui has also been known to offer a family rate where up to two kids can fly free to Tahiti with two paid adults (check the latest offers at www.airtahitinui.com).

In most cases, however, a child discount will only apply to regular fares, not to deeply discounted special offers.

Tips for Finding Your Family's Best Overall Fare

When flying with infants or young children, a good way to find your family's best total fare is to use a booking search engine that takes your child's age into account and whether a child under 2 years will fly as a lap child or in a purchased seat. This will allow you to compare total fares for your family across the available airlines.

Booking Engines with Built-In Infant and Child Pricing:

- www.cheapoair.com
- www.expedia.com
- www.kayak.com

When you know which airlines are available for your route, it's always a good idea to double-check the pricing each airline's website directly as you may only see some infant or child discounts applied there.

Be aware that even when an airline offers a standard child's discount, the discount rate may not apply to special-offer ticket prices where there is already a dramatic discount given for the adult fare. In these cases you may still save money overall with less expensive tickets for all adults and the child's ticket at that same price.

Choosing the Airline

Not all airlines are created equal in the eyes of traveling parents. Which airline you fly can greatly impact your experience when traveling with babies and small children, from the prices you pay for your child's seat to the services received before and during your flight. When you have a choice, choose well. Consider how some of these differences between carriers could impact your travel plans.

Some airlines do, some don't:

- Offer infant fares (see pg. 237) for children under 2 years old flying in their own seats
- Offer children's discounts for flyers between 2 and 11 years old
- Give lap children a baggage allowance
- Provide diaper-changing tables in lavatories (usually determined by the size of the aircraft)
- Warm bottles and baby food for passengers
- Offer pre-boarding for families (and pregnant women)
- Provide infant formula and/or baby food in flight
- Provide baby, toddler, or children's meals on request
- Provide toys, games, or coloring books for children
- Provide special in-flight programming for children (music, DirecTV, etc.)

To see how the airlines you may choose between compare in the family-friendly amenities they offer—or don't—be sure to see the airlines comparison table (pg. 244).

Flying the Foreign Skies

When given the option, you will most likely find the best family-friendly perks and amenities come from non-U.S. airlines. (No hard feelings, American, who once managed to give the five of us a block of eight seats together on an overseas flight!) Of course, one of my favorite perks of flying foreign carriers is that you may feel your travels have already begun before you even leave the runway. The flight crew and fellow passengers are more likely to speak in other languages and even the meals and programs shown in flight often reflect your destination.

Yet when you travel with small children, you will really begin to note the differences between carriers. For example, one U.S. airline charged us for meals and gave away our originally reserved window seats, then tried to reseat us across the aisle from one another in spite of our having a lap child who got to crowd the space of a stranger no matter which of us she sat upon (we were lucky—our honeymooning neighbor couldn't even see her spouse in his new seating assignment, and they'd made their original reservations several months in advance). Flying foreign airlines in both Europe and Asia, we've been greeted with care packages including everything from baby food and teething biscuits to toys and diapers, and offered a bottle of formula mixed and warmed in time for our takeoff. Thai Airways even offered us use of a bassinet if we wanted it—during a mere one-hour domestic flight.

Sure, you're far more likely to hear the horror stories about airlines where babies and young children are concerned. But where some families have been removed from flights for insisting on using a rear-facing car seat, refusing to cover a breastfeeding child, or failing to calm a frustrated toddler, there are airlines going above and beyond to help make sure the smallest passengers onboard—and their parents—are content as can be.

Flying Gulf Air, you may look forward to the assistance of a college-certified "Sky Nanny" who will meet you at the gate, help you board the aircraft with your child, arrange separate meal times for your child so you can eat in peace, and even help entertain and look after your child for you while you rest during long-haul flights.

Japan Airlines will provide you with baby food and diapers for your flight and install a complimentary child safety seat for your child younger than 3 years old flying in his own seat—plus, they can provide you with a complimentary stroller to use in Japan's major airports.

Asiana even has its own "Happy Mom Service" for parents flying with children under 2 years, which includes a separate check-in counter for families, a care kit for mom and baby with a nursing cover for those who want, use of child safety seats for children 6 months to 2 years flying in their own seats, and in case there are more babies on board than bassinets (and with service like this, why wouldn't there be?), they have baby slings for parents to use during the flight. Need I mention they grant a baggage allowance of one free checked suitcase up to 50 lbs for a lap child flying to or from the U.S.?

So be sure to consider your options carefully when you travel internationally with your child. To see which airlines may be available for your route, start with a booking engine like those with built-in child and infant pricing as listed on pg. 238. Then be sure to compare the benefits of each airline shown in the Airlines Table (pg. 244). When you take into consideration the various perks and discounts available, sometimes you can get *more* than what you pay for by choosing the right airline.

Notes on a Few "Exceptional" Airlines

With rare exception, you can count on the same basic truths to apply to travel with infants and small children across the airlines and around the world. Here are a few of the exceptions I found that you should be aware of when flying any of these airlines with babies and young children.

Exceptions for infants in seats:

Aer Lingus will not allow infants younger than 6 months to fly in a purchased seat (or car seat—see car seat exceptions for more).

Air Canada only allows children under 2 years to fly in their own seats when an approved car seat is used.

Ryanair will *not* allow infants (children under 2 years) to fly in purchased seats. Children younger than 2 years may only fly on an adult's lap.

Exceptions for lap child fares:

For international flights, a lap child fare is *almost* always calculated as 10% of the adult fare, and children under 2 years *almost* always fly free on laps for domestic flights. Here are the exceptions I've found:

AirAsia has a system of fixed-rate infant fares determined by the route.

EasyJet charges a flat rate of 20 £ each way for a lap child.

JetBlue charges a small fee for a lap child on international flights, which varies by destination.

Ryanair charges a flat fee of €30/£30 each way for a lap child.

Exceptions for car seats (child safety seats or CRS):

Aer Lingus does not allow car seats to be installed rear-facing on its aircraft, including all infant car seats and toddler car seats that may be installed rear-facing. Only car seats that can be installed forward-facing are permitted, and these may be used only for children younger than 36 months. Aer Lingus does not allow children over 3 years to fly in a car seat.

AirAsia only allows one car seat per group of three airplane seats.

China Airlines does not permit children over 40 lbs to use a car seat.

Easy Jet allows infants 2 years and older with a paid seat to use an approved car seat, but only allows forward-facing car seats.

Emirates, Gulf Air, and Singapore Airlines do not allow car seats to be installed rear-facing on their aircraft or to be used by infants less than 6 months old. Children 6 months up to 3 years may use approved car seats installed forward-facing in paid seats.

Ryanair does not allow car seats to be used in its aircraft (and charges a fee to check yours).

Other exceptions to note:

AirAsia does not allow children under 12 years to sit in the "Quiet Zone" of rows 7–14 on its AirAsia X flights.

American Airlines does not allow jogging strollers or any strollers weighing over 20 lbs to be checked at the gate. These strollers must be checked at the ticket counter and travel through the airport baggage system, and the airline is not responsible for damage (use a protective travel bag or rent a jogging stroller at your destination).

Malaysia Airlines does not allow infants in First Class, and children under 12 years are not permitted on the upper deck of its largest aircraft.

Planning to use your child's car seat onboard? Make sure you use a cabin-friendly car seat and check for car seat exceptions among any of the airlines you might choose (see pg. 241).

Table 1: Airlines Comparison Table[1]

Airline	Infant Fares (0-2 years)	Child Fares (2 years +) % of adult fare	Free lap child luggage allowance	Flyers beware!	Bassinets on long-haul flights[2]	Diaper changing facility	Other perks (reserve in advance and reconfirm within 24 hours)[3]
Aeroflot www.aeroflot.ru 1-888-340-6400	Free lap or 50% seat on domestic, 10% lap or 33% seat internat'l	50% domestic, 75% internat'l	22 lbs (10 kg) checked	See section beginning pg. 241	Yes	Varies	Infant and children's meals, diaper kit for long flights
Aeromexico www.aeromexico.com 1-800-237-6639	$35 lap flat rate to/from U.S.	USA does not apply discount	One stroller, bassinet, or baby carrier up to 44 lbs (20 kg) or 45"				Kids entertainment kit, children's meals on international flights
Aer Lingus www.aerlingus.com 1-800-223-6537 *See note on pg. 241	10% lap long-haul or 20 Euros short-haul 90% seat	Yes on long-haul flights, varies by route	22 lbs (10 kg.) checked, + 1 diaper bag, collapsible stroller	See section beginning pg. 241	Yes	Yes	Child meals by request on flights to/from USA and Ireland

---

[1] Please bear in mind that some details may be subject to change, so always confirm critical information with the airline at time of booking.
[2] Airplane bassinets, "sky cots," or "carrycots" must be reserved in advance and are subject to availability. Please see details for airplane bassinets, pg. 201.
[3] Infant and child meals and other special offerings are usually provided by advance request only. Call your airline ahead of time to request and confirm.

Airline	Infant Fares (0-2 years)	Child Fares (2 years +) % of adult fare	Free lap child luggage allowance	Flyers beware!	Bassinets on long-haul flights[2]	Diaper changing facility	Other perks (reserve in advance and reconfirm within 24 hours)[3]
AirAsia www.airasia.com (no North American phone)	Fixed infant fare, varies by route	Yes, varies by route and special offer	Only stroller	See section beginning pg.241	Yes, on AirAsia X flights only; pre-assigned bulkhead bassinet seating is a paid upgrade	Yes	
Air Canada www.aircanada.com 1-888-247-2262	Free lap on domestic and to U.S., 10% lap internat'l 50% seat	100% domestic, Varies internat'l	Bags checked for fee, same rates as adult, + stroller, bassinet, car seat counts toward checked bag allowance	See section beginning pg. 241	Yes	Varies	Infant and children's meals, kids' fun packs
Air China www.airchina.com 1-800-882-8122	10% internat'l, applicable child fare for seat	Yes, varies	1 free checked suitcase up to 22 lbs for domestic flights, up to 50 lbs internat'l, + stroller or bassinet		Yes	Yes	Infant and children's meals

Airline	Infant Fares (0-2 years)	Child Fares (2 years +) % of adult fare	Free lap child luggage allowance	Flyers beware!	Bassinets on long-haul flights[2]	Diaper changing facility	Other perks (reserve in advance and reconfirm within 24 hours)[3]
Air France www.airfrance.com 1-800-237-2747	Free lap on domestic 10% lap internat'l	85% domestic 77% internat'l	22 lbs + lightweight stroller		Yes	Yes	Baby food and biscuits by special request (more than 24 hrs advance), toiletry kit
Air New Zealand www.airnewzealand.com 1-800-262-1234	Free lap domestic 10% lap internat'l 75% seat	75%	Same as adult, + car seat and stroller		Yes	Long-haul	Long-haul flights: infant and children's meals biscuits by special request (more than 24 hrs advance), formula, diapers
Air Tahiti Nui www.airtahitinui.com 1-877-824-4846	10% lap internat'l Same as child	Yes, varies by route	1 free checked suitcase up to 22 lbs + 1 folding stroller		Yes	Yes	Child meals on international flights
AirTran www.airtran.com 1-800-247-8726	Free lap, 100% seat	100%	1 additional carry-on for child's items (e.g., diaper bag) + folding stroller and car seat		No	Yes	

Airline	Infant Fares (0-2 years)	Child Fares (2 years +) % of adult fare	Free lap child luggage allowance	Flyers beware!	Bassinets on long-haul flights[2]	Diaper changing facility	Other perks (reserve in advance and reconfirm within 24 hours)[3]
Air Transat www.airtransat.ca 1-866-847-1112	Free lap or 10% depending on destination, seat is same as child fare	Available on most flights (not to Fort Lauderdale), varies throughout the day	No luggage, only 1 car seat + 1 folding stroller		Yes	Yes	Courtesy strollers for use between gate and baggage claim at major airports in Canada, infant care kit, "surprise bag" with games, Air Transat Kids' Club for Canadian residents
Alaska Airlines www.alaskaair.com 1-800-252-7522	Free lap 100% seat	100%	None, but car seat and collapsible stroller can be checked		No	Varies	
Alitalia www.alitaliausa.com 1-800-223-5730	10% lap, Seats for 2 years+ only	Yes, varies by route	Up to 22 lbs (10 kg) checked baggage + folding stroller		Yes	Varies	Infant and children's meals on intercontinental flights, diapers, games
American Airlines www.aa.com 1-800-433-7300	Free lap domestic 50% other	Varies by route	Diaper bag, umbrella stroller	See section beginning pg. 241	No	All wide-body aircraft	

Airline	Infant Fares (0-2 years)	Child Fares (2 years +) % of adult fare	Free lap child luggage allowance	Flyers beware!	Bassinets on long-haul flights[2]	Diaper changing facility	Other perks (reserve in advance and reconfirm within 24 hours)[3]
Asiana Airlines www.us.flyasiana.com 1-800-227-4262	Call reservations, available by phone only	Call reservations, available by phone only	Domestic one folding stroller only, routes to Americas one checked bag to 50 lbs (23 kg) other routes one checked bag to 22 lbs (10 kg)		Yes, and child seats for under 2's in paid seat	Yes	"Happy Mom Service" for travelers with children under 3 years, nursing covers for breastfeeding moms, baby carriers for use in flight, baby and toddler meals, child safety seats for use in aircraft for under 2's in paid seat
Austrian Airlines www.aua.com 1-800-843-0002	10% lap 67% seat	67%	Stroller		Yes	Varies	Baby food, bottles, diapers, children's meals
British Airways www.ba.com 1-800-247-9297	10% lap 50% seat	50%	1 carry-on, + 70 lbs checked + collapsible stroller		Yes, and toddler seats for 0 – 23 mos	Varies	Adoption fares, child meals, activity kits
British Midlands www.flybmi.com +44-0-1332-64-8181	10% lap 75% or child fare for seat	75% internat'l only	22 lbs checked + collapsible stroller		Yes	Yes on overseas	Early check-in, children's meals, Nintendo

Airline	Infant Fares (0-2 years)	Child Fares (2 years +) % of adult fare	Free lap child luggage allowance	Flyers beware!	Bassinets on long-haul flights[2]	Diaper changing facility	Other perks (reserve in advance and reconfirm within 24 hours)[3]
Cathay Pacific www.cathaypacific.com 1-800-233-2742	10% lap	75%	Flights to and from the Americas 1 checked suitcase to 50 lbs checked, but only 45" total measurements, other destinations 22 lbs + collapsible stroller		Yes	Yes	Baby food, children's meals, kid's fun packs, child restraint seats for 6 mos – 3 years in certain seats
China Airlines www.china-airlines.com 1-866-462-8678	10% lap, applicable child fare for seat	Yes, varies	1 checked suitcase to 22 lbs (10 kg) + collapsible stroller	See section beginning pg. 241	Yes	Yes	Baby meals, children's meals, baby care kit with diapers, toys
China Southern Airlines www.csair.com 1-888-338-8988	10% lap internat'l on lap	75% adult fare	1 checked suitcase to 22 lbs (10 kg) + collapsible stroller		Yes, for a fee		Baby meals on request
Czech Airlines www.czechairlines.cz 1-800-223-2365	10% lap 67% seat	Up to 50%	One small suitcase up to 22 lbs (10 kg) + collapsible stroller, or portable crib		Yes	Varies	Infant meals, coloring books, games, diapers and wipes kit with rattle

Airline	Infant Fares (0-2 years)	Child Fares (2 years +) % of adult fare	Free lap child luggage allowance	Flyers beware!	Bassinets on long-haul flights[2]	Diaper changing facility	Other perks (reserve in advance and reconfirm within 24 hours)[3]
Delta www.delta.com 1-800-221-1212	Free lap domestic 10% lap internat'l No discount domestic seat, international seat may qualify for discount - call	100% domestic flights, internat'l flights may qualify for discounts up to 50% - call to inquire	Only with 10% or 50% paid ticket, + collapsible stroller, +booster/safety seat, + bassinet		Yes	Varies	Ask. Baby food offered on some long-haul flights. Other perks when flight operated by a foreign airline
Easy Jet www.easyjet.com 0871-244-2366 (fee)	20 £ lap 100% seat	100%	2 of the following items free of charge: stroller, travel crib, and/or car seat	See section beginning pg. 241	No	Yes	

Airline	Infant Fares (0-2 years)	Child Fares (2 years +) % of adult fare	Free lap child luggage allowance	Flyers beware!	Bassinets on long-haul flights[2]	Diaper changing facility	Other perks (reserve in advance and reconfirm within 24 hours)[3]
Emirates www.emirates.com 1-800-777-3999	Varies, approximately 10% for lap, Child fare for seat	Varies, approx. 80%	Varies. Either one checked piece to 22 lbs when based on "piece concept," or one piece to 50 lbs when allowance based on "weight concept," + one carry-on diaper bag + folding stroller	See section beginning pg. 241	Yes	Yes	Baby and child meals, complimentary stroller service (including twin strollers) at Dubai International Airport
Eva Air www.evaair.com 1-800-695-1188	10 % on lap Seat varies	75%	1 checked bag of 45" total combined dimensions or 22 lbs, + stroller		Yes	Yes	Baby meals, child meals, diapers, children's TV
Frontier Airlines www.frontierairlines.com 1-800-432-1359	Free lap domestic	100%	One diaper-type bag for baby		No	Varies	

Airline	Infant Fares (0-2 years)	Child Fares (2 years +) % of adult fare	Free lap child luggage allowance	Flyers beware!	Bassinets on long-haul flights[2]	Diaper changing facility	Other perks (reserve in advance and reconfirm within 24 hours)[3]
Gulf Air www.gulfair.com 1-888-359-4853	10% lap Child fare for seat	75% certain routes	1 checked bag to 22 lbs (10 kg), + collapsible stroller, + infant car seat	See section beginning pg. 241	Yes	Yes	Baby food, child meals, diapers, assistance of a SkyNanny on select flights, use of GulfAir strollers on arrival at Bahrain airport
Hawaiian Airlines www.hawaiianair.com 1-800-367-5320	Free lap domestic 100% seat domestic 10% lap international 67% seat international	100% domestic 67% internat'l	No allowance, and checked car seat or stroller counts toward 2 pc. limit for adult		No	Varies	

Airline	Infant Fares (0-2 years)	Child Fares (2 years +) % of adult fare	Free lap child luggage allowance	Flyers beware!	Bassinets on long-haul flights[2]	Diaper changing facility	Other perks (reserve in advance and reconfirm within 24 hours)[3]
Japan Airlines www.jal.com 1-800-525-3663	10% lap internat'l, Child fare for seat	Varies, approx. 50% of the one-way fare	One checked suitcase with same linear dimensions + weight or less of adult's allowance (50 lbs economy)		Yes	Yes	Check-in at JAL Family Service counter at Narita and Kansai airports, diapers, baby food and child meals, free child safety seat (car seat) "rental" available for children under 3 years in paid seat, complimentary strollers at Japan's major airports and some overseas
JetBlue www.jetblue.com 1-800-538-2583	Free lap domestic Small fee lap internat'l 100% seat	100%	One diaper bag, stroller, and car seat	See section beginning pg. 241	No	Yes	DirecTV at all seats with family-friendly channels
KLM www.klm.com 1-800-618-0104	10% lap, Child fare for seat	Up to 50%, but does not apply to lowest-fare specials	One carry-on to 22 lbs + one checked bag to 22 lbs, + fully collapsible stroller		Yes	Yes	Baby food, children's meals, toys

Airline	Infant Fares (0-2 years)	Child Fares (2 years +) % of adult fare	Free lap child luggage allowance	Flyers beware!	Bassinets on long-haul flights[2]	Diaper changing facility	Other perks (reserve in advance and reconfirm within 24 hours)[3]
Korean Air www.koreanair.com 1-800-438-5000	Free lap domestic 10% internat'l	75%	One checked bag up to 20 lbs, + either collapsible stroller or car seat		Yes	Yes	Baby food and infant formula if booked in advance, child's menu
LAN www.lan.com 1-866-435-9526	10% lap internat'l, Child fare for seat	75%	One checked bag up to 50 lbs (23 kg.)		Yes	Varies	Child meals on international flights
Lufthansa www.lufthansa.com 1-800-645-3880	10% lap internat'l, Child fare for seat	75%	18 lbs carry-on OR One checked bag up to 50 lbs (23 kg) + umbrella stroller, + bassinet		Yes	Yes	Baby food, child meals, kids TV programming
Malaysia www.malaysiaairlines.com +44-603-7843-3000 (international fees apply)	10% lap, child fare for seat	75%	Up to 22 lbs (10 kg) checked baggage (can be combined as 2 items, e.g., bassinet + bag)	See section beginning pg. 241	Yes	Yes	Children's playroom and baby care rooms at select airports, child meals, activity books for kids 3 – 10, limited supply of baby food and diapers on large aircraft

Airline	Infant Fares (0-2 years)	Child Fares (2 years +) % of adult fare	Free lap child luggage allowance	Flyers beware!	Bassinets on long-haul flights[2]	Diaper changing facility	Other perks (reserve in advance and reconfirm within 24 hours)[3]
Ryanair www.ryanair.com + 44-871-246-0002 (international fees apply)	Flat fee of €30/£30 each way for lap child Seats for 2 yrs + only	No	One folding stroller only (car seat or bassinet checked for a fee)	See section beginning pg. 241	No	Yes	
Qantas www.qantas.com 1-800-227-4500	10% lap internat'l, 100% seat	100%	Internat'l flights only: 1 checked bag 45" total		Yes	Yes	Infant, toddler, and child meals, diapers for international, kids kits, complimentary strollers for use at major Australian airports
SAS www.flysas.com 1-800-221-2350	10% lap, 75% seat	75%	22 lbs checked + collapsible stroller		Yes	Yes	Baby food, toys, video games
Singapore Airlines www.singaporeair.com	10% lap, infant seat must be booked by telephone	Typically 75%	One checked suitcase with sum of length + width + height not exceeding 62 inches, + folding stroller + car seat	See section beginning pg. 241	Yes	Yes	Baby and child meals available on all flights except between Singapore and Kuala Lumpur, diapers and baby amenities available onboard

Airline	Infant Fares (0-2 years)	Child Fares (2 years +) % of adult fare	Free lap child luggage allowance	Flyers beware!	Bassinets on long-haul flights[2]	Diaper changing facility	Other perks (reserve in advance and reconfirm within 24 hours)[3]
Southwest www.iflswa.com 1-800-435-9792	Call reservations, available by phone only.	Minimal discounts by phone only, promo fares online are best when available	One folding stroller only.		Ask	Yes	
TAM Airlines www.tam.com 1-888-235-9826	10% lap international, seat same as child fare	Varies by flight	One checked bag to 22 lbs (10 kg) within South America, or one checked bag to 50 lbs international, + folding stroller and car seat		Yes, fee for international travel	Varies by aircraft	
Thai Airways www.thaiair.com 1-800-426-5204	Free lap domestic, 10% lap international Child's fare for seat	50% domestic 50% to 67% international	One checked bag up to 22 lbs (10 kg), + collapsible stroller or infant carrier or car seat		Yes	Yes	Diapers, baby food on request, "gifts" for children, child meals

Airline	Infant Fares (0-2 years)	Child Fares (2 years +) % of adult fare	Free lap child luggage allowance	Flyers beware!	Bassinets on long-haul flights[2]	Diaper changing facility	Other perks (reserve in advance and reconfirm within 24 hours)[3]
United Airlines www.united.com 1-800-241-6522	Free lap within U.S., taxes only for lap to Canada, 10% lap international 50% seat	100%	Only car seat and collapsible stroller can be checked		Yes, but very limited number available	On all 747 and larger aircraft	Domestic meals for purchase, baby food on request for international flights
U.S. Airways www.usairways.com 1-800-428-4322	Free lap in U.S. 10% lap internat'l, 100% seat domestic Discount seat available on some international fares	100% seat domestic Discount seat available on some international fares	Diaper bag + folding stroller domestic, + one checked bag to 50 lbs on international flights		Yes, but a very limited number available	Yes	
Virgin Atlantic www.virgin-atlantic.com 1-800-862-8621	10% lap most flights, 75% seat	75% adult ticket price	Yes, 1 checked bag to 50 lbs (23 kg), + 1 carry-on		Yes, and child safety seats for children under 44 lbs in paid seat	Yes	Complimentary child safety seats for newborns up to 44 lbs on international flights in paid seats, in-seat TV with children's programming, children's meals

Choosing the Flight

When you have a choice between flights, it can be difficult to decide which times and options may be best for your family. Yet the particular flight you choose can play a key role in how smoothly your trip begins and ends, especially when considering naptime flights, nighttime flights, or stopover flights, and taking into consideration the timing of your travels to and from airports. As your child progresses through various ages and stages, your flight preferences may also change. Here are some points to consider as you decide between flights:

Naptime Flights

Blessed are they whose children may sleep during a long-haul flight. Infants who nap more frequently and often for longer periods than their older counterparts will, in general, have an easier time napping during flights. Nursing or enjoying a warm bottle at takeoff can especially help to set the mood for a snooze. As well, some older children just respond well to the hum of the engines and the familiar comfort of their car seats.

However, some babies and toddlers may be too stimulated by the newness of the situation, the bright lights, numerous passengers with unfamiliar faces, engine noise, and announcements blasting forth from the speakers to actually nap during the flight. If your child becomes overtired from his overdue nap, this could prove to be an exhausting flight for you all, and it may be wiser to try and time your flight for another time of the day, when he will be well rested and able to better adjust to the new environment onboard—not to mention the challenges of getting through the airport beforehand.

Babies, toddlers, and preschoolers alike may respond more favorably to flying when they feel well rested and can instead use the time to look at books, play games, watch a favorite show, stroll around the cabin to look for other children, engage with a new toy, and eat their favorite snacks.

Nighttime (or Red-Eye) Flights

Overnight flights can be ideal when flying the long-haul with a child. Unlike daytime flights, where napping may prove impossible, "red-eyes" cater to a resting crowd with a period where cabin lights are dimmed and announcements are minimal. Sometimes these flights are less crowded, too, which can mean shorter waits for the lavatory and food or beverage service, and possibly more room onboard for your family to sprawl (but don't count on it).

Depending on the length of your flight, you may board in time for dinner, which can help set the mood for evening rituals and bedtime for your child, or you may not leave until the middle of the night, when everyone is thoroughly exhausted and will hopefully go right to sleep. The risk is that, if your child has trouble sleeping for some reason, you will all miss your nighttime sleep. And if your child voices his complaints or frustration with the situation, your neighbors onboard may also miss their nighttime sleep, possibly adding feelings of awkwardness or guilt to the challenges you already face.

To help ensure as smooth an overnight flight as possible, make sure your child gets plenty of exercise and stimulation in the hours leading up to the flight (e.g., is not stuck in the exersaucer watching mom pack and pay bills all afternoon). In the days leading up to an overnight flight with a toddler or preschooler, help him visualize how the flight will go, including the time the family spends sleeping. Anything that can make it seem more like bedtime—putting on pajamas, reading bedtime stories, snuggling a favorite stuffed animal or blankie, etc., can also help.

Stopover Flights

Sometimes flights with a stopover en route can save you some money— but not always. Generally passengers prefer nonstop flights, as they shave at least a couple of hours off the total travel time and reduce the risk of parting ways with their checked baggage. Parents of infants and small children also like direct flights because there is only one ascent and descent to challenge the ears.

There is your stomach to consider, too: If you're deciding between one long flight from your city of departure to a destination overseas, or flying cross-country first before connecting with an overseas flight, meal service most likely will not be included in the domestic flight segment (unless you buy food items onboard). The direct overseas flight, however, will provide you with meals and possibly provide a children's meal or baby food if the airline offers it and you've requested it in advance.

When flying with an infant on a direct flight overseas, you may also be able to reserve an airplane bassinet. But if you fly cross-country first, this service most likely won't be an option on the domestic portion of your flight.

And just as there are definite advantages to flying directly without a stopover, there can also be advantages to taking a break when flying with small children. First of all, children get a change of scenery and a chance to stretch their legs—something you may be very grateful for if your child is energetic or will not be sleeping during the flight. Potty-trainees who may be afraid of the airplane lavatory will have a chance to use grounded toilets. At major airports offering baby care rooms, moms may also have a quiet retreat where they can breastfeed in comfort and privacy in case this proves a challenge with the infant onboard.

In case you're still having trouble deciding whether you'd prefer the stopover or the direct flight, here's one more thing to consider: When switching airplanes, you can also trade in your neighbors in case things didn't go so smoothly in the first round.

Choosing Your Seats

Which seats are ideal for your family depends on a number of variables, namely the age of your child (see Anticipating Ages and Stages, pg. 19), his temperament (see pg. 107), the duration of the flight, the size of the aircraft, and how many of you will be flying together. In some cases, you can request your preferred seats in advance; in others, it may be a first-come first-served free-for-all in which it may help to have your strategy formed well in advance.

Before You Book Bulkhead Seating...

I am often surprised how many people recommend outright that you should always book bulkhead seats for flights with a baby or small child. Bulkhead seats can definitely have their advantages, especially if you want to use an airplane bassinet during your flight, but for parents with babies and toddlers, they can also present some serious drawbacks that are worth thoughtful consideration. To help decide if you want bulkhead seats, consider these points:

Why you might favor bulkhead seats:

- Bulkhead rows are sometimes the only locations in aircraft where an airplane bassinet (if available) may be used.

- If you need to install a rear-facing car seat, the bulkhead row may make it easier to achieve the degree of recline you need for an infant, or for a snoozing older baby, without the possible interference of a forward neighbor's seat.

- There is no risk of your toddler spending the entire flight kicking a forward neighbor's seat.

- Bulkhead rows usually offer extra leg room, making it easier to slip in and out to the lavatory for diaper changes or trips with a potty-training child, or to get up and pace the aisle with an overtired baby.

- Once you reach cruising altitude, you can also take advantage of the floor space on your row to set your tote bag full of toys or your diaper bag.

Why you might avoid bulkhead seats:

- On the downside, the armrests on bulkhead rows are usually fixed and cannot be raised if needed to accommodate a wider car seat or to ease the buckling of the safety belt during a car seat installation.

- Bulkhead seats usually have fold-out trays that are smaller than those at other seats, and are often too close to be used with a baby or toddler on your lap.

- There is no under-seat storage, so you will have to wait until the fasten seatbelt signs are off to access your carry-ons, and after that your feet may have to share space with them.

- As well, bright and flashing light from a projected movie (where those are still found on flights) may annoy sensitive sleepers, especially those in bassinets mounted at the bottom edge of the screen (trust me).

- Without a row of seats as a privacy buffer in front of you, you may feel more exposed when breastfeeding, especially if anyone is waiting for the lavatory.

- And finally, bulkhead rows on larger aircraft are usually opposite the food preparation areas and beside lavatories, so extra traffic, unfamiliar faces, and noise can also be a problem for light sleepers and babies entering that new "era of awareness" that often comes around 4 months of age.

So consider your situation carefully before you reserve bulkhead seats. With baby snoozing in the bassinet, you may be able to fly the long haul more comfortably. But think twice if your child is easily overstimulated, and if you will regret not having under-seat stowage each time you have to access the overhead bin.

Best Bet Airplane Seats with...

Infants (approximately birth to 7 months) – Window seats on non-bulkhead rows afford the most privacy for breastfeeding, and peace and quiet for sleeping babies. If you want to use an airplane bassinet for a long-haul flight, however, you may have to settle for bulkhead seating. Call the airline to ask where bassinets may be used in the particular aircraft you'll be in.

Older babies (approximately 8 to 14 months) – Your baby may need more wiggle room now, and if he thrives on smiles and coos from passersby, the bulkhead row of a large airplane may be just the place for him. But if you seek peace and quiet in flight, and hopefully a nap from your child if not overnight slumber on a red-eye, try to choose seats near the rear of larger aircraft, where side seats taper down from three to two. These highly coveted seats give you extra space between the window seat and the window where you can keep extra items handy or even let your 10-month-old practice standing, while the center seats in this portion of the aircraft are usually the last to be assigned and some are often left empty—until other passengers seeking more space or an extra seat claim them (this could be you). If you will be on a smaller plane with lavatories only in first class and in the aft, try for seats near the front of the aircraft as most of the coach passengers will have to pass to the back of the plane to use its lavatories.

Toddlers on laps (approximately 14 to 23 months) – The bulkhead row will give you more space to maneuver, and without the constant temptation to your child of flopping down the tray incessantly or pulling on your forward neighbor's hair. Once in the air, you can set a tote bag of toys and books at your feet where you'll be able to access them more easily than you would in other rows. However, on long flights the two of you may not fit behind the armrest-mounted tray during meals. For long-haul flights on a large aircraft, it may be best to request the seats near the rear as described in the last section.

Toddlers in seats – The bulkhead row offers three great advantages here. 1) Your forward-facing toddler will not be able to kick a seat in front of him. 2) On smaller aircraft, you will be served drinks and snacks much sooner than the passengers in the rear. 3) It is easiest to pop out of your seats for quick access to the lavatory during potty training, especially on larger aircraft when these seats place you right next to the lavatory. However, be prepared that your child may keep a running commentary on everyone else using the toilet!

Preschoolers – Once your child begins flying without a car seat and has mastered potty training, she can sit virtually anywhere on the aircraft other than emergency exit rows. However, she may still prefer to sit near the window for the entertainment value and to have you as a buffer between her and the other passengers on the aircraft.

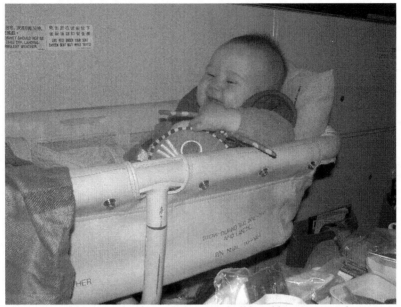

En route to Taipei with China Airlines: A bulkhead bassinet can be a great convenience during overseas flights with your lap-held baby—especially during meal times.

All About Airplane Bassinets for Babies

For overseas and other long-haul flights, many airlines offer special bassinets for babies that attach to the bulkhead wall (depending on the airline, these may also go by the name "infant cots," "sky cots," or "baby beds"). Some larger aircraft, like those operated by AirFrance, may even offer bassinets that attach beneath the overhead bins or in other locations throughout the aircraft. This convenience (free in most cases) allows parents to fly with babies at the lap-child rate, and also have a bed for their child—provided he is still small enough to fit in the bassinet and is not yet capable of climbing out of it. This benefit may prove invaluable as you negotiate your dinner tray or simply need to give your arms a rest.

Sizes of airplane bassinets vary, as do individual airlines' policies on age/height/weight limits for their bassinets. If your child will be 6 months or older during your travels, it's a good idea to call and ask the airlines you're considering about their bassinet policies *before* you purchase your tickets. Some parents have found out too late that a 10-month-old, for example, will not be allowed to use one airline's bassinet when a different airline's bassinets (or bassinet age policy) would have been perfectly suitable.

British Airways, however, has an alternative to bassinets that's available for children up to 23 months old (on a first-come, first-served basis, of course). This Britax "toddler seat" can also be installed on bulkhead rows, and it provides a seat with variable recline and a 5-point harness that is the envy of any parent flying a different airline with a lap-held toddler. While a handful of Asian airlines offer child safety seats for babies and toddlers, you must purchase a seat for the child using these (included in Airlines Table, pg. 244). For the time being, these toddler seats are still complimentary for lap children flying British Airways (see photo on pg. 266).

Since the number of bassinets (or toddler seats) per flight is limited and they are often only available for passengers seated in the bulkhead rows, be sure to make your reservations as early as possible to ensure you get the appropriate seats and a bassinet reserved for your family. Most airlines recommend reconfirming your seating and bassinet reservations within 72 to 24 hours of BOTH outbound and return flights. If your airline is in the practice of offering unconfirmed seats to passengers as they check in (as many are), you may lose your seating assignment, and therefore the privilege of having a bassinet, so always be sure to call ahead and reconfirm your seats. The one exception I've found to this is AirAsia X, which allows you to pay an extra fee to select your seating assignment in advance, including a bulkhead bassinet seating position.

Believe it or not, there is still one more way you could lose your rights to a bassinet you've already reserved for your flight. When all of the above is said and done, the bassinets are still provided on a first-come, first-served basis, and there are only a limited number of bassinets available on each airplane. So check in as early as possible to make sure one of them will be yours. Occasionally there are more babies onboard than bassinets.

Don't want to chance it? The FlyeBaby air travel hammock for infants can be used in most ordinary (non-bulkhead) seating positions throughout an airplane, creating a soft and secure spot for baby to lounge while keeping mom's hands free. More details about the FlyeBaby on pg. 69 and also at www.TravelswithBaby.com.

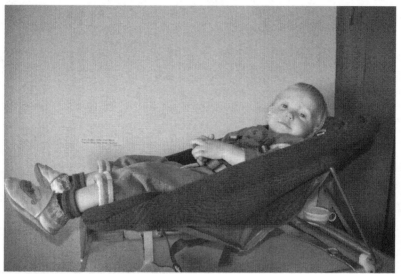

En route to London with a British Airways "toddler seat," the king of bulkhead-mounted bassinet options, which can be used for children 3 months up to 23 months (more on pg. 265).

✔ Airplane Bassinet Checklist

- ☐ Call airline BEFORE booking tickets to confirm bassinets are available on the flights you want, and that your child is within size/weight/age limits to use those available on that flight.
- ☐ Purchase seats at a bassinet position on the airplane (not all bulkhead seats are for bassinets, remember, and confirm locations with the airline if you are uncertain).
- ☐ If you purchased your tickets online, follow up with a phone call to reservations to put in your bassinet request (and any optional perks for your airline; see Airlines Table, pg. 244).
- ☐ Call your airline 24 hours in advance to reconfirm your bassinet request.
- ☐ Check in as early as possible for your flight to ensure you are one of the first families to receive the available bassinets on your airplane.

ON THE WEB:

At **Seat Guru** you can see a seating chart of the actual plane that will be used on your flight (barring last-minute changes), including the restroom and galley locations, a guide to which are considered the "good seats" onboard, and details such as diaper changing stations and availability, and locations for airplane bassinets. www.SeatGuru.com

CHAPTER 16

Countdown to Takeoff

Required Documents for Air Travel

In your pre-parent life, you may have whisked off to the airport with little more than a carry-on bag in your hand, your driver's license already in your wallet, and your e-ticket awaiting its printing for you at the airport kiosk. You may need to reprogram your thinking for air travel with your child, and not just because of the amazing increase in baggage.

Domestic Air Travel

Children flying within the United States are not technically required to have photo ID for flights unless they are traveling alone as unaccompanied minors (not generally allowed before 5 years of age). However, your airline may still require proof of age any time he'll be flying on your lap free of charge or in a seat at a reduced rate based on his age. For this, airlines require, at minimum, a certified (with raised seal) copy of a birth certificate.

Oftentimes, agents will not ask to see the birth certificate unless they are uncertain whether the child may be 2 years old, which creates the unfortunate impression among many parents that they don't need this documentation when flying domestically with a baby. However, if you were not asked for a birth certificate for a previous flight, it could be different the next time around. And once your child begins walking, it could be a tough call for agents having limited experience with children.

Be forewarned, the delays and chaos that can result from not having the proper paperwork when requested are simply not worth the risk. Parents have both missed flights because of this and been forced to buy on-the-spot tickets for babies and toddlers without proof of age.

Although a lap child does not need or receive an individual ticket for the flight, she must either have an "infant boarding pass," which will be issued upon check-in, or be annotated on one of the parents' boarding passes. In spite of the convenience of e-tickets and time-saving Web check-in options, most airlines still require parents flying with a lap child to stop by the counter.

Documents for International Air Travel

In the past, children traveling with their parents to most destinations within the western hemisphere did not need passports. Now, however, all U.S. passengers that travel by air to or from Canada, Mexico, Central and South America, the Caribbean, and Bermuda are required to have a valid passport—whether they've sprouted teeth yet or not.

As before, your child will need a passport for air travel to any other countries outside of the western hemisphere as well. Information on obtaining passports for infants and children begins on pg. 126.

Children Flying with One Parent or Other Caregivers

If either parent will be flying internationally with a child *without* the other parent, or if the child will be traveling with a grandparent or other caregiver instead of his or her parents, the traveling adult will need a notarized letter of permission or power of attorney from the absent parent(s). This applies even when crossing the U.S. border to Canada or Mexico. More information, along with a sample "Letter of Consent for One Parent Traveler," can be found on pg. 133.

Be aware that some countries are even more rigid about this documentation than the U.S., so always be prepared if traveling abroad without both parents present. If you have sole custody of your child, you will also need to be prepared to present the applicable verification: a sole custody order, death certificate, adoption decree, etc.

If you and your child, or your partner, have different last names (or hyphenated variations that differ from one another), be sure to read the section on Parents with Different Names, pg. 132.

Packing for Your Flight

When you are traveling with a baby or toddler, how you've packed can make as much of a difference as what you've packed.

The more items you can check in upon arrival, the fewer items you will have to lug through the security line, run through the X-ray, and carry all the way to your gate. However, most airlines will charge you for each checked item on domestic flights, which can get expensive for a family of travelers (see which items your airline will allow you to check or carry on extra items for your lap child for free in the Airlines Table, beginning on pg. 244).

Your car seat and a diaper bag of some sort may already be necessary carry-on items. Your stroller may also play a critical role in getting your child and some of her gear to the gate (it can carry the child, diapers and/or a daypack, or possibly even the car seat), and you may also need it to help her sleep during a layover or simply to help keep her contained while you use the restroom or out of harm's way as you collect your checked baggage. That's already three items to get through security, plus yourself and your child. Now, take off those shoes.

If packing for your flight is beginning to feel like a logistical nightmare, just keep the following pointers in mind, and by all means remember this: Of all the things you pack for your trip, the most important may be your sense of humor. Pretty much everything else can be improvised if needed or found along the way.

Formula, Bottles, Baby Food, and other Excess Liquids for Your Child's Flight

As long as you are clearing security *with* your baby or toddler, you are permitted to bring aboard liquid items including baby food, expressed breast milk, formula, medicines, juices, and shelf-stable milk boxes, in what the TSA calls a "reasonable quantity" based on your travel itinerary (note to international travelers: some countries may still require you to taste breast milk, formula, and/or boxed milk at security check points, though this is not the current practice at U.S. airport security).

For simplification at security, I recommend you place all of these excess liquid items for your child in a clear plastic gallon-size zip-top bag, which will be easy to present at the check point (just lay it on top of the items in your bin) and will also help contain any leaks or messes as you travel.

For travel within the U.S., you are also allowed to bring gel-filled teething toys and ice packs needed to keep breast milk and other baby essentials cold. These should also be presented with your child's excess liquid items, in the same large zip-top bag if possible.

Remember, any extra formula, breast milk, baby food, or other accepted liquids beyond what might reasonably be used during your flight itinerary should go into your checked suitcase. Otherwise, it may be confiscated at security.

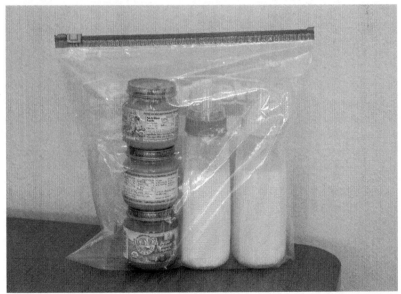

Prepared bottles and sealed jars of baby food ready to present to security in a clear plastic zip-top bag. The bag will also help contain any dribbles or leaks during travel—and you can throw your child's dirty spoons in there for clean up at a later, more convenient time.

Your Child's Travel Kit for Carry-On

While you can bring formula, baby food, and other approved liquids for your child into the cabin in quantities beyond the 3-1-1 rule, there are other liquid and gel essentials you might also be very glad to have onboard for your child. Here's what I recommend packing in your TSA-compliant "child's travel kit for carry-on."

I've found it very helpful to keep this small travel kit intact for use even at home and for brief outings. It's a nice way to keep these sometimes critical things organized and accessible.

Sample modified travel kit for carry-on with 3-1-1 liquid restrictions:

- Infants' Tylenol, 1 fl. oz.
- Infants' gas relief drops, 1 fl. oz.
- Small tube of diaper cream, 2 oz.
- Small tube of teething gel, .33 oz.
- Sample tube of healing cream (from doctor's office), .25 oz.
- Saline nasal spray, 1.5 fl. oz.

Pack your child's travel kit as you would pack your own liquid and gel items, with containers holding no more than 3.4 oz. (or 100 ml.) stored in a quart-size clear plastic bag with slide-lock top. All products should fit easily into the closed bag and lie flat when passing through the X-ray conveyor belt.

Perfecting Your Carry-On Diaper Bag

How many diapers should you pack in your carry-on diaper bag or backpack? You will obviously need enough diapers with you en route to cover your entire time spent traveling between home and your destination, plus a few extras for good measure. Then add a few more in case a flight delay finds you camped out at the airport for untold hours. As one father discovered while stranded overnight in an airport with two toddlers, even airport shops (and restaurants) close for the night. Now add the corresponding number of baby wipes, and your diaper bag may already be bursting at the seams.

As I prepared for my first long-haul flight as a parent, I loaded up the largest diaper bag we had with plenty of diapers and wipes, that extra change of clothes, a couple of receiving blankets, small toys, her travel kit, and a few other things to help pass our travel time. I proudly slung the 25 lb, almost-completely-zipped bag over my shoulder and boarded the flight thinking we were prepared for anything.

I'm not sure how many passengers felt the whap of that diaper bag the first time I lumbered down the aisle to the lavatory with my babe-in-arms, but imagine my surprise when, once inside, I couldn't shut the door. Still worse: The cumbersome catch-all didn't fit beneath the airplane seats and had to be stored in the compartment above our neighbors' heads.

While an official "diaper bag" filled with all your child's sundries may be helpful when running around town, leaving your child with a caregiver, or undertaking a road trip, it's not necessarily the best diapering solution when flying.

The Birth of the "Diaper Purse" – A few flights later, my daughter's carry-on diaper bag had transformed into a small backpack that fit neatly beneath the airplane seat in front of us (or at our feet during the cruising portions of flights on the bulkhead rows), and beside it fit what I called the "diaper purse." The diaper purse had just the essentials we might need in the lavatory. I wore the long purse strap across my body to where the bag hung conveniently at my hip, enabling me to reach into it one-handed as I tended to her on the changing table or on the toilet seat. Having at least one hand free to hold onto your child during in-flight diaper changes is not just helpful, but it can be critical for your child's safety, too.

The Case for the Dad-friendly Diaper Sling – If your mate is not willing to sport a "diaper purse" to the lavatory (as mine was not), you might consider the new messenger-style "diaper slings" that can be worn cross-body like the diaper purse, also keeping those diapering essentials within easy, one-handed reach. One dad-friendly diaper sling has even been named "the Diaper Dude." Just don't over-pack your messenger diaper sling or you'll find yourself wearing all of your baby's carry-on cargo to the lavatory for a mere diaper change. And I won't be held responsible if you can't get the door shut either.

The Wisdom of the Diaper Waist Pack – As another hands-free, space-saving alternative, consider using a waist pack (like a fanny pack, but with better marketing), which can store a few diapers and diapering essentials in an easy-to-access pouch you won't have to find space for in the lavatory. You can keep the waist pack in your larger "diaper bag," backpack, or messenger sling, and easily clip it around your waist when you need to stroll down that aisle with your child for the next diaper change. Keep your extra supply of diapers in the larger carry-on bag and refill the waist pack when needed.

What to pack in your streamlined diaper purse, sling, or waist pack:

- **A few diapers** – always at least 2 in case one is UAR (used on arrival).

- **Travel size diaper wipes** – Keep a back-up pack of diaper wipes in your larger bag.

- **Diaper cream** – Even if your child doesn't generally need it at home, he'll likely be doing longer-than-usual stretches in the same diaper during travel.

- **Thin, wipe-clean changing mat** – You want one that will fit compactly in your diaper purse/sling/pack and can be folded with one hand.

- **Antibacterial hand wipes** – These may be easier to use than the lavatory sink while juggling your baby, and can also be used to quickly clean any surfaces that may need it, including your wipe-clean changing mat.

- **Diaper disposal bags** – Lavatories are challenged enough. Seal up your stinky diapers.

- **Small toy or mini board book** – It's always helpful to have a hand-held distraction for your child during diaper changes, but especially when you don't want them touching the sullied surroundings of a lavatory.

Organizing Your Carry-On Backpack or Bag

Backpacks may be easily worn through the airport and help keep hands free; they also generally fit well beneath airplane seats. However, you'll want to consider the organization of yours carefully, especially if it will be used for the items you'll want to access frequently in flight (toys, toys, snacks, books, toys—see tips for planning your in-flight entertainment, pg. 282).

Reconsider using one for the items you'll want to access frequently in flight, like a changing array of toys, since you will be bending over and trying to maneuver the zippers each time, opening the pack nearly all the way between you and your neighbor's feet to find the one or two items you seek. In the meantime, other items may spill out the sides.

For your child's toys, snacks, books, and other items you'll need to access throughout your flight, you may fare better with a small tote bag. One light in color will make it especially easy to see the items inside, and there will be no zippers or Velcro to make noise if you need to access it as your child sleeps.

I have sometimes packed a loaded, small tote within a backpack so that I could easily remove it, ready to go, after we reached our seats.

As for the items packed inside, you can subdivide and conquer by using clear, slide-lock food storage bags (or other containers) to group like items in your carry-ons. It makes it much easier to find what you need en route (toys in this pouch, snacks in that pouch, travel kit there). Plastic storage bags also make it easy to pack a fresh change of clothes very compactly by squeezing the extra air out of the last half-inch of the "zipper" as you zip it. Also, be sure to pack an empty plastic bag for soiled clothing.

The Go-Hybrid forward-facing car seat and booster folds up to fit in its own travel case, and is much safer traveling through the airport baggage system than traditional hard-shelled car seats. See more in the full review at www.TravelswithBaby.com.

Checking Bags and Baby Gear

The first order of business is to know your airline's baggage restrictions and limitations. If you are flying with a lap child, check the Airlines Table, pg. 244, to see if your airline grants lap children a checked baggage allowance. Generally, a collapsible stroller and/or car seat checked at the gate do not apply toward your baggage allowance.

Also, be aware of the airline's weight limit for checked items. The standard 70 lbs per bag of the past has been reduced to 50 lbs by most airlines (some still offer a 70-lb limit in first or business class), and although it may be far simpler for your family to transport one suitcase at 59 lbs rather than juggle two separate, lighter suitcases, it may cost you an extra $25 or so each way to do so.

To avoid surprises, visit your airline's website to see their baggage policy or call their toll-free telephone number (both are listed in the Airlines Table, pg. 244). It may work best for your family to use multiple suitcases that can "piggyback" so you are able to roll, for example, two or three separate pieces with only one hand. For more ideas on cutting costs while packing your family's checked bags, see pg. 280.

Also, be sure to tag all items you will check *before* you leave for the airport, including the stroller, car seat, etc. This will save you from scrambling for pens, airline tags, etc., while juggling all your items and children through the line at check-in.

Before You Check Your Car Seat...

If you're traveling with your child's car seat but aren't planning to use it on the airplane, there are two important reasons I recommend you bring it to the gate rather than check it in at the counter. First, you are far more likely to arrive at the same airport at the same time with your car seat. Second, car seats, like bicycle helmets, are made to withstand the forces of one accident, one time, after which the manufacturers advise replacing the car seat (and most insurance companies foot the bill).

If you turn the typical car seat over or remove its cover to see where the harness straps feed through, you might be surprised to see how thin the plastic is at these important places. Just the strain of a "fender bender"—or possible collisions with 50-lb or 70-lb suitcases in the baggage system—can create cracks so thin you cannot see them with the naked eye.

That said, I realize lugging your car seat through the airport when you don't even plan to use it on the plane still may sound terribly inconvenient. In addition to the Seven Easy Ways to Get Your Car Seat to the Gate you should be sure to read (pg. 276), I offer these suggestions.

- **The Radian RXT folding car seat by Diono** (formerly SunshineKids) has a steel alloy frame, folds for travel, and has an optional carrying bag with shoulder strap or backpack straps. It is also FAA-approved for use in airplanes (in car seat mode only), so you would still have the option of using it onboard if you change your mind.

- **The Safety 1st GoHybrid Booster** is a forward-facing car seat (later converts to a booster) that also folds up for travel and comes with its own carrying case. Because of its unique design, the harness straps don't feed through a plastic shell, making it another safer bet for checking through the airport baggage system (with a few extra things in the carrying case, of course). It is not designed for use in aircraft, however, so you would not have that option.

- **The RideSafer Travel Vest** – This lightweight car seat alternative, for children 3 years and older, is a great solution when your car seat needs will be minimal (taxis, shuttles, driving to and from the airport). More about the RideSafer travel vest on pg. 68 and at www.TravelswithBaby.com).

- **You could also opt to rent a car seat at your destination.** When we arrived in Phoenix, for example, a local baby gear rental agency met us at the car rental counter in SkyHarbor Airport with the car seats we needed and a few extra items for our stay. You may be able to rent a car seat from the car rental company, too, though for longer stays, though you may have better odds of having a clean car seat the right size for your child—and possibly a better price—if renting from a baby gear rental agency. See more in Renting Car Seats on pg. 225, and in Baby Gear Rentals, pg. 82.

If you still must check a car seat through the baggage system, be aware that airlines don't always provide plastic bags for these, so be sure to tighten and fasten the straps, and stow away any loose LATCH equipment or tethers to help prevent your car seat from catching in the baggage system. You may be glad to have a protective car seat travel bag to help protect your car seat on its journey (see recommended car seat travel accessories, pg. 66).

Before You Check Your Stroller...

If for some reason it is easier for you to check your stroller on arrival, rather than at your gate, keep in mind that it will be far more vulnerable traveling through the airport baggage system than it is when left (and later retrieved) at the gate. Again, you may want to use a carrying bag or case to help protect your gear. If your stroller didn't come with a "travel bag," manufacturers often sell model-specific bags you can purchase separately, or you can choose from a variety of other stroller bags made to fit the standard sizes (recommendations at www.TravelswithBaby.com). Since strollers can generally be checked for free, take advantage of any extra space in your stroller travel bag for additional items you won't need in flight.

Before You Check a Pack 'n Play or Play Yard...

Play yards (a.k.a. Pack 'n Plays) can be very helpful in providing a safe space for your child in un-childproofed settings and a familiar place for him to sleep away from home, but traditional play yards are among the bulkiest and potentially heaviest things a parent might consider taking on a trip. Not to mention, the vast majority of airlines will charge you to check it (or count it toward one of your free checked bags). Before you haul a play yard to the airport, consider these alternatives:

- **If you'll be staying at a hotel, resort, or vacation property, ask if a crib is available for you to use** during your stay. Many hotels and resorts have a small number of cribs or play yards they can provide for guests on request. Some hotels will charge a small fee for this (as they might a rollaway bed for an older guest), though most do not.

- **For infants, portable co-sleepers** like the Snuggle Nest, which goes in the center of a large bed between parents, are also a convenient option that can pack into a checked suitcase and possibly a carry-on suitcase.

- **You may also be able to rent** a play yard, crib, bassinet, or toddler bed, along with any other equipment that would be of help, at your destination (more on this in Baby Gear Rentals, pg. 82).

If these alternatives still won't with your travel plans, it will probably be much easier for you to travel with a baby or toddler travel bed (sometimes called a "travel crib" or "travel cot"). Whether you want tall sides and structure similar to a crib or play yard, or simply want a soft extra bed for your toddler with raised sides to prevent roll-off, there are several flight-worthy models of travel beds available for young children. See specific recommendations in Travel Beds, pg. 76 (and at www.TravelswithBaby.com).

Some brands even include carrying straps or extra pockets for storage, and the infant models may even fit in the bottom of your suitcase. If you must ultimately bring your play yard along for the trip, make sure to pack it as carefully as possible. You may want to remove any wheels ahead of time to prevent them from breaking off in the baggage system. The carrying sacks they come with often don't always completely cover the ends, in which case you may want to use heavy-duty garbage bags and strong tape to ensure no pieces will be lost.

Five Money-Saving Tips for Checking Bags as a Family

1. **Stuff your car seat and stroller travel bags** – With very rare exception, airlines allow car seats and strollers to be checked for free, either at the check-in counter or at the gate for your flight. If you bring a protective travel bag for your stroller or car seat, add any jackets, sweaters, or other items you may want on arrival but won't need in flight. Extra stuffed animals you don't want taking up expensive space in your suitcase? Stuff them in these. (See recommended car seat and stroller travel bags at www.TravelswithBaby.com).

2. **Know what *not* to check** – While car seats and strollers generally fly free, baby and toddler travel beds/cots/cribs, bassinets, play yards, and baby backpack carriers generally do not. If you will need any of these items at your destination, it may be much cheaper to

rent them there for your stay than to pay additional baggage fees (more about baby gear rentals on pg. 82). If you still need to bring a baby or toddler travel bed with you, choose one that will pack compactly inside of a suitcase you're already checking, or is small enough it can count toward one of your personal carry-on items. Our Phil&Teds travel bed, for example, has traveled in the bottom of our large drop-bottom duffel to several destinations. (More about the Phil&Teds and other recommended travel beds on pg. 76 and at www.TravelswithBaby.com.)

3. **Choose an airline with a generous lap child luggage allowance** – If you're flying with a lap child, be sure to use the Airlines Table (pg. 244) to compare lap child luggage allowances for the airlines you're considering. For example, U.S. Airways grants one free suitcase up to 50 lbs for lap children on international flights. United, however, gives no baggage allowance for a lap child flying internationally.

4. **Get a frequent flyer credit card with baggage benefits** – Some airlines' frequent flyer credit cards give a free baggage allowance when you purchase tickets using the card. For example, American Airlines grants me and up to four of my traveling companions each one free checked suitcase on domestic flights when I purchase our tickets with their credit card. (Traveling as a family of five now, that makes a big difference!)

5. **Check your weights and measures** – When loading a suitcase with baby wipes, sun block, formula, baby food, favorite kid snacks, or other essentials, it's easy to go over the typical 50-lb maximum allowance for checked bags. Be forewarned that airlines rarely accept a weighted "average" between a family's checked bags, and you may end up stuck with a hefty overweight surcharge for a bag that weighs 54 lbs when your other two were much less than that. Likewise, be careful filling that largest suitcase you could find with all of the fluffy, lightweight bulky items you want to bring (Diapers? Snow coats? Baby blankets? Stuffed animals?). Always make sure a very large suitcase will be within your airline's size limits (generally 62 linear inches, length + width + depth). Fines can be in the neighborhood of $75 per offending suitcase!

Showing off his new hat made from an airline napkin and decorated with markers and Band-Aids by his big sister for all passengers to see.

Planning Your In-Flight Entertainment

Rather than bombard your child with every toy you've brought onboard at once in the hopes that something will attract his interest more than the freckled scalp in tantalizing view above the seatback in front of you, plan a strategic rotation of toys, books, and activities to keep things interesting—and under control—throughout your flight.

Like preschools, you may have your best results when you are prepared to give your child a new "activity" about every 20 minutes, which might sound daunting if you're setting out on an overseas flight! Nevertheless, some activities will be given during your flight, like eating, snacking, walking to the lavatory, and possibly sleeping. Here are some extra activities you can build into your flight plan.

The "Bag of Discovery" – Great for babies and young toddlers.

I've used various small purses and gaudy cosmetic bags for this, which give the added benefit of an intriguing bag in itself, and sometimes just a quart-size clear plastic slide-lock bag, which can work well with babies who might be entertained for some time just staring at the contents. In either case, I load the bag with a random assortment of small toys and gadgets for my children to open in flight and work their way through the contents. I've had my best results from the most random collections, rather than a collection of "like items." For long flights, I recommend bringing two different Bags of Discovery. And for your return flight, you'll want to switch a few items between bags, if not throw a few new things into the mix. Ideas: Finger puppets, measuring spoons, a small whisk, a teething toy for a baby, a couple of pipe cleaners for a toddler, small dolls, plastic dinosaurs, a mini board book, plastic Easter egg with Cheerios inside.

The "Creativity Kit" – Great for toddlers and preschoolers.

We use clear plastic vinyl zip cases for this, which are durable and make it easy to see and access what's inside. Ideas: Lacing boards, Wikki Stix, pipe cleaners, travel-size magnetic drawing board (Doodle Pro), pocket-size spiral notebook or hotel notepad, crayons or colored pencils, a postcard or two, small stack of coffee stir sticks or straws (you can ask your flight attendant for these), small stencils or tracing shapes. When your child is ready, you might add a few sheets of colored paper, toddler-safe scissors (yes, even the metal variety with blades shorter than 4 inches are now allowed on aircraft), small piece of aluminum foil, plain envelopes to decorate, glue stick.

Get Moving – Even in your seats.

There's no use denying it: Children need to move. In fact, from three years old through adolescence, they may experience the subtle (or not-so-subtle) urge to move their legs continuously as a response to growing pains. The best way I've found to help keep them from moving those legs continuously in the direction of the forward passenger's seat is to 1) Go for a walk every so often throughout the flight, whether it's just to the lavatory, to ask a flight attendant for a cup of ice water, or to go do some stretches together near the rear of the aircraft, and 2) Channel the rest of that energy into physical activities that can be done even with the seatbelt on, such as using those Wikki Stix or pipe cleaners to make 3-D objects, playing with a lacing board, or working with a small set of tangrams to create animals or other shapes and designs.

Babies also need physical activity for their own comfort as well as their development. On long flights, try to work in some of the routine exercises you probably do at home already—riding the bicycle, playing patty cake—which can be done on your lap, on the floor of the bulkhead row, in the travel bassinet, or on a spare seat (if such a thing exists on your flight). If your baby is pulling up or cruising, remember that she would probably enjoy the chance to stretch her legs as much as you would, so try to work in a lap together (holding her hands and letting her walk) when you make trips to the lavatory.

Screen Time – Use it, but don't abuse it.

If your airplane doesn't already have a screen built in before every passenger, you now have the ability to play video games and watch TV shows and movies on your own laptop, iPod, tablet, or possibly even your phone. When trapped in an airplane with a toddler, it can be tempting to (and even a frightful challenge not to) let the games begin—and never end until you touch down.

If you're on a short flight, that may be a fine solution, but if you've got long flights in your future, be warned that children who don't shift gears mentally or physically for long periods of time will likely just be bottling up that unused creative and physical energy for a later—and inconvenient—time. My advice? Treat the movies or shows as a special event that will happen at designated times in your flight, and be sure to communicate that plan to your child in advance. For example, you can explain that you have some fun surprises to share after takeoff, and that you're bringing a special movie to watch *after dinner* on your flight. You can see some of our screen-free favorites to help keep kids entertained on the airplane in the list on pg. 285.

Remember: The best toys are found.

Last of all, don't forget this traveler's motto: "The best toys are found." It's amazed me how fascinating the illustrated flight safety brochures can be to small children (I also hear this repeatedly from other surprised parents), and the empty plastic cups, and the crinkly packets of pretzels, and the reading lights, and the in-flight magazines, and just the fellow passengers who may be all too happy to play peek-a-boo or smile and wave at your child (we'll hope).

Five Screen-Free Favorites to Help Keep Kids Entertained in Flight

Here are some of our family's favorites for air travel without electronics. You can see photos of these and other travel recommendations at www.TravelswithBaby.com.

1. **Tangrams.** These usually wooden tiles are available in so many sizes, shapes, and colors, with sets suitable from children 3 years old and up. While there are many kits or box sets available in travel-friendly sizes, my kids have most enjoyed having a baggie full of the pieces and a booklet of animals to make using the various shapes. They follow the patterns as well as create their own imaginary scenes, sometimes laying the design flat and other times stacking them for a 3-D effect. Sets will vary in age appropriateness depending on the size of tiles.

2. **Wikki Stix.** If you haven't yet added Wikki Stix (or a similar product) to your travel toolbox, these can be a great activity with no mess or cleanup required (just don't let that cute Wikki Man melt into the dashboard of your rental car). They are bendable, reusable, and can be used to make simple flat designs, or rolled and wrapped to make 3-dimensional objects. Most sets include idea cards that show simple ways to make a design. Recommended for children 3 years and older.

3. **Travel Doodle Pro (Tag Along).** Our travel-size Doodle Pro has played a helpful part in so many of our family journeys that I wrote a poetic ode to it you can read for yourself in the Travels with Baby Tips blog. It's handy for even the youngest scribblers and is always ready for more.

4. **Log cabin art with coffee stir sticks.** This one is free, reusable, compostable, and so much fun that you'll want to build a two-dimensional log cabin all your own. Don't forget to swipe a handful of complimentary wooden stir sticks from the airport café before your flight (with plenty of extras for yourself).

5. **Crayola No-Mess Watercolors.** For best results, don't let your child use them at home or until well into your flight, when the freedom to paint feels most unexpected—and appreciated! Pack along a spiral drawing pad or just use airline-issue napkins.

Want more screen-free alternatives to help keep your kids busy during travel? There are dozens of tips, ideas, and inspiration in *Take-Along Travels with Baby*.

Five Tips to Help Prepare Toddlers and Preschoolers for the Flight

Even if your child has flown several times before, it may be difficult to remember all the nuances of the past experiences in his young mind. It may be very helpful, and comforting, to discuss these details in the weeks leading up to your flight, and answer any questions that (it may surprise you) are on his mind. Consider your child's unique temperament (pg. 107) as well, which may help you pinpoint any special concerns or situations it will be helpful to address ahead of time. For example, a very cautious child may travel much more happily after practicing clearing security, step by step, several times at home. A very active child may benefit from thinking through how he can manage his energy while standing in a long line (e.g., hopping on one foot as many times as he can, then the other—setting the ultimate airport one-foot hopping record). Here are the five main topics I suggest you cover.

1. **Security Checkpoints** – Security screenings can be a little unnerving for any of us, but for a toddler or preschooler it can be especially disconcerting. Help your child know what to expect at the airport, including lengthy lines for check-in and security, as well as what you will all need to do to pass through security (e.g., Yes, even the teddy bear must pass through the X-ray machine—but it's a quick ride). If your child is old enough to walk on his own, explain how you will each walk through the metal detector by yourself, and that you'll be right behind him. You may even want to talk about the jobs the TSA agents are performing, especially the ones who get to use "X-ray vision" to look inside everyone's suitcases—some kids find this very fascinating!

2. **Airplane Noises** – Although airplane noise can soothe some children right to sleep, the roaring engines and the exciting sensation of lifting off the ground may frighten more sensitive children. Likewise, some children find the landing portion a little unnerving to begin with, and the sudden KUH-KLUNK of the wheels coming down can be terrifying if they don't know what's happening. Just mentioning the various sounds the airplane makes—and the things you can listen for together during the flight—can be helpful for noise-sensitive and cautious children.

3. **"Airplane Ear" and Changes in Air Pressure** – "Airplane Ear" (a.k.a. the funny feelings you can get during changes in air pressure) is another good topic to discuss in advance, including how our ears will all need to adjust to the changes in air pressure, and what we can do to help. Just be sure to explain the terminology people use concerning the subject. As I learned on one excruciating flight when my toddler daughter would not do anything to help her increasingly painful ears adjust, it turned out she was more terrified of what would happen if her ears actually "popped" than she was of the pain she was already feeling! For more on helping ears adjust in flight, see pg. 308.

4. **Time and Timing of Flight** – Discuss the amount of time you will spend in the aircraft during your flight and how you will spend this time. Older children may enjoy contributing their own ideas, too, as you discuss possible books and toys to bring, snacks, games, etc. If a meal will be served in flight, talk about the procedure of getting

served and eating at your seats (and how it may require a little patience waiting for the food to come—and to return the trays). It may be helpful to discuss the length of the flight in terms of TV shows (e.g., "We'll be in the airplane for as long as it takes to watch TWO episodes of *Sesame Street*"), or through what activities you would otherwise be doing at home during that same time (e.g., "At home we would be eating dinner, getting ready for bed, sleeping all through the night, and still having BREAKFAST before we land in Frankfurt…but we get to do that all on the airplane!).

5. **Toilet Time** – For those in potty training and beyond, the aircraft lavatory may be a little intimidating—and that's before they even hear the unnerving rocket-flush. Again, help your child know what to expect ahead of time, including the need to wait to use the toilet, as is often the case during travel, and the importance of telling you as early as possible when he feels the urge. Also, consider modifications you may make to the aircraft toilet—a folding travel seat you can practice using at home, or perhaps even a folding practice potty. In early potty training, it may be simplest and safest to use diapers or disposable training pants during the flight, especially in the event that turbulence or other conditions may require all passengers to remain seated at length. If your child hasn't been wearing training pants most of the time, talk about why this might be a good idea—just during the flight. See more tips for travel with potty trainees beginning on pg. 98.

CHAPTER 17

At the Airport and on the Plane

Clearing Security with Small Children (and a Small Mountain of Gear)

Many a parent has tried to slip through the scanner with a sleeping infant in his car seat or stroller—unsuccessfully. Be prepared to put all of your gear, and I do mean all of it, onto the X-ray belt—right along with your shoes and anything else that would normally go through the scanner. Here are some tips for dealing with the main items requiring your attention as you all shuffle through security.

Baby carriers and slings

Wearing your child through the airport can free up your hands for the other items you're transporting—and can even free up your travel stroller to help transport a few other items (or another child). While I have occasionally walked through security "wearing" my baby, and doing so is allowed much more often at present than it was a few years ago, be aware that the TSA still reserves the right to ask you to remove any child carrier, soft pack, or sling and run it through the X-ray—even if it is entirely fabric without buckles or snaps, and even if your baby is sound asleep in it. Just be aware that while you may breeze through the first airport without ever removing your child from the Ergo, the TSA agent at the second airport may have different thoughts as you approach the metal detector and you will be expected to comply.

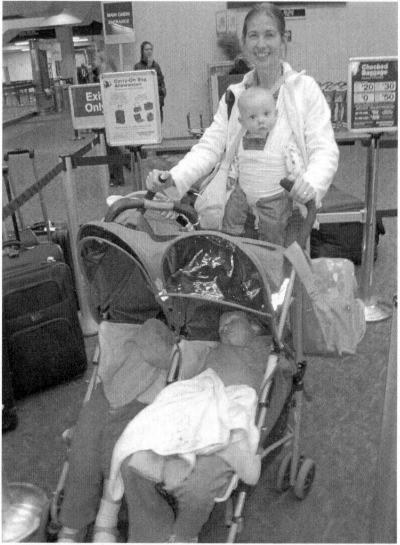

Midnight at San Francisco International Airport: Never underestimate the value or utility of a good travel stroller. Here, a twin travel stroller transports sleeping older siblings, two backpacks, and an infant car seat. Better still? It folds compactly enough to ride through the X-ray machine without security batting an eye.

Strollers, Prams, and Pushchairs

Although I've been allowed to push my child on through security in a stroller once or twice in other countries, with both being scanned by a hand wand, that is not the practice in U.S. airports or in most countries. In nearly every airport, children are required to come out from their strollers at security, and the strollers should be collapsed and placed on the conveyor belt to pass through the X-ray scanner. However, when unwieldy prams, tandems, twins, and jogging strollers arrive on the scene, they are generally sidelined and scanned by hand (and very much frowned upon) if they cannot fit through the X-ray scanner (you will want to budget for extra time).

American Airlines no longer accepts jogging strollers or strollers weighing over 20 lbs at the gate, so you will need to check these at the ticket counter, and preferably in a protective travel bag as they aren't responsible for damage. Consider using a lightweight travel stroller instead (recommendations at www.TravelswithBaby.com), and/or renting a jogging stroller at your destination (more about Baby Gear Rentals on pg. 82).

When traveling with a baby or young toddler, it's usually easiest (and safest) to leave them in the stroller until everything else is situated on the belt and ready for the X-ray. If you're traveling with another adult, have them pass through the metal detector first and begin collecting your other items, then buckle your child safely in his stroller as soon as it passes through to the other side, so you'll be able to use both hands to help finish collecting your things and can safely wheel him out of the path of hurried travelers while doing so.

Car Seats

All car seats must be placed on the conveyor belt to pass through the X-ray (without children in them!). Often, the larger toddler car seats, when faced with surprisingly small X-ray machines, will fit best facing down. If your child is passing through the airport in his car seat, whether it's an infant car seat or a toddler car seat attached to a car seat trolley (see pg. 70) or carry-on suitcase (as with the Traveling Toddler strap, pg.70), you may want to wait until the last moment, after all other items are ready to go through the scanner, to remove him from the car seat and place it on the belt.

Liquids and Gels

Rather than shuffling through different carry-on bags to retrieve your personal 3-1-1 bag of travel-size liquids from one place and your child's travel kit from another, it may be easiest to keep all family members' personal 3-1-1 bags together to present at security. If you are flying with excess liquid items for your child, such as baby food, medicines, or prepared bottles, make sure these are also easy to retrieve and lay on top of a bin as you pass through (see tips for packing your child's excess liquids on pg. 270).

Family members

With all of your bags, gear, shoes, and jackets placed on the conveyor belt, you will finally be allowed to stroll through the scanner with either your baby in your arms or your child walking on her own two feet. Once children can walk by themselves, they will be expected to do so through the metal detector. You or your partner may want to go first to help encourage them to pass through and alleviate any anxiety about what awaits on the other side (at Denver International, it may be a smiling TSA agent with a sticker for your child!), but if you are traveling solo with your child, you may want to send your child first in case you beep and require further scanning. (Doh! The metal grommets on my back pockets—I should have seen it coming.)

Four Ways Flying with Babies Has Actually Become Easier in Recent Years

1. Since early 2013, children under the age of 12 are no longer required to remove their shoes at U.S. airport security, leaving those unpleasant moments of instruction to remove soft-soled booties from infants' feet at security checkpoints a funny footnote in aviation history.

2. Babies are more often than not allowed to pass through U.S. airport security without being removed from their child carriers and slings, allowing swifter passage of family travelers who can use both hands to manage their gear.

3. Gel-filled teething rings, to the great relief of parents flying with teething infants—and the relief of the infants themselves—are once again permitted in the airplane cabin (pack and present these with your child's liquid items at security).

4. Family lanes have been introduced at many major U.S. airports (look for the green sign at security), and while they're not always open or available, they can sometimes speed a family through security much faster than the other passengers, and with agents who are more accustomed to inspecting baby items.

Tips for Swift Passage through Airport Security

Remember, the fewer items you have to shuffle at security, the better. You may feel inundated already with just the items for your child, so the less you have to carry or slip on and off for yourself the more manageable the procedure will be. Consider these tips for traveling parents:

- Pack your jacket that would have to be removed at security and wear a pullover sweater instead.

- Only travel in slip-on shoes (no laces, no buckles).

- Do not wear a belt when traveling, or keep it in your carry-on until you've passed through security.

- Pack your watch and only necessary jewelry in your carry-on to put on after clearing security.

- Use a backpack or over-the-shoulder bag that you can sling on and off easily and will keep your hands free to contend with other items.

- Consider letting your diaper bag double as your purse, or bring a purse that is small enough to keep in the diaper bag or daypack until it's needed.

- Wear a neck security wallet to keep your boarding passes and ID handy while keeping your hands free.

- Avoid wearing your baby in a frontpack carrier or other type of carrier that requires two hands to remove and/or resume wearing in case you are asked to do so.

- Consider taking twins or young siblings in separate travel or umbrella strollers, rather than in a cumbersome double stroller.

For the latest information about airport security requirements, visit the Transportation Security Administration online at www.tsa.gov, or call them at 1-866-289-9673.

Seven Easy Ways to Get Your Car Seat to the Gate

1. **Use a stroller or stroller frame** – Infant carrier car seats that "ride" on strollers as a "travel system" or on simple stroller frames are fantastic for travel. While your child still fits in his infant car seat, your best option may be to simply bring your infant-in-car-seat and stroller or stroller frame all to the gate. If you are using the car seat onboard, just check the stroller or stroller frame at the gate, getting the necessary tag from the counter there. If you are unexpectedly offered a free seat for your infant flying as a lap child (doesn't happen as often as it used to, but it's not entirely unheard of), you'll have the car seat with you to use during your flight.

2. **Use the handles of your travel stroller** – If you have a stroller with two separate handles (umbrella-style or similar), you may be able to put the carrying handle of your infant car seat in the farthest back position and "hang" it over your stroller handle. If traveling with a convertible or toddler car seat, you may be able to lengthen the straps of your car seat and loop them over the handles with the car seat facing your stroller. Just remember, if your travel stroller is very lightweight, you'll want to remove the car seat before removing your child to avoid a tip over (the same goes for when you hang that heavy diaper bag or daypack on it).

3. **Carry the car seat on your back** – You may be able to wear the car seat over your shoulders by lengthening the straps, which keeps your hands free for rolling the suitcase or pushing your stroller, though if your car seat isn't a good fit for you, you may change your mind about this plan somewhere around Gate 47. A better solution is a purpose-built car seat backpack carrier like the Pac Back or any of the various car seat carrying cases that include backpack or shoulder carrying straps (especially if you'll be traveling alone with your child or with more than one child).

4. **Use a protective car seat travel bag with wheels** – JL Childress and Brica both offer protective car seat travel bags that fit a wide variety of toddler car seats and come with backpack carrying straps or inline skate wheels (Brica's model offers both). See more advantages of using car seat travel bags on pg. 280.

5. **Use a car seat transporter or trolley** – Still wondering what to do with your *child*? Several models of toddler car seats can be attached to the GoGo Kidz Cart or Brica Roll 'n Go transporter, which makes it possible to wheel your child right to the gate in his own car seat, and possibly right down the aisle of larger aircraft (no promises here, however). Read more about the GoGo Kidz TravelMate on pg. 70 and at www.TravelswithBaby.com.

6. **Wheel your child, car seat, and carry-on suitcase in one** – Or for a more economical solution, the Traveling Toddler car seat strap can be used to attach your child's car seat to your rolling carry-on, enabling you to roll your child strapped in her car seat along with one carry-on suitcase at the same time (more on pg. 70 and at www.TravelswithBaby.com).

7. **Consider the Sit 'n' Stroll car seat** – If you'll be traveling much by airplane and/or taxi with your baby or young toddler, you might also consider the Sit 'n' Stroll convertible car seat that converts to a stroller (can be used from 5 lbs to 40 lbs, rear- and forward-facing; more on pg. 67 and at www.TravelswithBaby.com).

Awaiting yet another red-eye at San Francisco International. Unless it's nearly boarding time or you're waiting to be paged, go spread out at a vacant gate and get those ya-yas out.

10 Ways to Entertain Your Tot in the Terminal

If you dread spending time awaiting your flight with your toddler, or surviving a layover with your preschooler, fear not. Airports can be far more interesting to a child than they are to the rest of us. In fact, when my brother-in-law once panicked, unsure of how to keep his three- and four-year-old entertained on a rainy afternoon, he asked them where they would like to go: "To the movies? To the mall?" They both exclaimed excitedly, "To the airport!" And off they went. Here's a sampling of some of the fun to be had inside the terminal.

1. Ride the escalators.

2. Ride the elevators.

3. Play "I see a blue coat, I see a black coat" (or some version of "I spy with my little eye").

4. Count backpacks.

5. Have a picnic at a vacated gate.

6. Watch the airplanes taxi and take off.

7. Watch the airplanes descend and applaud the smoothest landings.

8. Fill water bottles for your flight at a water fountain.

9. Befriend airline personnel also awaiting your flight with questions like, "How many times have you flown on an airplane?" and "Have you ever seen Santa Claus up there?"

10. Get some quality physical activity in like practicing yoga, doing calisthenics, or dancing the Hokey Pokey at a vacated gate—that's what it's all about! If you're traveling with a baby, put down a blanket and let her roll, rock, or crawl, practicing all her latest moves.

For more ideas and inspiration to help keep your child entertained on the go, don't leave home without the companion guide to this book: *Take-Along Travels with Baby: Hundreds of Tips to Help During Travel with Your Baby, Toddler, and Preschooler.*

The Great Pre-boarding Debate

As airlines vie for the steadier, more lucrative repeat business of business travelers, many have done away with pre-boarding for families with young children (which might imply to the other passengers waiting to board that the airline favors travelers with babies and young children). If "family pre-boarding" is offered on your next flight, don't be surprised if your call to pre-board actually comes after all of the frequent flyer members and business class travelers have boarded the aircraft (this could be one good reason to join the loyalty program if you haven't already). Whether or not you are better off pre-boarding is another matter, and the answer is likely to change as your child develops and grows.

When to pre-board:

- If your child is slow to adapt to new situations, pre-boarding can be a good way to help him adjust to his new surroundings and make himself comfortable before takeoff.

- If you are flying with a car seat (especially for the first time), pre-boarding might allow you the extra time and attention from the flight crew to help get your car seat installed and settle into your seats. It is also much easier to carry a car seat down the aisle before passengers are blocking your path and resting their elbows on the aisle seat armrests.

- If you are flying a carrier that does not have pre-assigned seating, pre-boarding may be the only way to ensure your family gets seats together and ones that will be appropriate for car seats. (On Southwest Airlines, priority boarding may only be available with a paid upgrade. With AirAsia, you may choose to pay more to choose your own seats in advance.)

- If you are flying alone with your child, pre-boarding will help ensure you get the assistance you need folding your stroller at the gate, storing your baggage, installing your car seat, etc., all while taking care of your child.

- If you are boarding a large aircraft or traveling on a very full flight, pre-boarding will help you get to your seats expeditiously without getting trapped in a slow-moving line of passengers struggling to store their carry-on baggage—possibly bumping you or your child in the process.

- If you are traveling on a large airplane with a lap child and have seat assignments near the rear (where any remaining seats will most likely be found), you may want to board early to "squat" on an extra seat near yours in case you can claim it—or make a trade with someone for another vacant seat.

When not to pre-board:

- If you have an extremely active child, it might be best to let her burn off her energy outside of the aircraft and not board until the last moment possible.

- If you have a toddler that will be traveling on your lap, it may be best for the whole family to wait until the last moment possible to settle into your seats.

Tip: Airlines don't always agree, but it doesn't hurt to ask if one of the adults in your family can board in advance with the car seat to get it installed while the other adult lets the toddler burn off a little more energy. *Sometimes* they'll allow it.

Using a Car Seat (CRS) on Aircraft

According to FAA regulations, infants (children under 2 years) flying in purchased seats rather than on laps must be secured in their car seats as they would be in an automobile. As for children 2 to approximately 4 years and weighing less than 40 lbs, the FAA "strongly recommends" the use of an FAA-approved CRS (Child Restraint System, which is airline-speak for "car seat"), though it is not required. However, some airlines may request that you hold a smaller child that doesn't have a car seat in your lap during takeoff and landing. If you are undecided about bringing your car seat on board, keep these benefits in mind:

- Children are safest flying and landing in their car seats.

- Children are often more comfortable in their car seats than on a lap or in the adult-size airplane seat.

- You will likely be more comfortable with your child riding in his car seat, especially if you plan to eat or otherwise use your tray during the flight.

- You may both be more likely to snooze during the flight.

- Your car seat will be best protected from damage traveling in the cabin.

To be certain your car seat will be accepted by the airline, look for red type on the label that clearly says, "This restraint is certified for use in motor vehicles and aircraft." If your child's car seat does not have this statement on its label, be prepared to have your car seat checked for you at the gate. Some toddler car seats that start with 5-point safety harnesses and later convert to belt-positioning booster seats do not include this statement on the label, but instead explain in the user's manual that the seat is approved for use in aircraft as a car seat with harness only—so be sure to have your manual tucked into its storage place on the car seat as you travel in case there is any question.

Otherwise, car seats may be used on aircraft similarly to how they are used in automobiles throughout the U.S.:

- Children under 20 lbs – a rear-facing car seat

- Children 20–40 lbs – a forward-facing car seat

- Children over 40 lbs – a forward-facing car seat with a suitable upper weight limit for use as a car seat with the harness, not as a booster.

In some cases, your airline may even be able to provide you with a CRS for your child during flight. For example, British Airways and Virgin Atlantic now offer a limited number of CRSs for its seated passengers under 2 years old—jolly good if you'll be riding the tube or train on your vacation and won't otherwise need a car seat (see Airlines Table, pg. 244, for all airlines offering similar benefits).

Five Tips for Installing Car Seats on Airplanes

1. Because a CRS can be an obstacle to other passengers en route to the lavatory or, more importantly, when exiting in the event of an emergency evacuation, you will need to place the CRS in the least obtrusive seat possible—either a window seat or in the middle of a center row on wide-body aircraft.

2. Your CRS installs with the airplane seat belt just as it would with the lap belt of an automobile, though you may find it helpful or even necessary to turn the buckle so that it may be opened away from the armrest after your flight.

3. If possible on your row (armrests are usually fixed on bulkhead rows), lift the armrests out of the way to help ease your installation with the airplane safety belt.

4. If you're having trouble getting the safety belt buckled behind your car seat, ask a flight attendant for a seat belt extension, which may make it easier to get the belt latched before adjusting the slack.

5. Finally, if you have one of the more commodious, full-featured car seats for your child, perhaps one that boasts being the only car seat your child will ever need from birth through college, consider leaving it at home. It will likely be more trouble than it's worth.

What can you do when your child's car seat doesn't fit in the airplane seat?

Even if your car seat is approved for air travel and your airline permits them (see Exceptional Airlines, pg. 241), you might suddenly find yourself in a situation known to many veteran family travelers—the same car seat that fit in the last airplane you took doesn't fit this time around.

It's easy to get frustrated, especially as you struggle to get the seat into place while shielding your child from other passengers hoisting lead-weight carry-ons over your heads and flight attendants urge you to either get that car seat in place or gate-check it so everyone can get on their way (yes, we pay for this service). One mom who tried to stand her ground about using her child's car seat on a U.S. carrier was even told to get off the airplane altogether.

I hope you never find yourself in a tough situation like this, but in case you do it will be helpful to know your rights—and a couple of tips ahead of time that may help you avoid having to exercise them.

- Never fly with a car seat over 18" wide (16" is recommended by the FAA but practically nonexistent among car seats). Some infant car seats have bases that exceed this, but most can also be installed safely without their bases using the airplane safety belt (see your manual).

- Use a car seat with a narrow footprint and raised base to ease installation between armrests with the safety belt.

- If you want or need to install your child's car seat rear-facing, reserve bulkhead seats to ensure an adequate degree of recline without running into a forward passenger's seat—but make certain you follow the first point since armrests on bulkhead rows typically cannot be raised to allow for extra room.

If the bottom line is that your child's car seat simply won't fit as needed in the original seat you have purchased, don't panic. According to an advisory circular from the Federal Aviation Administration (Sept. 2010, AC No: 120-87B), the airline is obliged to help you find a seat that will work for your FAA-approved car seat—provided it's in the same class of service (no first-class upgrades for bringing big car seats onboard, sorry). Here's the actual text:

> **f. Operators Prohibiting CRS [child restraint system or car seat] Use.** *No aircraft operator may prohibit a child from using an approved CRS when the parent/guardian purchases a seat for the child. If an approved CRS, for which a ticket has been purchased, does not fit in a particular seat on the aircraft, the aircraft operator has the responsibility to accommodate the CRS in another seat in the same class of service. The regulations also permit an aircraft operator to use its discretion in identifying the most appropriate forward-facing passenger seat location, considering safe operating practices. For example:*
>
> **(1)** *A CRS with a base that is too wide to fit properly in a seat with rigid armrests can be moved to a seat with moveable armrests that can be raised to accommodate the CRS.*
>
> **(2)** *An aft-facing CRS that cannot be installed properly, because of minimal pitch (distance between seats) between rows, can be moved to a bulkhead seat or a seat in a row with additional pitch.*

Of course, if the car seat won't fit in *any* seat in coach, you will still be obliged to gate-check it for the flight (and a few airlines have actually written their own disclaimers to trump these if they feel like it). But if there is another viable option, it's up to the airline to help you—and possibly other passengers—make the switch to seats that will work.

Why No Booster Seats Onboard?

Although a safety booster could certainly improve a young child's view out the airplane window, they are not approved for use on aircraft. Whether or not a booster seat used with an airplane safety belt actually makes a child *less* safe during air travel than flying with the airplane safety belt alone is a topic I've yet to see addressed, but for now the explanation holds that safety boosters are made to properly position shoulder belts on children, and are not supposed to be used with lap-only belts including those found on aircraft.

Using the CARES Child Aviation Restraint

The FAA has approved a flight "safety device" designed as an alternative to car seats for children over 1 year old and weighing between 22 and 44 lbs. The CARES device (Child Aviation Restraint) is basically a harness that goes around the adult airplane seat back and attaches to the passenger lap belt. It helps protect against "turbulence and other incidents" by converting the airplane's seat belt into a safety harness.

I have used CARES with all three of my children now, and I can tell you that, weighing just 1 lb and packing into its own 6" stuff sack, it clearly has its advantages over hauling a car seat through the airport. However, it can have its drawbacks that you should be aware of. Before you buy CARES for your child, consider the pros and cons:

The pros of CARES:

- CARES is much easier to carry onboard than a car seat.
- It takes up far less space in a cruise ship cabin, train compartment, or a small hotel room than a car seat will.
- It is much safer than flying with your 1-year-old on your lap and, unlike the Baby B'Air and FlyeBaby, can be used during taxiing, takeoff, and landing.
- Using CARES instead of a car seat will make it much less likely that your toddler will be able to kick the seat in front of him (at least while buckled!).

Although CARES is not a perfect solution for all children, it can— at certain times and with certain children—feel darn near close.

The cons of CARES:

- CARES cannot be used in automobiles (though you may be able to rent a car seat at your destination, pg. 82, or use the RideSafer travel vest, pg. 68).

- Your child will still have the airplane's easy-open safety belt buckle right on his lap (I recommend buckling it with the lift flap facing him, but they usually figure this out).

- Even with the safety buckle fastened, there is no crotch strap to prevent escape artists from exiting through the airplane's lap belt.

- Your child will be strapped upright in a grown-up-size seat and may have trouble sleeping in it, if needed, during the flight.

One final note on CARES: You may be able to rent CARES by mail from select baby gear rental companies if you expect you'll need it for only one trip, or if you want to "try before you buy." However, if you use your purchased CARES at least twice, it may pay for itself. For more photos and details on my own family's experiences using CARES flight harness, go to www.TravelswithBaby.com.

Lap Child Safety

Because turbulence is unpredictable and is the leading cause of injuries on commercial aircraft, lap-held babies are among the most frequently injured passengers on turbulent flights. Some airlines outside of the U.S. may offer you a special safety belt for your lap child that goes around her waist with a second loop for your own seat belt to pass through to help protect against turbulence. A few airlines, like Austrian Air and British Airways, may even require you to use one of these safety belts for your lap child.

In stark contrast, these safety belts for lap-held babies and toddlers have actually been banned from use in commercial U.S. aircraft. At this time, the Baby B'Air flight safety vest is the only safety device specifically designed for lap children and tested for use on aircraft, and approved for use during cruising portions of your flight (remember that frontpack carriers and infant slings are not permitted for use in aircraft seats by the FAA).

This little red vest straps around the child's waist and between the legs, with a loop on the back where it connects to your airplane safety belt. Note that the Baby B'Air vest is not approved by the FAA for use during takeoff, landing, or taxiing as it is designed to help protect against turbulence only, not the motion or risks associated with landings. Nevertheless, it is a far safer alternative to merely holding your child on your lap, and certainly makes it easier to relax during your flight (you can even nurse your child while using it). See more about the Baby B'Air at www.TravelswithBaby.com.

What About All Those Germs?

The prospect of hundreds of air passengers, some inevitably sick with colds and possibly worse, coming together in cramped conditions with little vents spewing forth recycled cabin air can be especially disconcerting for parents traveling with babies and small children.

The good news is that the air itself that is circulating—and re-circulating—in your aircraft may actually be healthier than the air in your child's daycare, preschool, or even at the library. Most commercial aircraft now re-circulate the cabin's air every three to five minutes through state-of-the art HEPA filters. In a *20/20* special report by ABC News, an air filtration expert reported that these HEPA filters can capture up to 99.9% of small bacteria and viruses—even the SARS and bird flu virus.

Although the cabin *air* may be relatively free of illness-causing viruses and bacteria, the surfaces inside the airplane and the airports may be a different matter. Germs like to travel, too. If you had a microscope handy you could follow them on their course through the airport to their connecting flights as well. They tend to hitchhike from one surface to the next via droplets of moisture, particularly those coughed and sneezed onto hands that share railings, elevator buttons, armrests, trays, and lavatory doors.

What's your best defense? Wash your hands, and often. Better yet, keep a travel-size pack of antibacterial hand wipes (like Redi-Wipes) handy in your diaper bag or carry-on to use when washing hands isn't an option—especially after changing diapers in the lavatory where it may be impossible to safely wash your hands while your child is on the changing table. You can also use the wipes to quickly wipe down the armrests and trays at your seats as you settle in for your flight.

Ear Pressure, Pain, and Relief

While it can be very helpful to breastfeed or give a bottle to babies during takeoff and landing to help the ears adjust, traveling parents quickly learn that the timing doesn't always work out for this.

With any delays in boarding for your flight or taxiing to the runway, you may be faced with a hungry baby who wants to nurse now, thankyouverymuch, and will let you and every other passenger hear about it if he's put off for too long (stressful for both of you, and no way to start a flight). On a short flight, your baby may already have a full tummy and be snoozing blissfully as you begin your descent, leaving you with the difficult question of whether or not you should wake a sleeping baby.

In addition to the advice in "Preparing Toddlers and Preschoolers for the Flight" (pg. 287), here are some things you can do to help avoid unnecessary stress around the issue of ear pressure and pain when flying with your child.

- **Don't sweat the takeoff.** With healthy, functioning Eustachian tubes, the ascent is not as challenging to the ears as the descent before landing, although a child unfamiliar with the sensation may be uncertain how to respond, and the added engine noise during takeoff may also frighten some children. To help rule out an upset caused by anxiety (rather than ear pain), don't postpone breastfeeding or bottle feedings for hungry babies, show your child your own calm example throughout the takeoff, and use a soothing voice.

- **Keep everyone well hydrated.** Make sure your child (and all members of the family) stays well hydrated leading up to the flight, as this will help thin any mucus that may be present in the Eustachian tube and prevent blockages or reduce restrictions that could make it more difficult for the ears to adjust.

- **Get the doctor's stamp of approval.** If your child has experienced allergy symptoms, a cold, or an ear infection in the last couple of weeks before your flight, there is a chance that mucus or swelling in the Eustachian tubes may make it more difficult for his ears to adjust. You may want to consult your pediatrician to make sure "all ears are in the clear" before your flight, and ask if there are any remedies she might recommend to help make sure they stay that way.

- **Remember that drinking liquids is not the only way to help ears adjust.** When your child shows no interest in breastfeeding, bottles, or sippy cups, don't despair—and certainly don't show anxiety if you can help it. Just move on to the other ways you can help his ears adjust as you make your descent.

- **Embrace Mother Nature.** If your child does begin to cry, don't panic. Remember that even crying gets the jaw moving and can help equalize ear pressure.

Fifteen Ways to Help a Child's Ears Adjust in Flight

1. Breastfeeding

2. Bottle feeding

3. Cup feeding—even for infants

4. Sucking pacifiers

5. Chewing on a teething toy

6. Mouthing a washcloth with an ice cube inside

7. Rubbing teething gel on an a baby's gums

8. Yawning (fake it to make it)

9. Snacking

10. Using EarPlanes (for ages 1 – 10) to help regulate air pressure in the Eustachian tube

11. Licking lollipops

12. Chewing gum (for those old enough)

13. Talking

14. Singing

15. Laughing (give a tickle!)

Tip: Sometimes a bit of novelty is all it takes to turn a child's attention from the funny feeling in her ears to a jaw-moving activity that will relieve the pressure forming there. We've marveled many times how a simple small cup of water (or water with ice) placed against our babies' lips will be more interesting than any bottle (or breast) offered. Just be sure you have what you need before the airplane begins its descent and you can no longer access overhead baggage or move about the cabin.

Changing Diapers at 30,000 Feet

For many parents contemplating a flight with an infant or small child, how to handle diapering en route is a top concern. I wish I could tell you not to worry, that you can rest assured that your plane's lavatory will be equipped with a changing table, and that flight attendants won't tell you to get back in your seat because of a risk of turbulence—though the risk of a blowout is imminent. But life is full of surprises, and so is air travel with children. In addition to your "perfected diaper bag for carry on" (be sure to read pg. 273), here are a few ways you can be a better prepared for dealing with diapers on airplanes.

Finding the diaper changing table

Whereas some airlines such as JetBlue offer a changing table in every single airplane in their fleet, you shouldn't always expect this when flying carriers with smaller, "commuter" or regional aircraft. As a general rule, airplanes that have three or more lavatories onboard will have at least one equipped with a changing table, usually one at the back of the aircraft. If you look closely at the lavatory doors, you may see a picture of an infant or other clue that you've found the right lavatory. Ask a flight attendant if you aren't certain where it is.

When there is no diaper changing table onboard

Parents faced with diaper changes on aircraft not equipped with a changing facility have made use of their seats, the floor, the top of the toilet, and even their own laps in some cases. Needless to say, none of these situations is ideal. Chances are you know how messy the lavatories can become as the hours pass, and how little space a toilet lid affords a reclined baby or toddler. Be sure to come equipped with plenty of antibacterial Redi-Wipes and a large piece of flannel-backed vinyl to protect your seats from your baby—or your baby from the lavatory. Once your child can stand securely, it may be easiest (and most sanitary) to let her stand on the toilet seat or floor and change her diapers in the vertical.

Making the change
If you have the good fortune of flying aboard a plane with changing tables, be prepared to work without elbowroom. Chances are you will be most efficient by taking only the essentials into the lavatory with you. An over-the-shoulder purse or a waistpack may actually be handiest for your in-flight changes (again, see details on pg. 273), as it will keep a couple of fresh diapers, wipes, and cream handy at your hip without getting in your way or requiring (nonexistent) space on the (almost assuredly wet) counter or toilet seat. Also, be sure to bring plastic bags along in your diaper bag for disposing of or possibly storing dirty diapers until you reach your destination (lavatory trash space is limited, as is the air supply). And one final warning: If you find yourself with a dirty diaper in your hand, don't even think of passing it off to a flight attendant. As members of the food service, they are not permitted to handle human waste—not even from the cutest humans they've ever had the pleasure to have served. Instead, ask them where you can dispose of the diaper yourself.

Feeding Babies and Children on Airplanes

Breastfed babies have it easy when dinner is up in the air (see tips for Breastfeeding on the Go, pg. 97), but their bottle-fed friends and solid-food seniors may have a more interesting time of it.

Preparing Bottles During Air Travel
Some breastfeeding moms may find it helpful to have an extra bottle of breastmilk along for the journey in case their babies are too distracted by the new surroundings on the aircraft to focus on the breast for that first feeding. Formula-feeding parents will probably find it easiest to travel with single-serving packets of prepared liquid formula to use

during the flight (details on getting these through airport security on pg. 270).

Warming Bottles on Airplanes

On the larger aircraft and during longer flights, flight attendants will almost always warm bottles for passengers—though you should ask during your airline reservations if you have any question. Otherwise, you can bring your own large travel mug onboard and request hot water (as available for tea), or bring along a thermos that will fit around your child's bottles (the hot water provided on the airplane may keep long enough in the thermos for a second use). Take great care with the hot water around your child, and if she's at an especially "grabby stage," try to warm the bottle while your partner takes her for a diaper change or a walk around the cabin. If time allows, you might request hot water from an airport café or restaurant that keeps hot water for tea and begin warming your first bottle before your flight (or in a pinch, get hot water from the tap at the restroom).

Using Baby Food in Flight

Strained or blended baby foods are permitted in your cabin baggage, so long as they are in sealed jars and you are indeed traveling with a baby or a toddler (you will need to present them at security; see details and tips on pg. 270). As we quickly learn, baby foods can be quite messy regardless of where they are eaten. Some clever parents may color coordinate their child's meal to her travel attire ("Her favorite color is carrot!"), and others will opt for less visible fare, like bananas or pears. Jarred baby foods that are blended with oatmeal or rice have a slightly thicker consistency, which makes them a little easier to keep on the spoon. Remember to avoid feeding your child any gassy foods (and yourself if you're breastfeeding) during your flight and for at least 24 hours before takeoff. Aside from the obvious beans, you might want to steer clear of baby foods made with peas and/or turkey, for example.

Encouraging Self-Feeding and Snacking in Flight

Once your child is old enough to enjoy Cheerios, puffs, and other small finger-foods, this can be a great way for her to pass some time during the flight. You might like to bring along a travel tray that will work with her car seat (see pg. 78), which will be useful whether her car seat is installed facing forward or rearward. When not eating, the travel tray will also be useful to help keep other activities in easy reach as well. Another handy product may be the "Drink Deputy," which can attach to your child's car seat at one end (or overall strap, etc.) and her baby bottle or sippy cup at the other to keep it from falling to the floor and possibly rolling under your seats.

Meal Service for Children

If you are flying internationally, don't forget to check if your airline offers baby or child meals (see Airlines Table, pg. 244), and be sure to reserve yours in advance. When flying domestically, don't count on in-flight meals for purchase to include kid-friendly fare, and be sure to bring back-up food onboard for your whole family. Since the airlines don't usually expect all passengers to buy meals, they frequently run out before everyone is given the option.

Five Ways to Soothe a Fussy Baby in Flight

It's a great feeling to end the flight with a crew of smiling flight attendants and passengers praising your child for being such a great little traveler, and you for raising him to be that way. The older couple in row twelve may even turn their heads in surprise to say, "Oh, we didn't even realize there was a baby on this flight!" I hope it happens to you. But even when your child is an accomplished traveler, there may be times it simply doesn't go so well.

Teething pain can strike at any time in the first couple of years. A sudden new awareness of unfamiliar surroundings. An inexplicable dislike of strangers. Growing pains. Gas. The inability to sleep in airspace no matter how exhausted. And no matter what the reason, it seems there is always a chorus of strangers explaining to you that her ears haven't properly adjusted. It is stressful enough in times when you can't seem to soothe your child at home, but when trapped in an airplane full of fellow travelers it can be especially unpleasant.

For the time being, there is nothing to prevent you from bringing onboard a supply of chocolate kisses and ear plugs for your fellow passengers as a show of your goodwill. If you are feeling truly nervous about how things might go, pass them out with a smile as passengers take their seats and say, "Just in case—this is her first flight and we're a little nervous." Chances are things will go just fine, but in case she cries, you're bound to get sympathetic looks rather than dirty ones.

Here are some other tips for fending off a few difficult situations in case they present themselves during a flight:

1. **Bring two dry extra washcloths onboard,** one for dipping in a cup of ice water to help with teething (and keep the mouth busy), and the other to moisten with warm water from the lavatory to help clear a stuffy little nose if needed.

2. **Bring a supply of Hyland's Calms Forté 4 Kids** onboard to help relieve restlessness and irritability. Since the tablets dissolve almost instantly under the tongue, they can be given to toddlers and preschoolers, and also to babies with your pediatrician's guidance.

3. **Keep a crying baby in motion,** walking laps around the aircraft. Even if the motion fails to calm her, changing locations will at least spread the burden of noise among the passengers.

4. **Let digestion take its course.** Sometimes babies need to change positions or simply move their bodies to help their digestive systems do what they must. Playing "ride the bicycle" on your lap may help ease painful gas, or letting a baby who's pulling up or cruising at home stand and lean at your seats may get things moving in other ways.

5. **Create a canopy over your child with a blanket** tucked into the seat-back tray at one end, and behind your head rest, child's car seat, or your shoulder at the other end. It may help block out distractions and light, while helping your child feel more cozy and secure.

When all else fails, don't despair. Remember in the greater scheme of your vacation, the flight is just one little piece of the puzzle, which you will most likely be laughing and rolling your eyes about in the months to come. At some point, the flight will be over and, with any luck, you'll never see the other passengers again. But in case any of them really rub you the wrong way, you might offer the following:

- "She heard they were getting warm cookies in first class."

- "We tried to give her drugs for the flight, but she just said no."

- And to the real stinkers: "She's afraid of grown-ups who don't know how to smile."

For more on-the-go tips to help soothe babies, manage toddlers, and entertain preschoolers during your flight, be sure to pack your *Take-Along Travels with Baby* guide in your carry-on or upload to your Kindle.

CHAPTER 18

Special Situations

Fifteen Ways to Ease Flying Solo with Your Child

Flying solo with a baby or young child presents its own set of logistical considerations. For example, how do you get your carry-on bags, stroller, and possibly a car seat—oh, and your shoes, and your coat—onto the X-ray scanner while you juggle your child (and now they ask to see your boarding pass and photo ID for a second time)? How do you fold your stroller at the gate with your child in your arms? What do you do with your baby while you use the lavatory? And how do you install the car seat while wrestling your toddler and situating your carry-on bags? And if you're flying with a lap child, how will you eat your dinner when there may not even be room for the tray and your child in your lap?

Anything else to consider? How about negotiating baggage claim in an army of strangers slinging their heavy suitcases off the track? Traveling alone with a small child requires the swift dexterity of an octopus. Here are a few tips and strategies that may help:

1. If you haven't already purchased your tickets, it may be well worth comparing your airline options using the Airlines Table (beginning pg. 244) to see if any offer family-friendly perks that could make all the difference for you.

2. Take a "test drive" around your home (or around your block!) with whatever suitcase(s), stroller, backpack, baby sling, or other gear you plan to transport through the airport on your own. Don't wait until you get there to discover your plan needs a little fine-tuning...

3. Ask your airline if you'll have the option of curb-checking your baggage on arrival at either of your airports. This may help you avoid the hairpin turns and longer wait of the line inside the airport. An extra fee may apply (around $2 per item usually), but it could be well worth it.

4. If you want to wear your baby or toddler through the airport to keep your hands free for other things, keep it simple. Use a simple cross-body sling that will slip off and back on easily with one hand in case you are asked to remove it and put it through the X-ray (you'll also be less likely to get asked to remove a simple fabric sling).

5. Keep toddlers and older children buckled into their travel strollers until you have finished loading all other items onto the X-ray belt first. On the other side, collect your stroller first and strap in your child before collecting your other gear. It may take a few moments longer initially for your stroller to catch up to your other gear, but your child will be safer and you'll be much faster at getting the rest of it together when you have two free hands.

6. Consider using the FlyeBaby air travel "hammock" when flying solo with an infant on your lap, to help free up your hands (and ease your back) at least during some parts of your flight (more about the FlyeBaby on pg. 69 and full review at www.TravelswithBaby.com).

7. Instead of lugging along a car seat in addition to your child, you may prefer to use the CARES child aviation restraint (first read pros and cons, pg. 303) during your flight.

8. If traveling with your child's car seat, be sure to read the Seven Easy Ways to Get Your Car Seat to the Gate, pg. 276. Depending on your travel plans and needs, you may prefer to roll your child through the airport strapped into his car seat, and either check your stroller or leave it at home.

9. As you approach security, tell the first guard you see, "I'm going to need some assistance please," and expect it (and ask the second

guard you see, too, if you must). A security guard should help you get your items into the X-ray, and one will hopefully help you collect them again on the other side.

10. Keep your travel documents and those of your child, boarding passes, and your cash and credit cards in a necklace-style travel wallet. They will be easy to locate and access each time they are needed en route (even while you have a child in your arms), and will slip under your sweater or shirt when not needed for far greater security and convenience than carrying a purse or placing them in a carry-on.

11. When using airport restrooms, use the handicapped stall where there is plenty of room for your child to sit in his stroller and for you to park any extra gear. Many airports now have family restrooms, and some others offer baby care/nursery rooms for travelers with babies—visit your airport's website in advance to check for these and their locations.

12. When using aircraft lavatories, you can slip your baby into your over-the-shoulder sling (but remember flight crews in the U.S. will not allow you to hold the child in the sling during takeoff or landing).

13. Throughout your flight, don't hesitate to ask a flight attendant if you need help with anything, from assistance in installing your child's CRS to getting your bag into the overhead bin. Your seat should come equipped with a flight attendant call button—don't be afraid to use it.

14. At baggage claim, always keep a baby or toddler secured in his stroller or car seat, and aim for a less popular portion of the claim conveyor belt where the "suitcase sling zone" is not so frantic or crowded and other passengers will likely be more aware of your child.

15. Rather than wait in potentially long lines for taxis after your flight, check the rates for private car service at your destination. It may not cost much more to have a driver ready and waiting for you on arrival, and in some cases, they may also provide car seats or safety boosters for your child (see recommendations for private car hire

services with car seats for New York City and Paris at www.TravelswithBaby.com).

> **Don't forget:** Any time you will be crossing international borders with your child and without her other parent, even traveling from the U.S. into Canada, you will need a notarized letter of consent from the absent parent, or evidence that you are the child's sole legal guardian (see more on this topic and a sample letter of consent on pg. 133).

Flying with Twins, Multiples, or Multiple Children

Flying with More Than One Lap Child

Airlines do not allow more than one lap child per adult traveler, so if you are traveling alone with twins (or if your offspring outnumber you and your spouse) you will need to purchase at least one child's seat and plan to bring your car seat onboard (chances are you'll be glad to have extra space).

Generally, airlines do not allow for more than one lap child per seat row due to a limited number of oxygen masks, some of which may also need to be shared with cabin crew in the event of an emergency. This can vary by aircraft, so be sure to call and discuss your possibilities with the airline. In some cases, a family with twins on laps may sit on the bulkhead row, where there are sometimes extra oxygen masks. But most often, parents flying with more than one lap child sit in consecutive rows.

Flying Alone with Two Infants or with an Infant and Toddler

Be aware that some airlines will not allow an adult to fly alone with two infants, or an infant and a young child, even if a seat has been purchased for both children. This is usually addressed at time of booking—when the website won't allow you to continue your booking for one adult and two children or infants. If you encounter this problem, you may need to try a different airline.

Reserving Airline Seats for Multiple Children

Call your airline as soon as possible to notify them of any (and all) lap children that will be flying with you, as well as the number of car seats that will be coming on board with your family, and try to get seat assignments if possible. When purchasing seats for small children, remember that there are restrictions as to where child car seats can be placed on the aircraft. On larger aircraft, parents with two seated children may opt for the center row, with four seats together, where Mom and Dad can sit at each aisle and keep the children to the center seats. As always, be sure to call your airline 24 to 72 hours in advance of both outbound and return flights to reconfirm your seat assignments, as some airlines will reassign unconfirmed seats at check-in ("Would you prefer a window seat—or an aisle?"), and it is not unheard of for families to get split up on several U.S. airlines, even when they had chosen their own seats online at time of booking.

Flying with a Special Needs Child

Security Screenings

If your child has special needs, including medical equipment or mobility devices, be sure to plan for a little extra time at security checkpoints. As you approach the screening area, alert the security guard as soon as possible and explain that your child has special needs or devices, including any hidden disabilities that may affect his screening (e.g., a mental disability, hearing impairment, or if you have checked your child's wheelchair and he is riding in a stroller). This officer may help you or may contact someone else to help you with the screening process.

What you can expect during your child's screening:

- You will not be separated from your child during the screening, whether it occurs right at the metal detector, to the side, or in a private area.

- Infants will remain connected to their apnea monitors while they are screened.

- If you choose to carry your child through the metal detector, you will be responsible for removing him from his mobility aid. (The security officer will not do this.)

- A security officer will help you get your carry-on items onto the X-ray belt if needed (ask for help if you need it).

How you can help the screening go smoothly for your special-needs child:

- Tell your child what to expect ahead of time to minimize any anxiety during the process.

- Tell the officer all relevant information about your child's condition and medical devices.

- Tell the security officer if the child is likely to become upset and offer suggestions on how to minimize an outburst.

- Explain what your child's abilities are, e.g., if he can walk through the metal detector or if he will need to be carried, or if he can stand slightly away from his equipment for a hand-wand inspection.

- If needed, the security officer can conduct a pat-down search of your child in his mobility aid and visually inspect the equipment.

Traveling with Mobility Devices

You will want to call your airline ahead of time or check the website to ask about its specific policies and procedures regarding mobility devices. The following is true of most major airlines around the world, but again, you should confirm any critical details with your airline.

Most major airlines:

- Accept and transport wheelchairs, including folding, collapsible, non-folding manual, and electric/battery-powered wheelchairs, as well as electric-powered carts.

- Have room for one collapsible wheelchair onboard (in addition to overhead and under-seat storage space where some collapsible wheelchairs may also fit).

- Accept non-collapsible and electric wheelchairs as checked baggage at the ticket counter or gate.

- Require at least 48 hours' advance notice and earlier check-in (usually 1 or 2 hours) when checking battery-powered wheelchairs and carts as extra time may be needed to prepare the chair for loading (provide written instructions or special tools if available). Some batteries are also subject to dangerous goods handling, which could take extra time. In some cases, the airline may need to contact the manufacturer for special instructions.

- Allow you to bring walkers and other assistive devices that may be collapsed small enough to fit in overhead bins and underneath seats into the cabin without counting toward your carry-on limit.

- Allow you to gate-check strollers, which may be easier and faster to use in airports while getting to your gate and making connecting flights at other airports.

Flying for an International Adoption

Adopted Children Flying to New Homes in the U.S.

These children do not need (and cannot yet be issued) a U.S. passport as they must first clear immigration upon arriving in the U.S. Generally, internationally adopted children arrive under one of two visas (the IR-3 or IR-4 depending on the particulars of their situation), and qualify for U.S. citizenship upon entry. Based on the Child Citizenship Act of 2000, children arriving with an IR-3 visa automatically acquire U.S. citizenship and should be issued a Certificate of Citizenship without needing to file any additional forms. Those with an IR-4 visa are considered legal permanent residents, but must file for proof of citizenship. In both cases, the adopted children will need their proof of their U.S. citizenship to apply for a passport before flying outside of the United States again. For more information, call Overseas Citizen Services at 1-888-407-4747 or the U.S. Department of State Visa Office at 1-202-663-1225.

Airlines' Minimum Age Policies for Newborns

The majority of commercial airlines require infants to be at least 1 week old before flying. Here are some of the exceptions:

- Alaska Airlines – No minimum age
- American Airlines – 48 hours
- British Airways – 48 hours
- Delta – 1 week OR letter from physician required
- Easy Jet – 2 weeks
- JetBlue – 3 days (with letter from physician if under 2 weeks)
- Korean Air – 2 weeks for international flights (1 week domestic)

Special Discounts and One-Way Adoption Fares:

Some airlines offer programs to assist adoptive families by providing lower airfares with little notice, one-way infant fares, and other perks to meet the needs of this special situation. These fares are not published online, however, and you must call your prospective airlines to ask if they offer an "international adoption fare" for your route, and get the details of the particular airline's rules and restrictions. Some benefits of an international adoption fare may include:

- Low airfares with flexibility
- No advance purchase required
- Available up to the last seat in main cabin
- No penalties for cancellation or changes

- Open returns and stopovers are permitted

If you are flying at the last minute, however, it could be worth it to double-check before committing to your reservation. A last-minute special offer fare from the airline or a competitor (with restrictions and little or no flexibility) may still cost much less than the flexible, "special" airfare offered by the airline—which is based on a full-price, last-minute ticket with few restrictions if any. If flexibility is essential to your plans, however, the adoption fare may be the best plan.

Part VI:

Travels by Train

CHAPTER 19

Deciding to Go by Rail

Advantages of Taking the Train

Once you've officially spent too many hours cramped in an airplane with your children, waiting for the drink cart to pass again before you can finally dodge to the lavatory aft (hopefully before the next round of turbulence) to change a diaper that needed attention well before takeoff, the prospect of traveling by train may become truly enticing. You can:

- Wave goodbye to the car seat.

- Avoid lengthy airport lines.

- Stretch your legs whenever you please.

- Forget about turbulence.

- Explore the various train cars and facilities.

- Watch the scenery change with each passing mile.

- Focus on the faces of your loved ones, not traffic and road signs.

With babies, traveling by train can also be much easier than driving or flying, as you can hold and rock, and bounce or walk your child as you please. For the toddler or preschooler, riding the train may even be the most exciting part of your vacation—be it an hour-long scenic excursion train or a cross-country rail odyssey.

Which brings us to an important point: Unlike flying, train travel isn't only a means of getting to and from destinations with suitcases in tow. You may decide to ride the rails with your child just for the experience itself, especially when it may be as memorable and fun as riding behind a historic steam locomotive on an enormous carved log car to visit a legendary logging camp in the redwoods (Yosemite Mountain Sugar Pine Railroad, pg. 332), viewing three spectacular glaciers from a heated view car (Alaska Railroad, pg. 331), or riding along in a vintage parlor car with its own potbelly stove for an afternoon jaunt along the shore (Old Colony Railway, pg. 335).

Want to go farther by rail? Take the train to the nation's capital or to a national park (Yosemite details pg. 344, Grand Canyon pg. 344), or travel all the way to the Polar Bear Capital of the World (pg. 359). Have a European rail adventure in mind? Read your bedtime stories in one culture capital and eat breakfast in the next without setting foot in an airport or a rental car.

On that note, family rail trips in Europe may become even more sensible when you consider that children can ride most trains free until their fourth birthdays (and beyond in some countries, see pg. 367)—and for half the cost of the adult ticket thereafter. Compare that with flying or filling up your European rental car with expensive petrol!

Coast Starlight: A three-course dinner in the dining car and beds to sleep the miles away in beat the heck out of an otherwise 10-hour drive.

Families with more than one young child may also find it less expensive to travel by train than to purchase airplane seats and check baggage, or to rent that larger rental car to accommodate everyone and everyone's gear (see Top Reasons to Travel by Train with Twins or Multiple Children, pg. 328; Amtrak's Infant and Child Fare Rules, pg. 346).

Still, a successful family train trip requires some thoughtfulness and planning. After all, as exciting as the train is, even energetic toddlers may be ready for a change of pace after so long, and as fun as traveling in a sleeper car may sound, in some circumstances it may cost far more to spend one night in a sleeper car than to stay four nights at a family resort (see pg. 351). These next sections of the book will help you plan your first family train trips with confidence.

Top Reasons to Travel by Train with Twins or Multiple Children

For parents traveling with twins or multiples, there are additional advantages to traveling by train, especially when compared with the option of flying:

- Seating is often more flexible for train passengers (excluding reservations-only trains and some busy trains during peak hours) and there are no restrictions for how many lap children may be seated in a row.

- Restrooms are generally larger on trains than they are on airplanes (even handicapped facilities are available on most Amtrak trains), which makes it worlds easier to manage more than one child in the restroom versus the cramped aircraft lavatory. Handicapped restrooms onboard most trains have room enough for a stroller, so you can keep one child strapped in while attending to the other, if need be.

- Most trains will allow you to check far more gear than traditional airlines will, which can be very helpful when you are bringing TWO of everything (or three, or four, or...).

- Long distances are covered far more comfortably by train than by a car crowded with multiple car seats and mountains of gear.

- Family sleeper cars will give your brood much privacy and space to set up changing, napping, and eating stations without interference from other passengers or their seats. One parent may even nap with a child or children in the quiet compartment while the other(s) enjoy the café or view car. (Or when it's play time in the sleeper, one parent may catch winks in an unreserved seat in coach.)

- Children ages 2 and older may travel less expensively by train than by airplane—a difference that really adds up when purchasing multiple children's tickets. For example, children 2 years and older travel half-price on Amtrak in the U.S. and on VIA Rail in Canada, whereas children's discounts are being phased-out by most airlines. As mentioned earlier, in Europe children also travel free on their parents' laps until their fourth birthdays (and beyond in some countries).

- When booking a sleeper compartment, you only pay one accommodation price (the sleeper supplement) for the whole family, regardless of how many passengers. Since the price for this on Amtrak includes meals for everyone for the duration of your trip, the more mouths you need to feed on your trip, the more valuable this benefit will be (however, the bigger the sleeper on Amtrak, the bigger the price tag).

Five Tips for Great Train Trips with Babies and Small Children

1. **Bring a sling or child carrier** for babies and young toddlers to help you keep your hands free as you move about the train, especially in case you need to brace yourself as the train starts into a curve or as you carry back goodies from the snack car.

2. **Plan for a meal or snack en route** even during shorter rides to make it an extra special occasion and help stabilize blood sugar levels. You can splurge in the dining car, if available, or just get a hotdog in the snack car. Or pack your own lunches of favorites to look forward to. When you arrive, no one will be hungry or have to go in search of food!

3. **Bring a lightweight stroller with a shoulder strap.** Not only will it help you climb stairs everywhere you will find them (and not escalators or elevators or ramps), but it will help you immensely as you get on and off the train holding your child or your child's hand—or while pushing commuters out of your way in case of a crowded station. When your child is ready to nap or tires of walking—or you tire of carrying him, you'll be glad to have the stroller with you.

4. **Choose destinations with great public transportation** and centrally located stations (or thru-way motorcoaches that take you to the heart of a city) so that you can avoid bringing the car seat along or needing a rental car or taxis.

5. **Pack good travel gear.** It is tempting to bring the kitchen sink, but with good travel gear, you won't need it. For example, inflatable bed bumper rails pack down to practically nothing but can be used with hotel beds or sleeping berths for babies and toddlers. (Find more ideas in Great Products and Gear for Travel, beginning on pg. 66, and online at www.TravelswithBaby.com.)

Get Started: Twelve Scenic U.S. Day Trips by Train

If you're not accustomed to traveling by train, or you're not sure how your child will handle a lengthier journey by rail, a scenic excursion train ride can be a great initiation. But more importantly: Scenic excursion train rides can be really fun! Throughout the United States, opportunities abound to take private rail lines for just an hour or for an afternoon.

What's more, many of these rail lines feature restored rail cars and locomotives that make the trip even more memorable as they venture through some of the most spectacular scenery in the nation. Want to make a special holiday or season even more memorable? Many of these rail lines offer special event and holiday trains, too. Here are just a handful of the great scenic rail opportunities that await your family across the U.S.

ALASKA: Alaska Railroad
Anchorage (Fairbanks, Denali, Spencer Glacier, and more), AK
1-800-544-0552 www.alaskarailroad.com
Board the Glacier Discovery Train mid-morning in Anchorage and head off toward what is called by many the most beautiful stretch in Alaska. First, you will travel two hours along the Turnagain Arm of Cook Inlet, where Beluga whales, Dall sheep, eagles, and moose are often sighted. Make quick stops at Girdwood and then Portage, where you may choose to connect to a Prince William Sound wildlife and glacier cruise before your return trip to Anchorage. Or stay onboard all the way to Grandview and see three spectacular glaciers from the comfort of your heated rail car: Trail Glacier, Bartlett Glacier, and Spencer Glacier. On your return trip, you will travel the segment from Portage to Anchorage by motorcoach, arriving in time for a late dinner. You may bring your lunch and snacks with you or buy them onboard in the snack car. You may also board at other points along this route with adjusted fares. Other routes and packages are available, including journeys with overnight accommodations at hotels or cabins along the way. Some packages and extensions include cruises, wilderness jeep safaris, riverboat journeys, Arctic Circle air tours, helicopter hiking, salmon bakes, and more. Other trains include the Denali Star, Hurricane Train, and Coastal Classic. For the Anchorage to Grandview Glacier Discovery route, children under 2 years are free, children 2 to 11 years are $58, and adults are $116.

ARIZONA: Grand Canyon Railway
Williams, AZ
1-800-the-train / www.thetrain.com
Day-long excursions take you from Williams to the Grand Canyon Village at the South Rim of the Grand Canyon and back. These vintage diesel engines run year round and some historic steam engines also run spring through early fall. Once at the Grand Canyon, you can shop and explore on your own or take their optional motor coach tour of the rim. Five classes of train travel are available. Coach rates: children under 2 free, ages 2 to 16 are $45, adults are $75. The new Polar Express train operates November through early January, with evening departures including hot chocolate and cookies with the telling of the children's story *The Polar Express*, before Santa Claus and his reindeer greet everyone at the destination: The North Pole. Polar Express tickets are

only available by phone; children 2 to 16 are $23, adults are $37. Packages including lodging at Williams are available.

Note: For a complete vacation by rail, you can take Amtrak's Southwest Chief (see pg. 344), which runs daily between Los Angeles and Chicago, and stops at Williams, AZ.

CALIFORNIA: Yosemite Mountain Sugar Pine Railroad
Fish Camp, CA
1-559-683=7272 / www.ymsprr.com

Just before the south entrance to Yosemite National Park, you can take a 1-hour trip through the woods on "The Logger," pulled by an authentic steam locomotive down narrow-gauge tracks while your family rides along in open-air cars, some carved from real logs. Bring along snacks or a picnic for a 15-minute pit stop at a picnicking area. 30-minute Jenny Car rides are also available, and throughout summer there are special moonlight dinner trains with barbecue steak dinners and live entertainment. Rides on The Logger are free for children 2 and under, $9.50 for children 3 to 12, and $19 for adults.

GEORGIA: Blue Ridge Scenic Railway
Blue Ridge, GA
1-877-413-8724 / www.brscenic.com

Enjoy a 4-hour excursion along the white waters of the Toccoa River, through the Chattahoochee National Forest and historic Murphy Junction. A 1.5 hour stopover at the border cities of McCaysville, GA, and Copperhill, TN, allows you to enjoy lunch and ice cream, shopping, and stretching your legs in these quaint sister towns. The train is comprised of restored passenger cars from the 1920s and 1930s, plus others, including open-air cars. Also offered: Holiday trains and Rest and Rail packages that include discounted rail tickets with a cabin rental. Fees vary by season. In summer, children 2 and under are free (without seats), ages 2 to 12 are $20, adults are $36.

Yosemite Mountain Sugar Pine Railroad, California: Ready to ride The Logger and enjoy a picnic break in the pines.

IDAHO: Thunder Mountain Line
Horseshoe Bend, ID
1-877-IDA-RAIL / www.thundermountainline.com

The popular Horseshoe Bend Route takes you along the scenic Payette River to the historic settlement of Banks along what was once an old wagon road. Choose from vintage 1950s parlor and passenger cars, or open platform cars, and visit the bar car for a snack. Holiday-themed rides and special event trains are offered throughout the year. For the 3-hour Wild West ride, which includes a performance by costumed characters, children under 2 are $10, ages 2 to 12 are $27, and adults are $35.

MASSACHUSSETTS: Cape Cod Central Railroad
Hyannis, MA
1-888-797-RAIL / www.capetrain.com

Pass by cranberry bogs, woodlands, and marshes on a 2-hour narrated ride from Hyannis to the Cape Cod Canal (with optional whistle stop in Sandwich) in vintage 1940s and 1950s rail cars. Also offered: Family Supper Train, Brunch Train, and special events trains, including a

Thanksgiving dinner train and Train to Christmas Town. For the 2-hour scenic ride, children under 2 ride free, children 2 to 11 are $15, adults are $20.

NEW MEXICO: Cumbres and Toltec Scenic Railroad
Chama, NM (and Antonito, CO)
1-888-CUMBRES / www.cumbrestoltec.com
Authentic Denver & Rio Grande steam locomotives charge along this historic, narrow-gauge railroad, and negotiate a steep 4% grade as they travel the Cumbres Pass (you may recognize the train and scenery from movies including *Indiana Jones and the Last Crusade*). As you travel along the border between Colorado and New Mexico, watch for eagles, hawks, mule deer, antelope, coyotes, mountain lions, and range cattle. Several options are available, including a 6-hour round-trip journey with a 1-hour stop at Osier (buffet lunch included in fare). Children under 2 years are free, children 2 to 11 years are $39, adults are $79. Trains run May through October, with itineraries originating from either Chama, New Mexico, or Antonito, Colorado.

NEW YORK: Saratoga North Creek Railway
North Creek, NY
1-877-726-7245 / www.sncrr.com
Ride along 50 miles of the first Wilderness Heritage Corridor, following the Hudson River into the Adirondack Mountains and ending at Gore Mountain. There are several options available, including seven possible stops along the way, and seasonal activities ranging from mild season hiking, biking, kayaking, and riding the scenic chair lift at Gore Mountain to snow play and skiing in winter months (kids under 6 years ski and ride free at Gore Mountain). The 4.5-hour rail journey includes a 30-minute stop for picnicking or visiting the Caboose Café or gift shop. Runs seasonally with some special events, including "Robbery Trains" and a holiday season "Polar Express" train. For the standard trip, children 2 and under are free (without seats), roundtrip prices vary by season from $15 to $25 for children 2–12, and $25 to $35 for adults.
Note: For a complete journey by train, you can connect to Saratoga Springs by national rail from Montreal or New York City (see Amtrak's Adirondack route, pg. 339).

NORTH CAROLINA: Great Smoky Mountains Railroad
Bryson City, NC
1-800-872-4681 / http://gsmr.com
The Nantahala Gorge train takes passengers on a 4.5-hour round trip journey from Bryson City with a crossing of the Fontana Lake Trestle, which spans 780 feet at 100 feet above the water (you may recognize it from various movies shot here like *The Fugitive*), and into the Nantahala Gorge. There is a 1-hour stopover at the Nantahala Outdoor Center where you can relax by the river or enjoy more sightseeing on your own. Other routes and special event trains are offered, including the Tuckasegee River train (4 hours with a 1.5-hour stopover at historic Dillsboro), The Great Pumpkin Patch Express, a holiday Polar Express train, and more. Meals are available in the cars and may be included based on class of service. For the Nantahala Gorge train, children under 2 years are free, ages 2 to 12 are $29, and adults are $51.

OREGON: Oregon Coast Scenic Railroad
Garibaldi, OR
1-855-842-7972 / http://ocsr.net
A restored 1910 Heisler steam locomotive chugs along Tillamook Bay from Garibaldi to Rockaway Beach at the Pacific coast, where you can make a quick sand castle and stomp in the surf, or enjoy an ice cream cone before your return. 1.5 hour round trip, including layover. A three-hour dinner train is also available, and special event trains include a 4th of July Fireworks Spectacular, Pumpkin Train, and Candy Cane Express. Children under 2 are free, children 3 to 10 are $10, adults are $18.

RHODE ISLAND: Old Colony Railway
Newport County, RI
1-401-624-6951 / www.ocnrr.com
Enjoy a 10-mile round-trip ride along Narragansett Bay in either a 1904 open platform car in fair weather or an 1884 parlor car heated on the chillier days by a potbelly stove. Or go first class in a separate parlor car, where all passengers ride in wicker chairs arranged to face the bay. Travel through the old navy base and look out on the sailboats and the natural beauty of the Newport shore. Departures on most Sundays year round with 11:45 a.m. and 2:00 p.m. departures. The ride is 1 hour 20

minutes round trip. Children 0 to 13 are $6, Adults are $10. Parlor Car (first class) seating is $13.50 and is reserved for ages 7 and older only.

WEST VIRGINIA: Potomac Eagle Scenic Railroad
Romney, WV

1-304-424-0736 / www.potomaceagle.info

Enjoy a 3-hour narrated ride along the South Branch of the Potomac River, where historic farms are glimpsed between a mix of hardwoods and evergreens. Bald eagle sightings are said to occur on over 90% of these excursions, and if you are lucky you'll catch one—with your camera, of course. Vintage 1940s and 1950s passenger cars wend their way through this scenic narrow mountain valley. In fair weather, open-air cars are often added to the assorted restored vintage rail cars. All-day trips are also offered, with photo stops and a midday rest in Petersburg. For the 3-hour trip, children under 4 years ride free, ages 4 to 12 are $20, and adults are $50.

CHAPTER 20

All Aboard Amtrak

Why (and why not) take the "A" train?

Amtrak's network can take you through some of the most picturesque country in the United States, whether up the West Coast on the Coast Starlight Express (pg. 342), through the Rocky Mountains on the California Zephyr (pg. 340), to the Grand Canyon on the Southwest Chief (pg. 344), along the shores of Lake Champlain on the Adirondack (pg. 339), and over to Glacier National Park on the Empire Builder (pg. 342).

You can also ride the U.S. Rail system to some of the most popular family vacation destinations in the country, including Disneyland and San Diego on the Pacific Surfliner (pg. 343) and Orlando with your own car in tow on the Auto Train (pg. 340).

However, if you have not yet traveled by Amtrak, and especially if you are traveling to the U.S. from countries where the rail system is one of the best ways for families to travel between cities quickly and cost-effectively, you should be forewarned that Amtrak journeys may actually take longer than driving would between many destinations—even by a day or more for some. And the cost of adding a sleeper car supplement for your overnight journey may leave you temporarily speechless.

There could be one other problem with simply taking Amtrak to your destination as well. Unless you are arriving for an urban adventure in one of the few U.S. cities that are easily navigable by public transportation, or are connecting with a private rail line that will take you directly to your destination (e.g., the Saratoga North Creek Railway connection to Gore Mountain resorts, pg. 334; or the Grand Canyon Railway connection to the South Rim of the Grand Canyon, pg. 344), you may still need a rental car do your family's sightseeing once you arrive.

Still, there are obvious advantages to traveling by rail with babies and small children, even in the U.S. What's more, the journeys themselves can be unlike any others you'll undertake with your family—and the sheer novelty of a U.S. trip by train can make it all the more fun for everyone. This chapter will help you plan a good journey that fits your interests, your timeline, the ages and stages of your children, and your pocketbook.

Tips for Planning an Excellent Amtrak Adventure with Young Children

- **When traveling with one baby,** take advantage of the Superliner Roomette option for an overnight adventure. This is the least expensive private sleeper option you'll have in the U.S. when traveling with children—and once your child turns 2 years old, you'll no longer be able to book the three of you into this accommodation. This could be an ideal time to arrive by train in a culture capital for an urban adventure (see tips for Urban Adventures on pg. 42).

- **When traveling with a toddler,** plan to journey by rail in short segments, choosing a rail line with interesting destinations to stop and enjoy along the way whether you travel to one destination for your vacation or visit several along the route. Plan to spend your nights in hotels rather than on the train, where the extra space for your child to play in the room (and bath tub, and private bathroom) may be more appreciated than the romance of a cramped sleeper car. A swimming pool where he can burn off energy may also be very helpful.

- **When traveling with preschoolers** who can be entertained for longer periods by watching the passing scenery and playing games en route, plan a journey with longer segments through scenery that will capture his imagination, and with stopovers where he can get out and experience it firsthand by hiking along the canyon or river, playing on the beach, or visiting historical sites.

Amtrak's Most Notable Routes and Highlights

While I wouldn't recommend every family ride the rails nonstop from end to end (e.g., Chicago to San Francisco is 51 hours *without* getting off to set foot on terra firma), these overviews will help give you an idea of the major stops and points of interest along each of Amtrak's major routes, and the amenities available on each train. For a more detailed explanation of Amtrak's onboard amenities and sleeper options, see pg. 348; and for a list of Amtrak stations connecting with U.S. airports, see pg. 354.

ACELA EXPRESS: Boston – New York – Philadelphia – Washington, D.C. Travel up to 150 mph with limited stops helping you speed between cities in record time. Service is hourly during peak commute hours. However, fares are business and first class, and most discounts including children's do not apply during weekdays. Overhead storage bins, plus additional stowage for strollers or oversized items near exits of most cars. Café car onboard, Wi-Fi, and electrical outlets at all seats. Approximately 6½ hours total run one way. (Note: To travel for roughly half this fare and add only about 30 minutes to your journey, you might take the Northeast Regional instead. See pg. 344.)

THE ADIRONDACK: New York, NY – Albany – Saratoga Springs – Ticonderoga – Montreal, Quebec. Daily trips from NYC to Montreal, through the Hudson Valley wine country, the Adirondack Mountains, and along the shore of Lake Champlain. Travel in either direction with a morning departure and arrive at the final destination city in time for dinner. Snack car, reserved coach seats available. Approximately 10 hours total run. (Note: For a total journey by rail, you can transfer to the Saratoga North Creek Railway at Saratoga Springs; see pg. 334 for more details.)

AMTRAK CASCADES: Eugene, OR – Salem – Portland – Tacoma, WA – Seattle – Vancouver, B.C. Travel up the Willamette Valley, cross the Columbia River Gorge, and enjoy views of the Cascade and Olympic mountain ranges. Multiple daily departures. Train amenities include lounge, checked baggage at staffed stations, bistro car, feature movies, reserved coach seats, roomettes, family bedrooms, and bedrooms. Note: Some portions of the journey may be on a Thruway motorcoach depending on your departure, so look closely at the current schedule before booking. Eugene to Seattle is approximately 6.5 hours by train; Seattle to Vancouver B.C. is a final 3 to 4 hours. Additional info at www.amtrakcascades.com.

AUTO TRAIN: Washington, D.C. (Lorton, VA) – Orlando, FL (Sanford). This option makes it really easy to check your car seat—just leave it in the back seat of your car, along with all the extras you might want for your visit to Orlando. The Auto Train takes your family and its car nonstop on the 900-mile journey from the Washington, D.C. area to Florida (passengers must have a vehicle in order to take the Auto Train). Reserved coach seats, roomettes, bedroom suites, bedrooms, and family bedrooms are available. Lounge, dining car, and entertainment onboard. Approximately 16 hours 30 minutes one way, overnight each direction.

CALIFORNIA ZEPHYR: Chicago, IL – Omaha, NE – Denver, CO – Salt Lake City, UT – Reno, NV – Emeryville, CA (San Francisco). Daily departures whisk you from the Windy City through the heart of the Rocky Mountains, with views of Colorado's Gore, Byers, and Glenwood Canyons. Then it's on to the Sierra Nevadas, and finally the San Francisco Bay (Thruway bus service from Emeryville to downtown San Francisco). Reserved coach seats, roomettes, bedrooms, bedroom suites, and family bedrooms are available. Also onboard: dining car, sightseer lounge car. Total trip one way is approximately 51 hours and 20 minutes.

CAPITOL CORRIDOR: Auburn, CA – Sacramento – Davis – Emeryville (San Francisco) – Oakland – San Jose. Multiple daily trains take passengers from the Sacramento area to and through the San Francisco Bay Area by way of scenic wetlands dotted with numerous egrets and wildlife. All trains on this route are equipped with a limited number of bicycle racks where you can stow your bike—or bulky stroller if you please. Snack car, bicycle rack, and quiet car onboard. Total trip one way is approximately 3 hours and 14 minutes.

CAPITOL LIMITED: Washington, D.C. – Pittsburgh, PA - Cleveland, OH – Chicago, IL. Travel through the Potomac Valley, past historic Harpers Ferry, over the Alleghany Mountains, then up and over toward the Great Lakes until arriving at Chicago. Daily departures. Reserved coach seats, roomettes, bedrooms, bedroom suites, and family bedrooms are available. Also onboard: dining car and lounge car. Total trip one way is approximately 18 hours, overnight service each way.

THE CARDINAL (HOOSIER STATE): New York, NY – Philadelphia, PA – Washington, D.C. – Charlottesville, VA – Cincinnati, OH – Indianapolis, IN – Chicago, IL. The Cardinal runs between New York and Chicago 3 days a week, and the Hoosier State line runs the segment between Chicago and Indianapolis daily. On the Cardinal, you'll enjoy views of West Virginia's white water as can only be glimpsed by train, plus the Shenandoah Valley, the Alleghany and Blue Ridge Mountains, and the Ohio River. Reserved coach seats, Viewliner roomettes, Viewliner bedrooms, and Viewliner bedroom suites are available. Lounge car/dinette onboard. Total trip one way is approximately 26 hours 30 minutes. (Note: For faster, less-scenic service between Chicago and NYC, take the Lakeshore Limited.)

CAROLINIAN/PIEDMONT: New York, NY – Philadelphia, PA – Baltimore, MD – Washington, D.C. - Raleigh, NC – Richmond, VA – Raleigh, NC – Charlotte, NC. Travel through a Who's Who of historic towns on the Carolinian, with daily service between Charlotte and New York City. The Piedmont makes additional daily trips between Raleigh and Charlotte. Total trip one way on the Carolinian is approximately 13 hours 30 minutes (no overnight service). Reserved coach and business class seats, with snack car onboard.

CITY OF NEW ORLEANS – Champagne - Memphis, TN – Jackson, MS – New Orleans, LA. Travel through the heart of the U.S.A., tracing the trail of its musical heritage all the way to New Orleans, the birthplace of jazz. Watch for photo ops en route of picturesque farms, cityscapes, plantations—and possibly even Elvis. Daily departures with overnight service. Total trip one way is approximately 19 hours. Reserved coach seats, roomettes, bedrooms, bedroom suites, and family bedrooms are available. Dining car and lounge car onboard.

COAST STARLIGHT: Seattle, WA – Portland, OR – Eugene – Klamath Falls – Sacramento, CA – Oakland – Emeryville (San Francisco) – Santa Barbara – Los Angeles. The "Sightseer Lounge," with its floor-to-ceiling windows, helps you enjoy unparalleled views of snow-covered mountains, forests, valleys, and the Pacific Ocean as you travel this route. Reserved coach seats, roomettes, bedrooms, bedroom suites, and family bedrooms are available. Also onboard: dining car, sightseer lounge car, and kiddie car where children can meet and play. Total trip one way is approximately 35 hours.

CRESCENT: New York, NY – Washington, D.C. – Greensboro, NC – Atlanta, GA – New Orleans, LA. Travel from the Big Apple to the Bayou by way of the nation's capital, Blue Ridge Foothills, and scenic towns of the Deep South. Daily departures with overnight service. Reserved coach seats, Viewliner roomettes, bedrooms, and bedroom suites are available. Dining car and lounge car onboard. Approximately 30 hours one way.

DOWNEASTER: Brunswick, ME – Freeport – Portland – Dover, NH – Exeter – Boston, MA. Travel along the New England shoreline through coastal marshes, villages, and quaint colonial cities. Reserved coach seats available. Snack car and bicycle racks onboard. Multiple daily departures. Approximately 2 hours total run one way. (Note: Passengers transferring to other Amtrak stations in Boston must make their own arrangements to get between these stations.) More info at www.amtrakdowneaster.com.

EMPIRE BUILDER: Chicago, IL – Milwaukee, WI – St. Paul, MN – Grand Forks, ND – East Glacier Park, MT – Spokane, WA – Portland, OR – Seattle, WA. Follow major portions of the Lewis and Clark trail as you set out across the Mississippi and travel over the plains and atop the spectacular Gassman Coulee Trestle. Then on through Glacier National Park. At Spokane, you may venture north to Seattle, or travel down the Columbia River Gorge to Portland with views of Mt. Hood. Daily departures with overnight service (two nights for total run). Reserved coach seats, roomettes, bedrooms, bedroom suites, and family bedrooms are available. Dining car and sightseer lounge car onboard. One way is approximately 46 hours.

EMPIRE SERVICE: New York, NY – Poughkeepsie – Schenectady – Syracuse – Niagara Falls, NY. Escape from New York (City) through the Hudson River Valley and travel on to the Finger Lakes region. You'll pass by way of Buffalo on to Niagara Falls. Frequent daily trains. Reserved coach seats are available. Snack car onboard. Approximately 7 hours total run one way.

ETHAN ALLEN EXPRESS: Rutland, VT – Albany, NY – New York. Spring wildflowers and fall foliage especially dazzle travelers along this route through the Hudson River Valley and on through the wilderness of upstate New York and Vermont. In winter months, a motorcoach connection can take you on from Rutland to the skiing action and snow play at Okemo. Reserved coach seats are available. Snack car onboard. Daily departures. Approximately 5 hours 30 minutes total run one way.

KEYSTONE: New York, NY – Philadelphia, PA – Harrisburg – Lancaster. Step aboard at New York's Penn Station and ride to Philadelphia or beyond to Pennsylvania Dutch Country. Onboard amenities vary by train, but for those traveling segments only between Philadelphia and Harrisburg, only unreserved coach seating is available. Approximately 3 hours 50 minutes total run one way.

MAPLE LEAF: New York, NY – Albany – Buffalo – Toronto, ON. Similar to the Empire Service Route, with most of the same New York stops, you will travel up through the Hudson River Valley to the Finger Lakes region, and near Niagara Falls (stopping on both U.S. and Canadian sides). As you cross the Canadian border, the route becomes officially operated by Canada's VIA rail and international land-crossing document requirements for U.S. and Canadian adults and children apply (see pg. 126 for child ID requirements and pg. 133 for letter of consent for minor to travel abroad with only one parent or other caregivers). Reserved coach seats are available; snack car onboard. Approximately 12 hours 30 minutes one way, traveling from morning with evening arrival (no overnight).

PACIFIC SURFLINER: Paso Robles, CA – San Luis Obispo – Santa Barbara – Ventura – Los Angeles – Anaheim – San Diego. Travel the coastline of southern California, from its "Sideways" wine country (PRB) to Disneyland (ANA) and right into San Diego's Old Town (OLT). No reserved seating. Café car and bicycle racks onboard. Multi-ride passes are available. Multiple daily departures. Approximately 5 hours 45 minutes one way.

NORTHEAST REGIONAL: Boston, MA – Providence, RI – Hartford, CT – New York, NY – Newark, N.J. – Philadelphia, PA – Baltimore, MD – Alexandria, VA – Williamsburg – Newport News – Virginia Beach. With several daily departures, the Regional is an easy way to travel between the hearts of cities and historic outposts throughout the northeastern U.S. (Tip: If traveling to Martha's Vineyard, you can transfer to the ferry from the Kingston, RI station using Little Rest Limo, which will provide car seats or boosters for $2 more than the shuttle fare. More info at www.vineyardfastferry.com.) Reserved coach seats are available, snack car onboard. Entire route one way is 12 hours 30 minutes.

SAN JOAQUINS: Oakland or Sacramento, CA – Emeryville (San Francisco) – Martinez – Merced (Yosemite) – Fresno – Bakersfield. Take this route from either the San Francisco Bay Area or Sacramento through California's agricultural center; the San Joaquins is your ticket to many great sites and attractions, including Yosemite National Park. Spring through fall, you can board a luxury motorcoach right at the Merced (and sometimes Modesto) train station, which will take you for a 2-hour scenic drive right to the Yosemite Lodge (enter station code YOS as your rail destination for Yosemite; your park entrance fee is included). Or ride to the Martinez station and board a Thruway motorcoach for a quick ride that drops you off right at the main entrance to Six Flags Marine World (use station code VMW).

SILVER SERVICE/PALMETTO: New York, NY – Washington, D.C. – Charleston, SC – Savannah, GA – Orlando, FL – Kissimmee – Miami. Not only do these lines take you through the scenic and historic southeast, but they will carry you on to the homes of Disney World and Legoland Florida as well. Viewliner sleeper cars, reserved coach seats, dining car, and snack car onboard. Several daily departures. Approximately 28 hours total run.

SOUTHWEST CHIEF: Chicago, IL – Kansas City, MO – Dodge City, KS – Lamy, NM – Albuquerque, NM – Flagstaff, AZ – Williams Junction, AZ – Los Angeles, CA. Travel the celebrated "Atchison, Topeka, and Santa Fe" route out west through historic Indian regions and captivating canyons. Cross the Mississippi on a double-decked swing bridge completed in 1927, see the prairies named for Spanish silver (la plata), and follow the Red Cliffs of New Mexico and travel through a canyon that's only a few feet wider than the train. Arrive at the southern rim of the Grand Canyon where you can take a Thruway bus to the Grand Canyon Railway with its scenic tours and lodgings. Or stay on to the end point at Los Angeles. Reserved seats, roomettes, bedrooms, bedroom suites, and family bedrooms are available. Dining car and sightseer lounge car onboard. (Tip: If, at the time of your vacation, the eastbound journey from Los Angeles puts you at Williams at an ungodly hour, such as 3:50 a.m., and you don't care to see the sunrise at the Grand Canyon, check the time of arrival from the westbound journey from Albuquerque which currently arrives at night, and consider visiting the canyon from the westbound direction on your journey instead.) Total run one way is approximately 40 hours. (Note: For a total journey by rail, transfer to the Grand Canyon Railway at Williams; see pg. 331 for details.)

Rates, Pricing, and Passes for Amtrak

Amtrak ticket prices may vary widely for the same journey due to a number of factors, including how far in advance you make your purchase, availability of seats or rooms on your dates, and any special offers that may be underway at the time of booking. The easiest way to search and compare fares is to visit www.amtrak.com, where you can also check the latest special offers and weekly deals, which generally offer discounts on one or more routes for travel within the next month.

Remember that if tickets are available for purchase or pick-up at your station of departure (via Quik-trak kiosk or agent), you should plan to do so or else you will have to pay an extra service fee for purchasing your tickets onboard. When departing from an unstaffed station, where no tickets may be purchased (or one where the electronic Quik-trak kiosk is out of service and no attendant is on duty), you will have no choice but to purchase your ticket onboard and will not have to pay an extra service fee for doing so.

One bit of advice when purchasing unreserved seats: If you have no need for a reservation on the route and dates you plan to travel (e.g., it's a slow season and non-commuter route), or if reserved seats are already sold out, and you can find a lower ticket price for your same journey on other dates—buy it. Tickets for unreserved seats are valid for one year from the time of purchase, and may be used on any train traveling the route, regardless of the actual price paid!

Amtrak Pricing for Infants and Children

- **Infants** – Children under 2 years travel free on their parents' laps.

- **Children** – Children 2 to 15 years old, accompanied by an adult, ride for 50% of the adult's ticket price.

This pricing applies to all Amtrak tickets for U.S. journeys, except for weekday travel on two eastern lines used heavily by commuters: the high-speed Acela Express (Boston to Washington, D.C.) and Metroliner service (New York to Washington, D.C.). These discounts do apply, however, to these two routes during weekends. The child's discount may also not apply to some rail passes, like the North American Rail Pass, where fixed prices apply for children (infants on laps are still free).

Amtrak's Infant and Child Fare Rules

Limitations also apply to the number of free infants and discounted children that may travel per paid adult. The fine print can be confusing, so if you are traveling with twins, or multiples, or multiple children, here is a quick guide:

- 1 adult may travel with… 1 free infant

- 1 adult may travel with… 1 free infant, 1 infant at 50% (riding on child's ticket)

- 2 adults may travel with… 2 free infants

- 2 adults may travel with… 4 children at 50 % each

- 1 adult may travel with… 2 children at 50% each… and/or 1 free infant

- 2 adults may travel with… 4 children at 50% each… and/or 2 free infants

Rail Pass Options and Multi-Ride Tickets

If you'd like to plan a multi-stop journey on Amtrak, or travel with greater flexibility, Amtrak also offers two rail passes, including:

- **The USA Rail Pass** – 15 days/12 segments, 30 days/12 segments, or 45 days/18 segments of rail travel within the U.S. on Amtrak. Sleeping car accommodations are an additional charge if you choose to upgrade on routes where they are available. Passes are set at a flat rate for adults and children 2 to 15 years (at time of writing $449 adult/$224 child for the 15-day pass).

- **The California Rail Pass** – 7 days of travel within California over a consecutive 21-day period. Eligible trains include the Capitols, San Joaquin, and Pacific Surfliner corridor trains, most connecting Thruway services (now including Thruway extensions to Reno and Las Vegas, NV), and the Coast Starlight between Los Angeles and Dunsmuir, California. As with the USA Rail Pass, this covers seats only, and sleeper car upgrades are extra where available. Passes are set at a flat rate for adults and children 2 to 15 years (at time of writing $149 adult/$79.50 child).

Be aware that with each of these passes you are required to make reservations for each segment you will travel, and have printed tickets before boarding, in addition to carrying your pass. See pass pricing details, restrictions, and any updates to these pass plans at www.amtrak.com, or call 1-800-872-7245.

Other Discounts Available from Amtrak

If your party includes any of the following, you may be eligible for additional discounts. Note that some discounts may not apply to the weekday Acela Express or Metroliner routes, or possibly the Auto Train, and most will only apply to the individual ticket holder's ticket (e.g., the AAA member himself).

- AAA members save 10%.

- NARP Members (National Association of Railroad Passengers) save 10% on Amtrak travel, and get additional discounts on

Canada's VIA Rail, Grand Canyon Railway, Alaska Railroad, and more.

- Veterans with a Veterans Advantage card save 15%.

- Students with a Student Advantage card save 15%.

- International Student Identity Card holders save 15%.

- Active-duty US military personnel, their spouses, and their dependents save 10% Students with Student Advantage card save 15%.

- Seniors 62 years and over save 15% on tickets (not sleeper supplements) and get 10% off the North American rail pass.

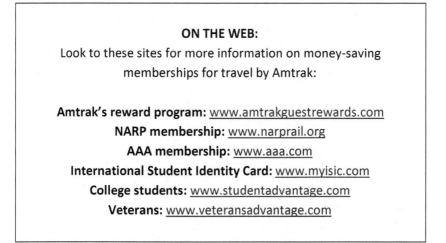

ON THE WEB:

Look to these sites for more information on money-saving memberships for travel by Amtrak:

Amtrak's reward program: www.amtrakguestrewards.com
NARP membership: www.narprail.org
AAA membership: www.aaa.com
International Student Identity Card: www.myisic.com
College students: www.studentadvantage.com
Veterans: www.veteransadvantage.com

Seats, Sleepers, and Onboard Amenities

Amtrak Seats and Sleeper Compartments

Although seat types vary by train and route, even Amtrak's short-haul coach train seats are still more spacious than airline coach seats (your baby or toddler can probably sit between you and your mate), and offer space enough on the floor in front of you to set your baby in her infant carrier or put down a small blanket to let your toddler play.

Unreserved Coach Seats are available on certain short-distance trains. They will still be larger than coach seats on aircraft, recline, have trays and reading lights, and most will have leg rests. On some trains, you may also have the option of table seating, with four seats facing each other and a large table in the center—a great option for families who can break bread, play games, color, and converse more easily facing each other than they would across the aisle. When traveling by day on a short-distance train, ask your conductor if there are any of these seats on your train if you don't see them in the first car you board.

Lower Level Coach Seats must be made available first to elderly and disabled travelers, but they do offer some advantages for travelers with babies and small children as well. First, it is easier—and safer—to board the train and get settled into your seats with your carry-on bags stowed without having to negotiate the steep stairs of Amtrak trains (you can always explore the train later without your hands full). Second, the handicap-accessible restrooms on this level are where you'll find the diaper changing stations.

Coach Seats on overnight trains are spacious and feature a deep recline with a leg rest—plus fold-out trays and individual reading lights. You will enjoy more legroom, more elbowroom, and more of a view from your large window than you could hope to on an airplane. Some newer coach cars also feature 110 outlets at the seats, but this is still not considered standard for coach seats. Check for amenities on your particular train online at www.amtrak.com or call 1-800-USA-RAIL to inquire.

The Superliner Roomette (formerly called "Budget Sleeper") is a great option when your child is still small enough to sleep comfortably beside you and doesn't need much room to play. By day, your private compartment has its own picture window and two wide seats with a table. At night, your attendant transforms it into two twin-size bunks, complete with pillows and linens. Passengers with a roomette are considered first-class passengers, and all meals during their journey are included. You will share a restroom with only the other passengers in your train car, as well as shower facilities (towels and soap provided in your room). See photo on pg. 350.

Coast Starlight: Traveling in our Superliner Roomette. At night, this seat becomes one half of the lower bunk.

A Family Room is less expensive than the traditional room for 2 adults (Superliner Bedroom), but it does not include its own private bath. Instead, it offers more space for playing, visiting, and sleeping. By day, your room provides two wide, reclining seats and a table (same as the roomette), plus a sofa, and views from two picture windows. Come nightfall, your room converts to two adult-size bunks and two smaller beds for children. Passengers with a family room are also considered first-class passengers, and all meals during their journey are included. Bathroom and shower facilities are shared, as described for the roomette.

The Superliner Bedroom is designed primarily for two adults, but can accommodate two adults and a small child if desired. It has three seats by day with two bunks at night (the lower bunk is slightly wider and may work for co-sleeping with your child between you and the wall). These cars include a private toilet, sink, and shower in the compartment, but at the expense of much space.

The Superliner Bedroom Suite is ideal if you will be traveling with friends, grandparents, or just a big family of your own. The "suite" is simply made up of two interconnecting Superliner Bedrooms, for a total of two separate rooms, each with its own private bathroom and shower. It is designed for four passengers, but can accommodate up to six. By day, each room has a large sofa with reclining sections and an easy chair. At night, the sofa converts to a bed and an upper berth folds down from above. Be sure to reserve your suite WELL IN ADVANCE as there are a limited number of rooms that may connect on each train, and any of them may be reserved as individual rooms. Unfortunately, there is no cost savings for booking two rooms as a suite, so you will ultimately pay the same price as you would for two separate rooms. You may need to call in order to book your Superliner Bedroom Suite: 1-800-USA-Rail.

A Note on Amtrak's (Amazingly Expensive) Sleeper Options

Before you get too enamored with the idea of overnight travel in a sleeper car on Amtrak, you should brace yourself for the "sleeper supplement" you will pay in addition to your passenger fare or rail pass. This is where your rail costs may suddenly skyrocket. As mentioned earlier, passengers with sleeper accommodations on Amtrak are traveling first class, with complete hot meals served in the diner, soap and towels and shower, a daily newspaper, bottled water, and nightly turn-down service. Sure, it's no weekend at an all-inclusive beach resort on the Riviera Maya, but your pocketbook might not know the difference.

Consider a trip on Amtrak's Coast Starlight, traveling overnight from San Francisco (Emeryville), California to Portland, Oregon, in low season (February). With advance planning, tickets for 2 adults and one child riding in reserved coach seats is $215 one way for the three travelers at time of writing. Now, if you don't want to spend the night sleeping in your coach seats (which is up to you), you can choose to add one of these sleeper options and pay an additional:

- $539   Two Roomettes (only 2 passengers over 2 years old are allowed in each)

- $771   Family bedroom (sleeps up to 4 in beds)

Given the current departure and arrival times, the only meals included at these rates would be breakfast and lunch. And guess what? You've still got to get home again.

Unfortunately, Amtrak doesn't offer a more affordable second-class sleeper option at this time, as is so popular in Europe and in some other countries. For now, you must choose between overnight coach seats or first-class compartments with all the trimmings—or perhaps more practically, do your rail travel by day and spend the night at a hotel.

Amtrak's Onboard Amenities

Each train is different, so to be certain of any critical onboard amenities for your journey, check with an Amtrak reservations agent by phone or look up your train's specs online at www.amtrak.com. Although you can expect roomy reclining seats with reading lights and trays on virtually all Amtrak trains, you may also be able to enjoy some of the following amenities:

Electrical outlets: 110-volt electrical outlets can be found in most first-class, business-class, and sleeper cars. Many of the newer coach cars feature outlets at the seats as well, but not all cars have outlets at all seats (watch for these when choosing your seats).

FREE Wi-Fi: Several Amtrak trains now offer wireless Internet access throughout the trains, while many others provide it in certain cars (look for hotspot stickers in the windows when boarding) and while in certain stations. You can see Wi-Fi availability in your search results when using www.amtrak.com.

Lounge, dinette, and café cars: You can expect at least one of these less formal dining options on most of Amtrak's trains, except on a small number of very short-distance trains. Get coffee, donuts, hot dogs, and the like, to eat at your seat, or possibly at a small table in this car.

Dining cars: Long-distance trains feature full-service dining cars, where you will most likely be asked to make reservations for your preferred lunch and/or dinner times. Reservations can be made from 11:30 a.m. to 3 p.m. for lunch, and from 4:30 to 9:00 p.m. for dinner, and you can simply tell the attendant passing through your car which time you prefer. If you have booked a sleeper car or roomette, your meals are included in your fare; otherwise, you will pay extra. Remember, if you are traveling with an "infant" even with overnight accommodations, your child is not guaranteed a space at the table, so to avoid eating with your child on your lap, book an earlier seating when the dining car will be less crowded. Ticketed children can order from the children's menu.

Diaper changing tables: Changing tables are available in most handicap-accessible restrooms found on the lower level of Amtrak Superliner trains and in select cars on older trains. Ask the conductor where you can find an accessible restroom if you are unsure where to look.

Showers: Showers are available to passengers with Roomette and Sleeper reservations. Facilities are shared only with other passengers traveling in their same car. Soap and towels are provided.

Bicycle racks: Some Amtrak trains include cars with bicycle racks just inside the doors. You may use this area to lock up your bike, place cumbersome strollers (even doubles—don't be shy), and other oddly-shaped or oversized items.

Amtrak's Baggage Policies

One of the great advantages of taking the train for families with small children is the incredible amount of stuff you can bring with you. Each ticketed passenger may bring aboard on two carry-on size suitcases, AND each passenger may also check two suitcases up to 50 lbs. Here are the details.

Accepted Carry-On Baggage:

- Two pieces per passenger, 50 lbs max each (23 kg), not to exceed 28" x 22" x 14" (70 cm x 55 cm x 35 cm). On Pacific Surfliner only, carry-on baggage is restricted to 28" x 22" x 11".
- Additional personal items such as briefcases, purses, laptops.

- "Infant paraphernalia," including strollers, diaper bags, and car seats, are allowed *in addition* to Amtrak's baggage allowance for travelers with children under 2 years.

Guidelines for Checked Baggage:

- Two pieces per ticketed passenger, 50 lbs max each, not to exceed 75 linear inches (23 kilos, 190 cm)
- Up to two additional bags may be checked, at $20 each
- Special items, including baby carriages, bicycles, golf bags, and skis are accepted as checked baggage, but may cost $5 for a special handling fee.

If you plan to check bags, first make sure your departure station actually checks baggage. This shouldn't be a problem at the larger stations, but some small depots and unstaffed stations do not offer this service; www.amtrak.com has details for all of its stations, including baggage service and hours. You can also call their toll-free number to inquire: 1-800-USA-RAIL. Bags must be checked in no less than 45 minutes prior to departure, and be clearly tagged. You will need to present valid photo ID to check your bags, and keep track of your claim check for pickup at your destination.

As for carry-on bags, just remember that space is limited, especially when trains may be at their fullest during peak times and seasons. When riding in standard passenger cars, you may need to store your bags in the space above your seats if the oversized baggage racks are already full, so carry on smaller suitcases that are sure to fit (and won't break your back). Space is also at a premium in sleeper cars and roomettes, so it may prove a far greater convenience to check everything you won't need during your journey.

Airports Served by Amtrak

If you'd like to connect to Amtrak from an airport, or plan your journey to coincide with a one-way flight, there are a handful of U.S. airports served by Amtrak, at least by a connecting Thruway bus. When checking schedules and fares to or from these airports, use the station code shown in parentheses after each airport name below to be sure your Amtrak fare includes service all the way to or from the airport. If you are planning to connect for a flight departure, be sure to plan your arrival time earlier than you would otherwise need to be at the airport as trains, like airplanes, do sometimes experience delays—especially in winter weather.

Baltimore Washington International Airport, MD (BWI) – Free bus transfers are available to and from Baltimore Washington Airport. Connect with the Acela Express, Regional, Metroliner, and Vermonter trains.

Burbank/Bob Hope Airport, CA (BUR) – Catch either the Pacific Surfliner from the airport, or take an Amtrak Thruway bus from this airport to Bakersfield, where you can catch the San Joaquins. You may also take the Pacific Surfliner (or Metrolink commuter train) from this airport to reach downtown Los Angeles.

Oakland – Coliseum Airport, CA (OAC) – This Amtrak station is connected by a pedestrian bridge with the Oakland Coliseum/Airport BART (Bay Area Rapid Transit) station, where you can catch an AirBART bus to the Oakland international Airport ($2 exact change or BART ticket). Connect here with the Capitol Corridor.

Milwaukee General Mitchell International Airport, WI (MKA) – The station is located at the western edge of the airport, with a free shuttle bus running between the two. This station is served by the Hiawatha line.

Newark Airport, N.J. (EWR) – Ride a monorail between the Newark Airport Stop station and airport with your fare included in the price of your Amtrak ticket (when the airport listed is the final destination on your ticket—other passengers purchase $5 monorail tickets from a vending machine). Connects with Keystone and Regional trains.

Palm Springs Airport, CA (PSP) – Amtrak Thruway bus service connects the Palm Springs Airport (PSN) with the North Palm Springs train station (PSN) where you can board the Sunset Limited.

Van Nuys Airport, CA – Connecting bus service at the Van Nuys rail station (VNC) and Van Nuys Airport Bus Stop (VNF). Catch the Coast Starlight or Pacific Surfliner.

Required Documents for U.S. Rail Travel

Domestic Rail Travel

Passengers under 18 years are not required to carry travel documents or ID when not crossing borders. Passengers 18 years and over must have valid photo ID when:

- Obtaining, exchanging, and refunding tickets
- Storing baggage at stations
- Checking baggage
- Asked for ID onboard as part of a random ticket/ID check per federal Transportation Security Administration guidelines.

A current state or provincial driver's license, military photo ID, or Canadian provincial health photo ID card is acceptable.

US-Canada Border Crossings

Anyone preparing to cross the U.S. border by train should plan to arrive at least 1 hour before their scheduled departure for verification of ID and possible customs clearance. Passports are required for all international travelers who are not permanent residents of the U.S. or Canada.

Please note that everyone traveling from Toronto to New York City must have tickets purchased before 8:30 a.m. on the morning of departure, as a complete list of all travelers must be submitted to U.S. Customs and Immigration at that time. Passengers who are not on the day's list will not be allowed to enter the United States.

U.S. and Canadian citizens 16 years and older who are crossing their shared border are urged to carry valid passports or passport cards, though adult citizens of both countries may instead present a Trusted Traveler Card (NEXUS, FAST, or SENTRI), or an Enhanced Driver's License, or an Enhanced State ID Card. Citizens of other countries must carry a valid passport and any applicable visas.

U.S. and Canadian children 15 years and younger are subject to the land crossing requirements explained on pg. 126. As when traveling out of the country by air, sea, or automobile, children traveling with only one parent must have a notarized letter of consent (see pg. 133). Remember, if at any time in your trip you plan to fly over the border, full passports will be required.

CHAPTER 21
Catching VIA Rail in Canada

VIA's Most Notable Routes and Highlights

VIA Rail is Canada's primary passenger rail system, with trains running vast distances across the continent, from Prince Rupert on the Pacific Ocean to Halifax on the Atlantic Coast, and from sub-arctic Churchill on the Hudson Bay (the world's polar bear capital) to Windsor at the southern tip of the Ontario peninsula (drive north and you're in Michigan). It can take you to the hearts of Canada's cosmopolitan cities, or to destinations so remote that no station even exists (a "special stop" can be wherever you please, but must be reserved at least 48 hours in advance).

THE CANADIAN travels from Toronto, ON, to Vancouver, B.C., by way of Edmonton and Jasper, and the Canadian Rockies. Passengers can enjoy views from dome cars and newly renovated Skyline and Park cars. Total run is 4 days.

THE OCEAN travels from Montreal to Halifax with an overnight journey along the St. Lawrence, scenic second day of travel for late afternoon arrival at Halifax. Along the way, passengers enjoy a "Maritime Learning Experience," which includes lessons on the culture and heritage of Canada's eastern sea coast. At time of writing, cabins offered on this route sleep only two people, with Economy class seats as the alternative. Total run is 1½ days.

THE SKEENA (Jasper – Prince Rupert) takes you from Jasper National Park in the Canadian Rockies to Prince Rupert with an overnight layover in Prince George (book your own hotel room). Total run is 2 days, including layover.

THE HUDSON BAY (Winnipeg – Churchill) takes you to the tundra in comfort and *warmth* to the small city of Churchill, the self-proclaimed Polar Bear capital (great viewing opportunities come in late October/early November). Total run is 2 days/2 nights.

THE MONTREAL-TORONTO LINE travels between downtown areas of both cities, with local and regional transit connections at both Montreal Central Station and Toronto's Union Station, greatly simplifying your travel between the two destinations and making for an easy start to an Urban Adventure in either city. From 5 to 6 hours total run.

Rates, Pricing, and Passes for VIA Rail

VIA Rail tickets can be compared with airline tickets, where you opt for varying degrees of flexibility and save accordingly. Generally, you have the choice between Regular Fares, Discounted Fares, and Supersaver Fares, each providing a greater level of savings and less flexibility in making changes to your ticket. There are a limited number of Discounted and Supersaver fares available for each journey as well, so they tend to sell out close to the departure time. It is also well worth checking the special offers online at www.viarail.ca. Promotions sometimes include free travel for children, free upgrades, and discounts on select routes.

VIA Rail's Pricing for Infants and Children

- **Infants** – Children under 2 years travel free on their parents' laps (may occupy seat when available). You must call 1-888-VIA-Rail to provide your lap child's name after booking your reservation. Only one lap-held infant is allowed for each adult.

- **Children** – Children 2 to 11 years travel at half price in Comfort class (Economy), and for a lesser discount (around 25%) off the adult ticket price in other classes (e.g., Sleeper class).

- **Students** – Children 11 to 17 years get student discounts of 35% off Comfort class fare or 10% other classes of service.

VIA Rail's Rail Pass Options for Families

Although children do get a standard discount on each of these passes, it is not nearly the 50% savings they receive on point-to-point tickets in Comfort class (Economy), so be sure to compare costs for your journey if you'll be traveling with a child 2 years or older. If you'll be traveling a great deal with a lap child, however, one of these passes may be your best option.

- **Canrailpass – System:** 7 one-way trips anywhere in Canada during a 21-day period, riding in Economy class. One complimentary stopover is allowed on each trip.

- **Canrailpass – Corridor:** 7 one-way trips anywhere within the Quebec City–Windsor corridor in a 10-day period, riding in Economy class. One complimentary stopover is allowed on each trip.

There is also a huge difference in pricing for rail passes to be used in high season compared with low season, so if you have flexibility to travel outside of summer months, you might want to do so. Traveling with rail passes in May instead of June, for example, could save a family of 3 around $1,000.

At time of writing, the Canrailpass – System is priced at:

- High Season, June 1 – October 15: $907 child / $1,008 adult

- Low Season, October 16 – May 31: $567 child / $630 adult

Other Discounts Available from VIA Rail

- **Full-time students** – Regardless of age, full-time students with an ISIC (International Student Identity Card) can receive student fares for travel throughout the VIA Rail system.

- **Seniors** – Travelers 60 years and over receive a standard 10% discount on Comfort class fares, even in conjunction with other special offers. No standard discount is given for Sleeper class, however.

The scenic Canadian charges alongside Moose Lake. ©VIA Rail

Classes of Service, Seats, and Sleepers

VIA Rail offers two basic classes of service on its trains: Economy class and Sleeper or Touring class. Economy is essentially coach seating—the lowest priced, most basic option available, and you will find it offered in all regions. No meal service is included in this fare, but you may purchase food onboard where available and reserve seating in the dining car where you will pay additionally for your meals.

All passengers with "bedded" accommodations, be they basic berths or private bedrooms, are traveling Sleeper class. In most cases, this means your meals will be included during your journey, and you will also have access to shared shower facilities (except in deluxe rooms, which include a private shower). Note that VIA Rail's bedrooms all include a private toilet and sink, which not only makes them rather expensive, it also greatly reduces the available floor space (to little more than leg room for the seated passengers).

If you'll be traveling with an active child who needs room to roam, it may be far more practical to reserve sleeping berths rather than a bedroom. With an upper and lower berth reserved (which you can and *will* have to share with your child as they aren't allowed to sleep alone in a berth), you will actually have cushy seating for four by day, plus any additional open seats that may be found around you—and no walls closing you in.

Here is what you can expect to find in each of Via Rail's classes and accommodations:

Economy Seats – Wide, roomy seats with head rests, reading lights, and fold-out trays. On most routes, seats recline and a pillow and blanket will be provided for overnight travelers.

Sleeping Berths – Passengers traveling with sleeping berth reservations travel by day on upholstered sofa-like seats that face each other (each seat is wide enough for two and so is quite comfortable shared with a child). At night, these seats convert to a lower berth (or bunk) with a privacy curtain. An upper berth folds down from above, with its own privacy curtain, but it has no view from the window. Lower berths cost slightly more than upper berths. Each berth is the size of a single bed, but may be shared by an adult and child or even by two adults, but be aware that young children are not allowed to sleep in a berth alone, and if the number of children traveling exceeds the adults (e.g., 3 kids with 2 parents), you will not be able to reserve sleeping berths. Six total berths (upper and lower) are located in a car. Unlike most couchettes found in Europe, there is no locking door to secure the compartment, just a privacy curtain for your bed. Restrooms and shower facilities are shared with the other travelers in your car.

Single Bedroom – This option features only one single bed, though you may share it. It includes a private toilet, sink, and mirror. However, the compartment is scarcely larger than the bed itself (6' 5" x 3' 7"), and when the bed is made, it blocks access to the toilet, so only share this with your mate *and* child if you like to sleep tight—*really* tight—and won't need extra room for playing.

Double Bedroom – Enjoy two armchairs by day (side by side, facing the bathroom with the window to one side) and two bunks by night, with your own toilet, sink, and mirror. A small closet, fan, and electrical outlet are also included. Shared shower with fellow passengers in your car.

Triple Bedroom – By day it offers two armchairs and a sofa. At night, it converts to two lower bunks and one upper. A small closet, fan, and electrical outlet are also included. Shared shower with fellow passengers in your car.

One other important consideration about booking VIA sleeper class with kids is that, although you *can* squeeze two adults and two children, for example, into a double bedroom (or even a triple), regardless of how many beds are included in your reservation, you will pay the much higher sleeper fare for each of your passengers.

For example, at time of writing, a family of 4 traveling one way on The Canadian from Vancouver, B.C., to Jasper, AB, in late May would pay:

- $137.55 CA for each adult and $74.55 CA for each child (before taxes) to ride in Economy on the overnight train.

Yet, for 2 sleeping berths, it climbs to:

- $404.25 per adult and $355.95 per child (before taxes)—even though the children are sleeping on the same single bunk with a parent.

- Please note: Unlike the Economy class fare, the children's meals are included in the sleeping berth fare, so be sure they eat plenty.

VIA Rail's Baggage Policies

Carry-On Baggage

Each passenger, including infants and children under 2 years riding on laps, is allowed to carry on either:

- Two small bags, each measuring no more than 21 ½ x 15 ½ x 9 inches (54 ½ x 39 ½ x 23 cm) and weighing less than 25 lbs (11 kg.), plus one personal article such as a laptop or small backpack,

- One suitcase not weighing more than 40 lbs (a surcharge applies for suitcases weighing between 40 lbs and 50 lbs) and measuring less than 62 linear inches (158 linear cm) plus one personal article. This option is not offered on sleeper cars because of space limitations.

- Strollers (pushchairs) are allowed as additional carry-on baggage if they can fold to 10 in x 36 in (25 cm x 92 cm), and purses do not count as carry-on bags.

- Larger strollers and prams and play yards can be brought onboard most trains, but will count toward the carry-on baggage allowance.

Checked Baggage and Baby Gear

Each passenger—including infants and children riding for free on laps—is entitled two pieces of checked baggage, with each not weighing more than 50 lbs (23 kg) or exceeding 62 linear inches (158 cm). Infant and toddler gear, however (including checked car seats, strollers, and play yards), does count toward the checked baggage allowance, and you will be asked to sign a liability waiver when checking these.

Airport and Other Connecting Services

VIA Rail has made it very simple to connect from most major airports and; for example, at www.viarail.com, you can now book your journey from Pearson International Airport to Kingston, ON, as one reservation, which includes your Airport Express shuttle from the airport to Toronto's Union Station.

Montreal-Trudeau International Airport: AirConnect Airport Service. VIA Rail provides a free shuttle service between its Dorval train station and Montreal-Trudeau International Airport. The shuttles run every 20 to 30 minutes, with AirConnect stops clearly marked outside the exits of both domestic and international airport terminals. When purchasing your Amtrak tickets, use Montreal-Trudeau Airport as your end (or starting point).

Toronto Pearson International Airport: Airport Express. Airport Express is not a free service, though it is free for children 11 years and younger. The shuttle runs between Toronto Pearson International Airport and a handful of downtown points, including the Fairmont Royal York Hotel, which is your stop directly across the street from Toronto's Union Station. Use Toronto Pearson International Airport as your end (or starting) point.

International Travel and Travelers

Please note that everyone traveling from Toronto to New York City by rail must have tickets purchased before 8:30 a.m. on the morning of departure, as a complete list of all travelers must be submitted to U.S. Customs and Immigration at that time. Passengers who are not on the day's list will not be allowed to enter the United States.

Information on identification and other travel documents required for children crossing the Canada–U.S. border can be found on pg. 356, and more information about passport requirements for children starts on pg. 126.

CHAPTER 22

Train Travel in Europe

Riding Europe's Family-Friendly Rails

In Europe, sophisticated and streamlined rail service delivers travelers to the smack-dab center of one city after the next, even "Chunneling" under water to whisk travelers from the mainland to Great Britain. Routes are planned (for the most part) intelligently, with overnight routes that are well established and served by trains that are suitably outfitted. It's efficient. It's affordable—especially when traveling with young children. And it can be a great way for anyone to see Europe, whether traveling with children or without.

Those traveling with children, however, can look forward these helpful perks of rail travel in Europe:

- Children may travel on trains free until at least 4 years everywhere in Europe, and until 5 and 6—and even 16 years when traveling with their parents in some countries (see Children's Discounts for Rail Travel by Country, pg. 370).

- Children from 4 years (or 5 or 6 where applicable) to 11 years (or 12 or 15 where applicable) travel for 50% of the adult fare (see pg. 370).

- In some countries, all of the children of a national rail pass–holding parent can travel free with that parent—even if they are all tourists. (See European Rail Passes Favored by Families, pg. 373.)

- Two parents traveling together at all times (or any 2 adults) save with the Saver Pass rail pass, which also entitles them to first-class travel (more on pg. 373).

- Budget-friendly "couchettes," the second-class sleeper option across Europe, are much more affordable than the sleeper options available in the U.S. or Canada, plus some trains have couchettes with only 4 beds, ensuring a family of 4 (with two paid children) can have the privacy of its own locking sleeper compartment at a bargain.

- Centrally located train stations and better public transportation can eliminate the need for additional taxis or shuttles to transport your family from outlying airports to the city center—which is especially helpful if you'll have to pay per person, need a car seat, or won't all fit in a single cab.

Of course, traveling by train in Europe affords families the same advantages as it does elsewhere, too: You can enjoy the changing landscape and architecture, you can stroll about the cabin with your child instead of politely asking him not to kick the seat in front of him. Seats are also much more spacious, and you can choose to either sleep the journey away and awaken at your destination, or enjoy observing every moment of the journey and stopping to experience points in between. And what better place to do all of the above with your child than on the continent best interconnected by rail: Europe?

European Rail Travel Reality Check

Okay, so I've painted a pretty rosy picture of families enjoying rail travel vacations across Europe, and you may feel ready to get out your rail map and start plotting your most amazing adventure by rail yet. Before doing so, I recommend you also consider the flip side of European rail travel as a family with very young children. While these points don't have to be deal breakers, you should keep them in mind as you plan your journey to help ensure safer, happier travels by train.

- Even where "porters" are said to exist, you may never see one. You will need to travel light and should expect to have to shuffle all of your gear in addition to your child(ren) through the station and onto your train, and manage it all as carry-on. Consider using backpacks (the trip-worthy kind vs. day-trip-worthy) and small rolling suitcases if you'll be traveling many legs by train. Smaller bags will also make it easier to take advantage of lockers at rail stations if you want to stop off mid-route.

- Those conveniently located rail stations in major European cities can get extremely crowded during commuter hours and are no places for toddlers to be shuffling around on foot while you juggle a stack of luggage. Although you might be tempted to leave it behind, having a lightweight travel stroller could be a very important safety precaution (recommendations at www.TravelswithBaby.com). However, if you'll be using many of the older stations or rail systems connecting with un-stroller-friendly local transportation (e.g., Paris Metro), a good child carrier for your front or back (or both) may be a better way to go (recommendations for child carriers for travel also at www.TravelswithBaby.com).

- Pickpockets love train stations—and crowded trains. Since you'll likely have your hands full and attention spent between gear and children already, always try to avoid peak travel times when possible, and of course, exercise good city smarts where your wallet is concerned (see tips in City Smarts for the New Parent, pg. 184). Traveling midday also makes for less stressful mornings as you leave your accommodations and less crowded trains as you travel toward your next.

- Train strikes happen. Despite your best-laid rail travel plans, a train strike could still ultimately thwart your itinerary and either ground you in one place longer than expected, or force you to rent a car for part of your journey instead (said the woman who got the next-to-last rental car out of Venice). Yet one more reason to get that travel insurance for your vacation (for more on travel insurance, see pg. 105).

Now that we got that out of the way, let's get back to the positives about rail travel in Europe with kids—like where exactly kids can travel for free with their parents or grandparents until their fifteenth birthdays (Germany), and better still: which trains have an indoor playground decorated with a jungle theme (Swiss Family Coaches).

Free Rides and Discounts for Children

If you ever need to make the case that Europe supports family travel by train, just start with the free rides granted to infants and children across the continent. For country-specific age details, see pg. 370.

- **Infants** – For train travel throughout Europe's international rail network, children under 4 years old may travel free on a paid adult's lap and in a shared sleeping berth or sleeper compartment. Within some European countries, children may also ride free up to 5 years or 6 years, though it does not entitle them to a seat if the trains are crowded. See free and discounted ages by country in the following table.

- **Children with rail pass–holding adults** – In Switzerland and Great Britain, children under 16 years may travel free when their parents have qualifying rail passes and an optional Family Card or pass (more in Rail Passes Favored by Families, pg. 373, and also Other Discounts for Families, pg. 375).

Switzerland: Forget airplanes and automobiles. Not only can children travel free on trains with pass-holding parents, they can pass the miles in a Family Coach (Familienwagon) outfitted just for them. © SBB CFF FFS

- **Children of adults with point-to-point tickets** – In Germany, as well as several other European countries noted in the following table, children under 15 years ride free whenever named on one adult's point-to-point ticket, so a standard German rail pass may actually be a less attractive option for families traveling with older children. At time of writing, families can also opt for a Sparpreis Familie (special price family) ticket, where, for $49 Euros total one way, two parents can travel domestically with up to three children, even on some long-distance and overnight trains ($8 reservation fee may apply, sleeper supplements additional).

- **Children 4 to 11 years** generally travel for around 50% of the adult ticket or rail pass price for international travel in Europe. For travel within individual countries on national networks, higher infant ages or child age limits may apply, as noted in the following tables with ages listed by country.

Depending on where you will travel and how often (or how little) you plan to travel by train, it may be most economical to purchase point-to-point tickets for domestic travel only where needed. Consider the following discounts by age and other available discounts for families in the countries you plan to visit.

Table 2: Children's Rail Discounts by Country

Country	Free Until Age	Child's Discount[4]	Other Discount
Austria	6 years	6 to 15 years	
Belgium	12 years[5]	4 to 12 years	
Bulgaria	7 years	7 to 10 years	
Croatia	4 years	4 to 12 years	Family Ticket, see pg. 374
Czech Republic	6 years	6 to 15 years	
Denmark	12 years[6]	12 to 16 years	
Finland	6 years or 16[7]	6 to 16 years	
France	4 years	4 to 11 years	
Germany	6 years or 15	6 to 15 years	No Pass at All, see pg. 373
Great Britain	5 years	5 to 15 years	BritRail Pass, see pg. 373
Greece	4 years	4 to 12 years	Greece Family Card, pg. 374
Hungary	6 years	6 to 14 years	
Ireland	5 years	5 to 15 years	Family Ticket, see pg. 375
Italy	4 years	4 to 12 years	Familia Offer, see pg. 375

[4] Child discount is applied beginning at the youngest age shown and ends when reaching the upper age limit shown in this column; e.g., 6 to 15 years means no child discount after the 15th birthday.

[5] One ticketed adult may take up to 4 children on Belgian Rail in 1st or 2nd class, with no children's tickets required. Additional children and kids over 12 years pay 50% of the adult fare.

[6] Two children up to 12 travel free for each paid adult.

[7] One child up to 16 may travel free for each paid adult, child discount for additional children. Children under 6 years are always free and do not count toward free child allowance.

Country	Free Until Age	Child's Discount[4]	Other Discount
Luxembourg	6 years	6 to 12 years	
Macedonia	4 years	4 to 11 years	
Netherlands	4 years	4 to 11 years	Railrunner ticket, see pg. 376
Norway	4 years or 15[8]	4 to 15 years	
Poland	4 years	Discounts only by special offer	
Portugal	4 years	4 to 12 years	Family Ticket, see pg. 376
Romania	4 years	4 to 11 years	
Serbia	6 years	6 to 14 years	
Slovakia	6 years	6 to 15 years	
Slovenia	6 years	6 to 12 years	
Spain	4 years	4 to 14 years	
Switzerland	6 years	6 to 16 years	Swiss Pass, pg. 374

Don't forget, some of the best discounts for rail travel can be found in the special offers sections of each national rail system's website.

ON THE WEB:

The Man in Seat 61 is a site I found and adored back when researching the first edition of this guide, but since then? He's become a father with two children of his own, and the site now includes a wealth of information and answers for parents planning European rail travel with babies and small children (and includes several other regions as well).

Find him online at www.seat61.com.

---

[8] One child up to 15 years always travels free with each paid adult.

The Best European Rail Passes for Families

There are many types of rail passes you can choose from when traveling to or through Europe, and in addition to saving you the time and trouble of purchasing individual tickets for each journey, you may also enjoy extra benefits, such as first-class travel, museum discounts, or free regional transportation, depending on your pass. In many cases, when two adults travel together at all times, they can save even more on rail passes with the Saver Pass (sometimes called "Twin") discount.

Still, depending on where you will travel and the ages of your children during your travels, it can be well worth comparing costs of rail passes side-by-side with regular tickets or discounted "family tickets" (see pg. 375). For rail passes in Europe for families, these are generally the best deals going.

- **No pass at all** – Depending on your travel plans and destinations, it may be more cost effective for you to buy point-to-point tickets, especially in Germany where children 5 years and younger always travel for free by rail, and from 6 years until their 15th birthdays they may still travel free when named on accompanying adult point-to-point tickets. In contrast, children 6 to 15 years must pay 50% of the adult price for German Rail Passes (more details follow in German Rail Passes on pg. 374). Most Eurail passes, including the German Eurail Pass (not to be confused with the German Rail Pass), are priced for children from 4 to 11 years, regardless of the country's free child age maximum. To run some price checks on the routes you're considering, and find out more about any special offers or discounts for families, visit the national rail site for the country or countries you'll be visiting in Europe. Also, see additional discounts for family rail travel in Europe in Other Family Discounts for Rail Travel, pg. 375.

- **BritRail Passes** – When you purchase any BritRail Pass in advance of your trip (but not a rail pass combining Britain with other countries), you can opt for one "Child for Free Pass" for each rail-pass possessing adult (formerly called the BritRail Family Card). With this pass, one child age 5 to 15 years may travel with each BritRail Pass–holding adult for free. Additional children (outnumbering the adults in the group) are 50% of the adult fare, as are grandparents who may also be traveling with your brood. The BritRail Pass is also valid on the Heathrow Express and Gatwick Express airport trains, and entitles pass holders (and families) to special Eurostar fares. More information at www.britrail.com.

- **German Rail Passes** – In Germany, two adults who will be traveling together at all times can opt for a "Twin" discount of 25% off any of the German Rail Pass options, ranging from 3 days to 10 days of travel in one month. However, you should really do the math before going this route. Children from 6 to 11 years pay 50% of the adult German Rail Pass rate (does not include the Twin discount). As mentioned before, with point-to-point rail tickets for the adults, as many as 3 children up to 15 years can travel free in Germany. More information at www.bahn.com.

- **Swiss Passes** – As with BritRail Passes, children under 16 years may travel free with Swiss Pass–holding parents and a Swiss Family Card. The Swiss Family Card is also free on request when you purchase your Swiss Passes in advance of your trip, and if you purchase your Swiss Passes through www.RailEurope.com, they will include the Swiss Family Card when sending your passes. More information at www.sbb.ch.

- **Saver Pass** – If you will be two adults traveling together at all times (or one adult traveling with one child), be sure to look at the Saver Pass options that will let you purchase certain Eurail passes at a savings and travel with first-class status. The percentage of savings you'll receive varies by country. Children under 4 years will travel free on your first-class lap, and older children may have their own Saver Passes for 50% of the adult price (except in Britain or Switzerland where they can travel free with your adult Select Saver Pass and the Family Card).

ON THE WEB:

RailEurope (www.raileurope.com) is a good resource for comparing rail passes available for the country or countries you'll be visiting, and for scoping out the various accommodations and their prices on popular overnight trains. **Rick Steve's website** also has a very helpful section on rail passes at www.ricksteves.com.

Other Family Discounts for Rail Travel

While some of these family discounts may be available any time you purchase domestic rail travel in the specified country, others may require an advance purchase of as much as a month or more. Be sure to visit the national rail website for purchasing details.[9]

- **Croatia Family Ticket** – When a minimum of three family members travel together and at least one is between 4 and 12 years old, a Family Ticket may be purchased, giving everyone in the party 40% to 50% off of their ticket prices. The Family Ticket may be purchased for any roundtrip journey within Croatia, on any of its passenger trains, in either first- or second-class seating. Children under 4 years always travel free by rail in Croatia and don't count toward the discount for three passengers. Grandparents may also be included in the Family Ticket. More information at www.hzpp.hr.

- **Greece Family Card** – The card costs 13 Euros at time of writing, but once purchased, a family with two people traveling together will save 25% on train fares, and a family of three or more people will save 50% when traveling together. Children under 4 years always ride for free in Greece, and children from 4 up to 12 years always ride for 50% of the adult fare, but this could at least save you 50% on the adult tickets if there will be enough of you traveling together (excluding infants under 4 years who do not count toward the minimum). More information at www.trainose.gr.

- **Irish Rail Family Ticket** – This option allows a family with two adults and up to four children ages 5 to 15 to travel together to a listed destination and back for one flat rate (children under 5 are free on Intercity lines and under 3 are free on Dart). For example, at time of writing, one Family Ticket from Dublin to Cork would cost €100 for a round trip with return that same day, or €140 for an open return. Family Tickets can be purchased at ticket offices or ticket vending machines in stations. More information at www.irishrail.ie.

- **Italy Familia Offer** – This option is for groups of three to five people who will be traveling together, with at least one child from 4

---

[9] Note that some countries offer a family discount only for permanent residents of that country and so have not been included here.

to 12 years old and at least one adult. The Familia Offer provides the 50% discount on children's tickets (30% in couchettes) as well as a 20% discount on the tickets of adults traveling with the child (or children). The number of seats they will sell with these discounts is limited per train, per day, and per class, so buy in advance when possible and if you can't get the discounts the first time around, try other times or days if you have flexibility. More information at www.trenitalia.com.

- **Netherlands Railrunner Ticket** – In the Netherlands, you can purchase an all-day ticket for children 4 to 11 years to travel with you for the flat-rate fare of €2.50. More information at www.ns.nl.

- **Portugal Family Ticket** – On weekends only, families of 3 to 9 people can save 50% on select trains. Read the fine print carefully, as some routes may require a return by midday Sunday, for example. More information at www.cp.pt.

Classes of Service, Seats, & Sleepers

European Classes of Service

First-class cars have fewer seats and better upholstery. For parents, this translates to more space for luggage and lap children, and often a cleaner travel environment. When traveling first class on "premier" trains, a meal is sometimes included. If you travel with a Saverpass, you are entitled to ride in first class.

Second-class cars accommodate far more passengers, and seats are generally fixed in place (no reclining). If you are traveling on point-to-point tickets, second class will be your least expensive option.

Seats and Sleeper Compartments

Coach seats – On European trains, coach seats generally refer to seats situated on either side of an aisle, much like on an airplane. In first class, these seats may be larger and there may be only one seat on one side of the aisle with two on the other to compensate for the use of space.

Compartment seats – On many trains in Europe, you'll find compartment seating, where a corridor passes along one side of the train car, with doorways into individual compartments. These compartments may seat up to six or even eight people. With unreserved seating, you may walk along and choose the least crowded compartment.

Couchettes – These are usually the second-class option for lying down flat to sleep on an overnight train. Like compartments (which some of them are by day), you will walk down a corridor at one side of the train car with couchette compartments on the other side. Couchettes may contain up to six bunks stacked three high on each side, so be sure to arrive early to ensure you get a lower bunk—hopefully both lower bunks for the greatest comfort and convenience while traveling with your child. A pillow and blanket are provided. You may be sharing the couchette compartment with strangers, but the compartment door should lock for general security at night.

Sleepers – These may be offered as first-class accommodations, usually with beds for 1 or 2 people (and sometimes a very small optional 3rd bed suitable for a child), or as second-class accommodations, with beds for 2 to 4 people. In either class, there is usually a sink provided in the compartment, an outlet, reading lights, and linens. Where "deluxe" first-class sleeper accommodations are available, they may include a private toilet and shower as well.

European Airports with Railway Stations

These major airports have built-in train stations, which can help whisk your family to the city center or help you get on your journey most efficiently. Ending your rail journey at the airport of your return can also be quite helpful, without need of taxi or shuttle, or the car seat.

Amsterdam Schiphol (AMS)
Berlin Schönefeld (SXF)
Brussels National (BRU)
Düsseldorf (DUS)
Geneva, Cointrin (GVA)
London, Heathrow (LHR)
Malaga (AGP)
Munich, Strauss (MUC)
Rome, Fiumicino (FCO)
Stuttgart, Echterdingen (STR)
Zurich (ZRH)

Barcelona Prat (BCN)
Birmingham (BHX)
Copenhagen (CPH)
Frankfurt am Main (FRA)
London, Gatwick (LGW)
London, Stansted (STN)
Manchester (MAN)
Paris, Charles de Gaulle (CDG)
Stockholm (ARN)
Vienna, Schwechat (VIE)

Part VII:
Travels by
Cruise Ship

CHAPTER 23

Before You Book Your Cruise

The Case for Cruising as a Family

A family vacation with a major cruise line is for many the ultimate, all-inclusive dose of rest and relaxation. For parents that want to escape it all, lift nary a finger for meal preparation, eliminate the risk of getting lost on the way to the next destination, and never be more than a moment away from some form of entertainment, a snack, a restroom, or even a doctor—cruising is where it's at. Those who have planned any kind of trip with a baby or small child can appreciate the ease and simplicity a well-chosen cruise vacation may offer.

Top Reasons to Cruise as a Family

- **"All-inclusive" pricing** – You can plan to eat often and well, without guilt, even when ordering multiple side dishes to appease a picky toddler. And when cruising abroad, your price will be locked in, in spite of exchange rate fluctuations that could cause a land-based vacation budget to jump.

- **Convenience** – All of the restaurants and facilities are an easy walk from your cabin.

- **Safety of a closed community** – Between ports, you know that everyone on board is a ticketed passenger or hired staff, and there are miles of deck to stroll and explore without need of crossing streets or dodging cars. And while you are onboard, you don't even need to carry a wallet with you—most things are included, and any extras are charged to your room.

- **Multiple destinations** – See a number of different destinations without the need to repack or schlep baggage, and without the frustration of losing extra time in transit, stuck in seats. If you sign up for any of the ship's organized excursions, you can even be escorted right from the gangway to the best highlights at your port, complete with a guide.

- **A drop-off nursery or children's program** – When you choose the right cruise, you can leave your child in the qualified hands of registered staff onboard while you explore an exotic port, go on the dive trip, enjoy a late show, or decompress in the steam room.

- **A doctor in the house** – You have the added comfort of knowing a doctor is onboard, should you need one, along with a small supply of prescription drugs and over-the-counter remedies (antibiotics, ear drops, etc.).

- **Exotic and remote locales** – You can satisfy your appetite for adventure by visiting destinations you might not feel so comfortable exploring independently with a baby or small child, with safe water and food onboard, secure accommodations, and a registered organization ensuring you're safely at home each night.

But before booking that next best bargain cruise you see advertised, make sure the cruise line really provides all the pluses you're hoping for—including an environment where your family will feel comfortable and welcome. Remember, not all cruise lines cater to families with babies or small children. Some don't even allow children younger than 12 years onboard, and others may allow only a limited number of children or infants on each sailing. Not to mention, a cruise line with strict dining protocol or absolutely nothing to offer the family with an under-3-year-old other than a full-price 3rd/4th passenger fare does not a happy family vacation make. This section of the book will help you determine which cruise lines and cruises are the best fit for your family's ages, stages, and interests.

Cruisers Beware: Some Cruise Lines Do, Some Don't...

- Offer discounted pricing for infants and/or children
- Allow babies on board, or children under certain ages
- Limit the number of child passengers onboard
- Provide family-friendly cabins
- Allow children in swim diapers to use its splash pools
- Offer flexible dining options or children's menus
- Provide babysitting, childcare, or children's activities

As you shop for an enticing itinerary and the perfect price for your cruise, you'll want to be sure you also get the best possible amenities and perks for your family—and in an atmosphere that will be comfortable for everyone. In other words, you'll first want to know which cruise lines are the best match for your family's needs.

And even though 24-hour pizzerias, children's programs, and high chairs are lovely, the single most important factor for your family may be price—and that can vary dramatically depending on a cruise line's passenger rate policies and special promotions.

Cruise Discounts for Infants and Children

Unless otherwise noted, the cruise prices you see advertised are quoted as a per person rate, based on two people traveling together and staying in a room designed to fit no more than two passengers. Virtually all cruise lines charge a fee for an additional person, called a third- or fourth-passenger rate, even if that person is not yet eating solid foods and shares a bed with his parents.

Third- and fourth-passenger rates are generally less than the primary passenger rates, but as you can imagine, they can make the cost of cruising with a baby jump—without giving you any additional cabin space or meals your child can actually eat.

Cruise Lines that Always Offer Children's Discounts or Free Passage

Obviously, the option of having your child cruise free or at a discounted rate should be carefully considered. At present, only two cruise lines allow infants or children to cruise free on every sailing, and one is holding on to very low flat-rate pricing for young cruisers.

- **Cunard Cruise Line always allows infants (specified as children under 2 years) to cruise "free,"** meaning for only the cost of port taxes and government fees. Once children reach their second birthdays, however, they must pay the same 3rd or 4th passenger rates as everyone else onboard. www.cunard.com

- **MSC Cruises always allows children through 11 years old to cruise "free"** (again, for port charges) on its cruises, and children 12 to 17 years receive a children's discount. www.msccruisesusa.com

- **Disney Cruise Line always allows children under 3 years to cruise at a drastically discounted flat rate** based on the length of cruise (and not by accommodations), and gives a children's discount for kids from 3 to 12 years. www.disneycruise.com

However, your best *total* price for your family may still come from a cruise sale (e.g., a deeply discounted last-minute offer) where the rate for the first 2 passengers is already substantially lower than what you might pay for regular adult fares. So it can definitely pay to price out multiple cruises for your entire family before making your final decision.

Cruise Lines with Occasional Children's Promotions

A handful of other cruise lines run special promotions with discounted rates for children that are better than the standard third- and fourth-passenger rates, but these offers only apply to certain sailing dates or itineraries. Depending on the offer, the discount may include infants under 2 years or all children up to 17 years. Since these deals are not always widely advertised, you may want to check the cruise lines' websites for possible upcoming children's specials, and make note of the specific sail dates and ship names.

The discounts should be automatically reflected in your quote from a cruise specialist or online agency, so long as you are prompted for the children's ages at the time of the cruise. Here are your best bets to check for bargain sailings with your child.

Best-bet cruise lines to watch for special family offers:

- Carnival Cruise Lines www.carnival.com 1-888-Carnival

- Costa Cruises www.costacruise.com or 1-888-249-3978

- Disney Cruise Line www.disneycruise. com 1-800-951-3532

- Holland America Line www.hollandamerica.com 1-877-SAIL-HAL

- MSC Cruises www.msccruisesusa.com 1-800-666-9333

- Norwegian Cruise Line www.ncl.com 1-800-327-7030

- As well, the vacation discounter site www.vacationstogo.com makes it easy to scan your cruise vacation search results for any "kids free cruises" by labeling these offers in the right-hand column (email registration required).

ON THE WEB:

While other cruise lines may have seasonal offers and special promotions where children can cruise free or for a greatly reduced rate, these cruise lines always offer this special pricing:

Children under 12 years always cruise "free" with:
MSC Cruises – www.msccruisesusa.com

Children under 3 years always cruise at a discounted rate with:
Disney Cruise Line – www.disneycruise.com

Children under 2 years always cruise "free" with:
Cunard Line – www.cunard.com

Other Cruise Discounts

Depending on the cruise line, point of embarkation, and some other factors, you may be able to get an additional discount on your cruise. When getting a cruise quote online or over the phone, you may be asked for additional information to see if you qualify for any of these possible discounts. Some possible discounts include:

- **Past passenger discount** – If you have cruised with the same cruise line in the past.

- **Resident's discount** – Sometimes having residency in a certain state may qualify.

- **Military discounts** – Several major cruise lines offer discounts to active members of the U.S. military. Some cruise lines also extend these discounts to retired members and veterans as well.

- **Interline discounts** – Airline employees may qualify for discounts on select sailings with certain cruise lines.

- **Police, fire fighters, and teachers** – Occasional discounts may be offered.

- **Group discounts** – Most often your group will need to book a minimum of eight cabins to qualify, but occasionally (in the low season) fewer cabins will qualify. This can be a clever way to plan family reunions or cruise with several other friends or family members. You will need to call the cruise line or a cruise specialist to discuss requirements and group discounted rates for your select sailing.

Minimum Age Requirements

Although some cruise lines are welcoming babies and toddlers on board with open arms and ample amenities, cruise lines still vary widely in their policies regarding the minimum ages required for infants and small children. While some cruise lines, such as Disney, allow infants to cruise from 12 weeks minimum, Clipper Cruise Line does not allow children under 9 years to sail, and Viking Cruise Line insists cruisers be at least 12 years old (cruise lines not serving children under 5 years or offering family amenities are omitted from this book).

Other cruise lines, such as Celebrity and Princess, effectively discourage children from cruising on most itineraries by charging full-price third- and fourth-passenger rates (no children's discounts) and limiting the number of children onboard each cruise; Crystal and Silversea specifically reserve the right to limit the number of children under age 3.

The itinerary may also affect whether or not an infant may cruise. For cruises calling on more than one country, there is often a minimum age requirement of 6 months, and for most exotic cruises (e.g., South America, Asia, etc.) infants must be at least one year of age and sometimes older. Minimum age requirements are included for each cruise line in the Cruise Lines Table, pg. 391.

Depending on your child's temperament and your own vacation wishes, there is one other factor that could determine whether or not she is old enough for the cruise vacation you envision: Is she old enough to qualify for the onboard babysitting or children's activities? For many parents, this may make or break a cruise deal; if you're one of them, consult the cruise table for details about babysitting with each of the major cruise lines.

Babysitting and Children's Programs

Be warned: A cruise line that says it offers "babysitting" does not necessarily provide babysitting for babies! Most cruise lines offer childcare—be it in the form of babysitting or children's activity programs—only for potty-trained children (no pull-ups or training pants allowed), and for those over 3 years old. If you are depending on shipboard childcare to get the most out of your cruise, you'll want to be sure you choose a cruise line that will accommodate your needs.

Onboard Babysitting

Babysitting onboard cruise ships can be divided into three categories: formal drop-off nurseries, private in-room babysitting, and group babysitting. Disney, Cunard, and Carnival offer childcare for the youngest cruisers, caring for infants as young as 12 weeks. Norwegian will care for children 2 years and older, but requires parents to carry a beeper and come change the diaper themselves if needed (while in port, at least one parent must stay on the ship to do so). A handful of others are also noted in the Cruise Lines Table, beginning on pg. 391.

- **Formal drop-off nurseries** can be found on each of Disney's ships (12 weeks to 3 years, hourly fee). Cunard's ships also have a complimentary nursery, which is staffed with certified British nannies (6 months to 2 years, complimentary).

- **Private in-room babysitting** is offered on very few cruise lines and is usually subject to crew member availability, so book ASAP: Celebrity (6 months to 12 years), Crystal (6 months to 12 years), Holland America (no age specified), and Royal Caribbean (6 months to 12 years).

- **Group babysitting** is far more common on cruise ships and is usually offered during late night and port visiting hours: Carnival (4 months to 11 years), Celebrity (3 years + toilet trained), Costa (3 years minimum), Holland America (3 years to 12 years), Norwegian (2 years to 12 years), Princess (3 years to 12 years), Royal Caribbean (3 years to 12 years).

For any of these babysitting options, be sure to check hours of availability and book as far in advance as possible to avoid disappointment. More details about babysitting in the Cruise Lines Table.

Complimentary Kid's Programs for Toddlers

Children's programs have been added to many cruise lines to help give children a chance to socialize and stretch their imaginations, sometimes with arts or crafts, games, dance lessons, or special activities related to the itinerary. While Royal Caribbean includes a program for children 6 months to 3 years to attend *with* parents, most programs are designed for children to attend without their parents. At this time, those cruise lines offering supervised (i.e., "drop-off") activities for the youngest sailors to attend without their parents include:

- **2 years and older:** Carnival, Cunard, Norwegian
- **3 years and older:** Celebrity, Costa, Crystal, Disney, Holland America, P&O Cruises, Princess, Royal Caribbean

More details about children's programs are provided in the Cruise Lines Table.

Family Dining Options and Opportunities

Traditionally, cruise guests would be assigned one of two dinner seatings, and would have to report to the formal dining room at their appointed time. This option still exists on many cruise ships, and if you want to take advantage of gourmet, multi-course dining onboard, this may be your only chance to do so.

Fortunately for families, more and more ships are offering additional flexible dining options as well, a great help to the family that struggles to get out the door on time, or has a picky eater in tow, or a toddler who struggles to sit through a five-course meal. Here are some of the dining options and opportunities available from some cruise lines that may help make your family's cruise all the more enjoyable.

Flexible dining – Most large cruise ships now offer additional flexible dining options, like buffets or pizzerias that open earlier and let you come as you are and sit where you please whenever suits you. Norwegian and Disney offer multiple round-the-clock dining options with complete flexibility for families. This may serve your family well for most or all nights of your cruise, but if you want some time to enjoy the full-meal deal in the dining room (even Disney offers adult-only restaurants as a reprieve), be sure to check what babysitting options the cruise line offers before booking with them.

Child-friendly dinner times – Another innovative solution for the dinnertime dilemma has come from Carnival. They offer an earlier dinnertime (5:45 pm) each evening for children 2 years and older where they dine with other kids in their age group and youth counselor hosts. After dinner, the kids join in more activities with their age group while Mom and Dad can dine alone. Norwegian's youth counselors also take participating children to dinner at least one night of each sailing.

Room service – Having your dinner delivered to your door can also be a delightful way to enjoy the evening's meal…while your baby snoozes in her bed…or your toddler practices the delicate art of using silverware. Some cruise lines will charge additional fees for this service, whereas some others will include room service in the price of the cruise—a serious value if this option works well for your family.

High chairs – Even in the formal dining rooms on ships, you can expect a high chair to be provided for your child if needed. However, strap and tray configurations are not always ideal, so if your child is an escape artist or has special needs, you may want to consider bringing a portable dining booster you know and trust. In peak family travel times, there may also be more competition for high chairs, and they will be doled out on a first-come first-served basis. Hook-on chairs that mount to the table's edge take up little space while traveling, but beware that they should not be used on tables with table cloths—what you are most likely to encounter in a ship's formal dining room. (See recommended dining boosters for travel at www.TravelswithBaby.com.)

Bottles and baby food – In formal dining rooms and shipboard restaurants where you will be waited on at your table, feel free to ask for bottles or baby food to be warmed for your child. Regular milk will be available, but bring your own formula if you'll need it. In most cases, waiters will be more than happy to accommodate your special requests, and will be more than happy to receive your show of appreciation at the end of your cruise (do be sure to tip). In self-serve buffets and less formal eateries, you may need to ask for a mug of hot water (as for tea) to warm things yourself. Currently, Crystal Cruises and Celebrity offer baby food by special request for lunches and dinners in their dining rooms; otherwise, bring your own.

Table food for toddlers – Casual café-style dining may provide some good options for your toddler, like pasta, bread, yogurt, fruit, pizza, or French fries, but don't be afraid to make special requests in the dining room. Anything on your menu that sounds remotely like it may interest your child—mashed potatoes, rice, steamed vegetables, soup—is fair game. Feel free to ask for side orders, even served in a bowl, without salt or sauce, or whatever suits.

Children's menus – If you choose a cruise line that offers a children's menu, rest assured that your child will have his fill of pizza, chicken nuggets, French fries, grilled cheese sandwiches, and the like, as you might expect from a children's menu at any restaurant.

A New Parent's Guide to Cruise Lines

Deciding which cruise to take can be daunting for anyone, but the stakes are even higher when bringing a baby or small child along for the ride. You are not only committing to where you will vacation, but where and how you will eat, sleep, and entertain yourselves in one fell swoop.

Don't risk choosing a ship that isn't a fit for your family—where you might push your stroller through casino after casino only to wind up in the blaring discothèque with nowhere left to go but your cabin, or spend your nightly 5-course meals cringing as your toddler tosses breadsticks at your distinguished dining companions.

Instead, use the following table to size up which cruise lines are the best match for your family's high seas adventure. As you'll see, there are plenty of cruise lines ready to accommodate families with babies and small children. At a glance, this table will help you quickly size up which cruise lines may be best for your family now and in the years ahead.

Crib notes: All of these cruise lines state that they can provide a crib on request, though the number available on each cruise will be limited. Since they are all are available on a "first-reserved first-served" basis, be sure to reserve yours ASAP or bring along your own baby travel bed or cot (recommendations on pg. 76 and at www.TravelswithBaby.com).

Table 3: Cruise Lines Comparison Table[10]

Cruise Line	Min. age	Child discount[11]	In-room babysitting	Drop-off babysitting	Free children's programs	Flex dining	Child Menu	Room service
Carnival www.carnival.com 1-888-CARNIVAL	6 mos. Or 1 yr.[12]	No	No	6+ mos. on port days, $6/hr	2 yrs +	Yes	Yes	Yes
Celebrity www.celebritycruises.com 1-800-647-2251	6 mos. or 1 yr.[13]	No	1 year+, rate varies	3 yrs+ Potty trained $6/hr	3 yrs + Potty trained or w/parent	Yes	Yes, + baby food offered lunch & dinner	Yes
Costa www.costacruises.com 1-888-249-3978	6 mos.	Select itineraries	No	3 yrs + Free	3 yrs + Potty trained	Yes	Yes	Yes

---

[10] Please bear in mind that some details may be subject to change, so always confirm critical information with cruise lines at time of booking.
[11] Child discounts only apply when traveling as the third or fourth passenger with two fare-paying adults in same cabin.
[12] Infants must be 1 year for Transatlantic, Hawaiian, and South American cruises.
[13] Infants must be 1 year for Transatlantic, Transpacific, Hawaiian, Australian, and South American cruises/cruise tours.

Cruise Line	Min. age	Child discount[11]	In-room babysitting	Drop-off babysitting	Free children's programs	Flex dining	Child Menu	Room service
Crystal www.crystalcruises.com 1-800-804-1500	6 mos.	50% min. fare up to 12 yrs w/ 2 adults	6+ mos. $10 - $20/hr	No	Select sailings, 3 yrs +	Yes	Yes, + baby food	Yes
Cunard www.cunard.com 1-800-7CUNARD	6 mos. or 1 yr.[14]	Up to 24 mos. free[15]	No	6 mos. + Free	2+ years	No	Yes	Yes, 24 hours
Disney www.disneycruise.com 1-800-951-3532	12 wks.	Up to 3 yrs Flat-rate discount prices	No	12 wks to 36 mos. $6/hr (10 hr max per cruise)	3 yrs +	Yes	Yes	Yes, 24 hrs
Holland America www.hollandamerica.com 1-877-SAIL-HAL	12 wks.	Select itineraries	Yes, $8/hr	After hours is $5/hr, $8/hr other	Prinsendam is 5+ yrs. All other ships 3 yrs + potty trained	Yes	Yes, + baby food $1 ea. by advance request	Yes, 24 hrs

[14] Cunard requires 6 months for cruises in North America, Europe, Caribbean, Mexico, Transcanal, Australia, and New Zealand. Children must be 1 year old for the following cruise destinations: Africa, South America, South Pacific/Hawaii/Tahiti, world cruises, exotic cruises (Asia/Orient/Antarctica/Indian subcontinent), Transatlantic/Transpacific.
[15] "Free" meaning no passenger rate, but government taxes and port charges still apply for each passenger onboard.

Cruise Line	Min. age	Child discount[11]	In-room babysitting	Drop-off babysitting	Free children's programs	Flex dining	Child Menu	Room service
MSC Cruises www.mscruisesusa.com 1-800-666-9333	3 mos.	Up to 17 years cruise free[16]	No	$18/hr, 3 yrs + potty trained	Yes, 3 yrs. + or w/parent	Except dinners	Yes	Yes
Norwegian www.ncl.com 1-866-234-0292	No	Up to 24 mos. cruise free	No	2 yrs to 12 yrs while in port and after hours, fee varies	2 yrs +	Yes	Yes	Yes, 24 hrs
P&O Cruises www.pocruises.com 1-877-828-4728	12+ mos.	Select family cruises	No	After hours, fee varies	3 yrs + potty trained	Yes	Yes	Yes, 24 hrs
Princess www.princess.com 1-800-PRINCESS	6+ mos., 12 mos., 18 mos. [17]	No	No	3 yrs + potty trained, $5/hr	3 yrs. + potty trained	Yes	Yes, + baby food by request	Yes
Regent Seven Seas www.rssc.com 1-877-505-5370	1 yr.	50% min. fare 11 yrs. and under	1 year +, $25/hr where available	No	5 yrs +, select sailings only	Yes	Yes	Yes

---

[16] "Free" meaning no passenger rate, government taxes and port charges still apply for each passenger onboard.

[17] Princess requires 6 months for Alaskan and Caribbean cruises, 18 months for exotic cruises, and 12 months for other cruises.

Cruise Line	Min. age	Child discount[11]	In-room babysitting	Drop-off babysitting	Free children's programs	Flex dining	Child Menu	Room service
Royal Caribbean www.royalcaribbean.com 1-866-562-7625	6+ mos., 1 yr.[18]	No	1 yr +, $8 - $19/hr	3 yrs + potty trained, $8/hr	3 yrs + and potty trained, and 6 mos. to 36 mos. w/ parent	Yes	Yes	Yes
Silversea www.silversea.com 1-800-722-9955	6+ mos., 1 yr.[19]	No	No	No	No	Yes	No	Yes

[18] Royal Caribbean requires children to be at least 6 months for all cruises and 12 months for Transatlantic and Exotic Cruises.

[19] The Silver Explorer and Silversea Expeditions cannot accommodate infants under 12 months.

CHAPTER 24
Booking Your Cruise

Stateroom Types and Configurations

Your options for ship cabins or "staterooms" may vary widely. With large cruise lines, there may be numerous stateroom options available, ranging from the most economical interior stateroom to a sprawling multi-room suite complete with private butler service. As mentioned earlier, bathtubs are not considered the norm on cruise ships, nor are mini refrigerators, unless you are cruising with Disney Cruise Line or in a family cabin or suite that specifically states otherwise.

Interior Staterooms

The basic interior stateroom features few bells and whistles, and is likely to be the headlining price advertised for the cruise. Keep in mind that it will have no window and will most likely have two separate beds unless otherwise stated. Interior cabins are generally the smallest offered, and the beds may even be bunk style to save space (and not for a crib), so make sure you have the specifics for this type of stateroom on your particular ship before reserving it. Often the cruise line's website or online agency will have helpful pictures of most ships' basic cabins (if you're not seeing them elsewhere, try www.vacationstogo.com).

Oceanview Staterooms

A room with a view may be far more valuable to a family cruising with a baby or small child that will likely be spending more time in its cabin than some other passengers; not to mention, oceanview cabins are generally larger than interior staterooms. Oceanview cabins may have either a small porthole window or a larger window and often include more floor space—possibly even a pull-out sofa. When traveling as a family, it can be well worth the extra cost to upgrade to this cabin type if possible, especially if you would like to have a portacrib in your cabin. Sometimes cabins with an "obstructed view" or "partially obstructed view" are listed at a discount—be sure you have details about just how obstructed the view may be to avoid disappointment (lifeboats, columns, etc.). If you don't mind a room with a view—of a lifeboat—this may be a good option to help increase your floor space.

Deluxe Stateroom

What this means may vary by ship, but generally it includes greater square footage for your cabin, which may be especially helpful if you will be using a portacrib or need extra space for a child to play. It may also mean nicer furnishings and more of them, and you are more likely to find a king-size bed option in these rooms. Often a sofa with a pull-out bed is also included, which means more seating by day and an extra bed (if you need it) by night, which can be a far better option for cruising with young children than pull-out berths (a.k.a. elevated bunks).

Verandah/Balcony

Having your own private balcony off your cabin can prove invaluable during nap times. You and your mate can step outside to fresh air and conversation, or a good book, and continue to enjoy the views as you cruise. If you are picky about your view, or nervous about having deck access with your little adventurer, visit the cruise line's website to see photos of these cabins, or call to request a brochure. Some older ships have open bars spread wide apart to maximize the view, but most have added plexiglas to optimize safety. Some newer ships feature balconies with solid, clear walls that are far safer with small children and provide an even better view. However, some cabins may have a verandah made of a solid white wall—sturdy, but it blocks half the view from your cabin. Again, you can usually look up photos for the specific cabin type on the ship you are considering on the cruise line's website.

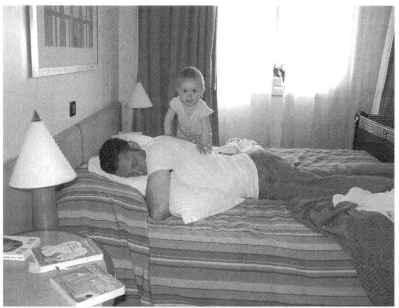

Close quarters: If your cabin is actually large enough to accommodate a portacrib, you may no longer be able to walk around your bed.

Triple/Quad+ Occupancy

A variety of staterooms (any of those mentioned above) may provide sleeping spaces for three or even four people, but how they do so is especially important to know if you'll have a small child using one of the beds. In interior staterooms and some of the other smaller cabins available, the third and/or fourth bed is usually a bunk that folds down from above (not practical for a toddler, so you and your mate can arm wrestle for it). In oceanview or deluxe rooms, it is more likely to be a sofabed. If you are planning to use a portacrib or travel bed in your cabin instead of a third bed, you will be more concerned with how much floor space you will have to work with. Generally, cabins with sofas/sofabeds will give you the advantage of extra space allotted for the sofabed.

Suites

One-bedroom suites can be found on most ships, and some two-bedroom suites can be had as well. You are much more likely to have a mini-refrigerator in a suite, and possibly even a wet bar. All of these details will vary from ship to ship and by stateroom category, so check with your cruise specialist for any deal-breaker details before you book this cabin type.

Family Staterooms and Family Suites

Some newer ships (including those from Carnival, Royal Caribbean, Costa, and Disney Cruise Line) offer cabins with beds for four or more people. Unless otherwise stated, these only include one bathroom, but there is more floor and storage space regardless. A few cruise lines, like Celebrity and Disney, offer family staterooms with privacy curtains or partitions between sleeping areas. Disney family suites have two bathrooms and include a bathtub.

Connecting Staterooms

A limited number of interconnecting staterooms can be found on most newer ships, but you will want to make your reservation before they sell out. This is also a great option if you'd like to travel with grandparents or friends—and the second bathroom, which you most likely would not have in a suite, may come in handy at times.

Getting the Most Room for Your Money

Whatever the cruise line, more space may be had for a price. But chances are you'll have plenty of other things to spend money on during your cruise. Here are a few extra tips for helping you get the most space for your money. Carnival offers some of the largest standard staterooms available, with interior staterooms up to 185 square feet—keep that in mind as you compare prices with other cruise lines.

You might also watch for free cabin upgrade promotions to help stretch your dollars. These and other "free bonuses" often crop up for last-minute cruises advertised online. If you're very claustrophobic, consider the cost of booking two interconnecting staterooms with low 1st and 2nd passenger fares for the first cabin and the 1st passenger + single supplement for the other—two such cabins may cost less than a suite booked for three or four passengers, and you'll have that second bathroom.

Selecting Your Cabin's Location

When booking a cruise online, you are often given the opportunity to choose which cabin you would like for your selected options and price category. As you peruse deck plans, try to think of the ship as a whole, not just the individual levels with cabins you are considering. Keep in mind:

- **Where are the elevators?** Not only will elevators nearby create extra traffic by your door, but you will also likely suffer through the conversations of strangers waiting for the elevators.

- **What's upstairs?** A theater, dance floor, or casino may provide unwelcome noise—and late into the night.

- **What's out the window?** If you're booking an ocean-view cabin, watch for footnotes that may explain you will have an obstructed or partially obstructed view. If you are looking at cabins on one of the upper levels, also watch out for rooms that may be on a deck with passersby outside.

- **Why go below?** The lower the cabin, generally, the lower the pricetag. You may also feel less motion riding low in the ship. But if you're looking at lower levels, steer clear of the fore and aft sections if possible. Although there's a chance the humming of engines at the rear may help soothe your child, it may also give you a headache. And when the anchor drops at the front of the ship, the jarring noises can wake small sleepers.

- **Why go higher?** Cabins, windows, and balconies are generally larger, and you have less of a trek to get to the restaurants, pool, and other facilities. You can also avoid lengthy waits for the elevator during peak times (dinner, shows) by taking the stairs instead.

- **Why aim for the middle?** Many cruisers think the middle of the mid-ship levels offer the best balance of convenience, quiet, and calm. Just watch out for the lifeboats that may be blocking your view outside.

Five Important Requests to Make in Advance

As you book your cruise, whether over the telephone with a specialist or through an online agency, you will hopefully be given the opportunity to make your special requests. If not, call the cruise line directly with your questions and requests regarding cruising with your child. This is the time to make it known if you'd like...

1. A crib/portacrib – All major cruise lines except Seabourn will tell you they can provide these, yet they only have so many onboard a given ship. So if you're counting on the cruise line to provide your baby's bed, don't take any chances. Make your request ASAP.

2. Baby food – If your cruise line offers baby food by request, by all means don't forget to put in your request. This isn't a standard staple on even the cruise ships that offer it, so give them plenty of advance notice if you'd like to take advantage of their offer.

3. Bed rails – Only Disney Cruise Line offers these to passengers, and like cribs, the number available is limited. Put in your request ASAP or bring your own (recommendations in Travel Safety and Childproofing at www.TravelswithBaby.com).

4. Babysitting – Ships offering private or after-hours group babysitting require advance notice, so the sooner you can put in your request, the better. If you have an idea of which days or evenings you would

like to hire a babysitter (based on your itinerary), ask how far in advance you can reserve the service, and don't take any chances.

5. Children's programs – Your cruise line may assume at the time of booking that, based on your child's age, he or she will be participating in the onboard children's program. However, during peak family travel seasons, space may be limited—particularly for popular children's events. Contact the cruise line well in advance to be sure your child will be able to participate.

CHAPTER 25

Preparing for Your Cruise

Researching Your Ports of Call

An exciting itinerary means little if you can't get off the ship and see the destinations firsthand. Whereas some ports will find you smack dab in the middle of the action, allowing you to stroll off the gangplank and into the action with your child at your side (or on your person), others may require a bit more planning and/or spending to get you and your family where you'd like to be.

For example, cruise ships calling on a San Francisco dock adjacent to Fisherman's Wharf offer an easy walk to the Pier 39 attractions, including restaurants, cable cars, Alcatraz and Bay cruise ferries, the Aquarium of the Bay, and also the Exploratorium. Cruise ships calling on Rome, however, actually drop anchor in a different town called Civitavecchia and require about an hour's drive (one way) to get to Rome itself.

Port-specific information is sometimes available through your booking agency or the cruise line's website itself, though these resources tend to lean heavily on the organized sightseeing activities and encourage you to pay for the excursions offered by the cruise line— which may be your best bet in some situations. If you are docking in a remote location, or where tourist services are few and far between, or where your personal safety is best ensured by using the business affiliated with the ship, an organized shore excursion might be best.

Fortunately, a visit to www.cruising.org will help you find a wealth of information about port destinations worldwide, including the docking location, what is within walking distance, how to find and use the local transportation to get to the major attractions, activities, and events, area maps, and even where to get medical assistance or exchange currency. It is well worth checking out your destinations on this site in advance, and also reading any advice they offer regarding taxis and local transportation.

Consider for each destination:

- Can you walk off the ship and see what you'd like on foot?

- If not, is public transportation easily accessible from the port, or will you need a taxi?

- Are there places where the shore excursions offered by the cruise line may be best—and worth the expense?

Sometimes, the size of the vessel also determines how closely you may dock to the port city you would like to see, so while certain smaller ships may dock within walking distance of some attractions, others may need to dock farther out and will require you to take a shuttle or taxi into town. When calling on some island destinations, like George Town, Grand Cayman, or Santorini, Greece, your ship may actually drop anchor at sea and ferry passengers in on a smaller vessel—exciting stuff for the kids onboard! When docking beyond a reasonable walk from the port attractions, most cruise lines offer reasonably priced shuttle buses to and from the town center, a far safer option than taking a taxi into town without a car seat.

Choosing Your Shore Excursions

When cruising with toddlers and preschoolers, especially, you may prefer an itinerary with many destinations that are quickly reached by foot or by shuttle bus, and where you may enjoy the flexibility of your own schedule. For example, when docking at Barbados (Bridgetown), you can simply stroll off the ship and walk to one of the most beautiful beaches there—perfect for a family day at the beach, complete with lunch and a diaper change back on the ship. But where the attractions and major sights are not so conveniently located, organized shore excursions can offer definite advantages over going it alone:

- The time in port is used to your best advantage, going straight to the sites of interest.

- The tour bus is ready and waiting with no need for lugging along a car seat.

- An English-speaking guide tells you everything you need to know to appreciate the sites.

- There is no worry of getting back to the ship in time for departure.

- You know you are with a trusted tour operator on land.

Before choosing any shore excursions for your family, you'll want to make sure there aren't any restrictions that may prevent your child from going with you. On more active excursions, such as rainforest canopy adventure tours, children must typically be at least 12 years old and 48 inches tall—no standing around taking turns holding your baby on these tours! However, on many if not most excursions, children and/or infants are allowed to come along for the ride, with infants riding on laps for free, and children sometimes paying a discounted rate (though not always).

Most cruise lines provide details of their shore excursions on their websites, including the physical activity level necessary to keep up with the tour, and recommended clothing or shoes, all of which can help you better gauge the suitability for your family. Cruise lines encourage advance booking, which is a good idea for the most popular tours that may sell out before the ship sets sail. You, however, may feel more comfortable waiting until you are on the ship and can speak directly to the cruise activities director about which excursions she would—and wouldn't—recommend for your family. If you are considering checking your child into the kid's activity program or onboard babysitting while in port, be sure to make the arrangements as early as possible. If you can't make arrangements for your child before the cruise, it's not a bad idea to stop by the purser's desk to make arrangements before the ship leaves port.

Savona, Italy: Destinations where you can simply walk off the ship and explore on foot have definite advantages when bringing along a small child or two.

Tips for Excellent Group Excursions

- Carefully consider excursions that require more than a half hour of uninterrupted driving to get to the destination (in addition to other drive time between sights). You may have the benefit of a tour guide providing background and commentary as you make the journey, but if your child isn't content with the situation, no one may be able to hear it. Shorter driving segments with fresh air and changes of scenery are safer bets.

- Use a frontpack or soft backpack carrier for your child rather than a stroller, which may become a tripping hazard to others in your group as they stop sporadically to gaze and take photographs. Your stroller may also be difficult to use over the changing terrain—not to mention it could become an annoyance in the bus. A soft backpack carrier that doubles as your diaper bag/daypack may be a great option for older children, and saves space over the framed (hiking) variety.

- Rest assured your group will make pit stops, and be prepared to make the most of them. In the event of an untimely diaper change, don't be afraid to check in with your guide for advice on where to change it, and be willing to sit out one round to take care of business, rather than risk holding up the tour while you negotiate diapers and wipes.

- Respect your fellow travelers' rights to an excellent group excursion, too, by being ready and willing to "take it outside" if your child becomes audibly unhappy with a tour or has difficulty respecting the boundaries at a given destination.

Taking Taxis in Port

There are times and destinations where your family may prefer some flexibility in its day—or the leisure of enjoying just one or two sites. Taking taxis can be a cost-effective way to get your family to its destinations, and at some destinations, like Antigua, taxi drivers are hailed as the most knowledgeable local guides available and are highly recommended for sightseeing. However, car seats (and the lugging of them) may be an issue, and going without is not recommended (for help, see Best Car Seats for Travel and Car Seat Alternatives at www.TravelswithBaby.com).

Your best bet may be to hire a "car and driver" for the day, whether it's one designated taxi driver who agrees to be your local guide (discuss the itinerary and price up front) or a local company that offers private sightseeing. You can strap in your own car seat and relax while someone else navigates, and you'll have an extra person to snap those family pictures with *all of you* in the shot. This is also a safer way to reach outlying destinations, as opposed to risking whether or not you will be able to get a return taxi when you need it, or finding yourself faced with drivers that insist your return trip will cost double: "You wanna get back to your fancy-pants ship or not?"

Hiring a car and driver may also be less expensive than organized ship excursions in some cases, particularly if you have to pay full price for your child. At ports where taxis are considered to be risky, some cruise lines will also offer a private car and driver option. Or you can check www.cruising.org for local sightseeing options including "car and driver hire" through a local agency.

If you take a taxi, be sure to have complete instructions in the local language as to where you want to go, or at least a map you can point to for clarity. But more importantly, have clear details of where you need to return to. Some cities have multiple docking locations or expansive harbors, so hard as it may be to believe, repeating the name of the harbor over and over again with an American accent, or saying "big boat" in the local language followed by the name of the cruise line, or even singing the theme song from *The Love Boat* may not be enough to get you back to your ship (just ask us).

Packing for Your Cruise

Packing Baby Essentials

If you'll be cruising for a week or more with a baby, it is not unreasonable to expect you will need an entire suitcase devoted to baby essentials. Really. Cruise lines do not stock baby food, formula, diapers, or wipes onboard, except in very rare cases (you may find a few diapers on Disney ships, but certainly not enough for every baby onboard).

For a fee, Holland America Line will arrange for you to have commercial baby food, diapers, and a mini refrigerator in the cabin (by advance request through the ship's services department). Disney Cruise Line has also partnered with Babies Travel Lite to make it simple for your order of baby supplies to meet you at your cruise ship cabin as well as your pre- or post-cruise hotel in select cities (read more on using baby supply delivery services, pg. 83).

In addition to the most basic supplies, you'll want to bring along any baby bottles or sippy cups, toddler utensils, bibs, and related paraphernalia you may need to help make it a comfortable voyage. Just remember, as your supply of diapers and baby food diminishes you'll be freeing up lots of room for souvenirs—which are much more fun to hunt for in port cities than diapers for your child.

You'd better bring it onboard:

- Diapers
- Swim diapers (if needed)
- Wipes
- Baby food
- Formula
- Bottles, nipples (or disposables)
- Sippy cups
- Toddler silverware, etc.
- Travel bottle of dishwashing soap, bottle brush
- Baby sun block
- Baby shampoo
- Preferred lotion
- Baby bathtub inflatable insert

Packing Your Carry-On Bags

You should arrive at your cruise ship no later than 2 hours before the departure time. The embarkation process itself may take around an hour, much of it reminiscent of waiting around an airport, though possibly with fewer comforts. During this time you will need to check in, check your luggage, and clear security.

Since your luggage may not be delivered to your cabin for a few hours, you will want to give some serious thought to what goes into your carry-on bags, which will accompany you to your cabin. Certainly anything you'll need for your first hours onboard should be there, but think of other things that can help kick-start your vacation, too. Depending on when and where you board, you may want sun block, swim suits, a favorite toy or game, or perhaps naptime essentials.

Make sure you have:

- Enough diapers to last you through bedtime, just in case
- Corresponding amount of formula and/or baby food
- Changes of clothes for each passenger
- Any necessary bottles or sippy cups
- A favorite book or two
- Trusted lovey or security blanket
- Medications (in your child's travel kit, pg. 61)
- Toiletries
- Your trusty travel stroller

At the end of your cruise, you'll want to repack your carry-on bags just as thoughtfully, since the rest of your luggage will likely need to be packed and surrendered the night before you disembark (placing it outside your door). In case there are not enough porters for passengers, as is often the case, be sure you have enough diapers and essentials to last you through a couple of hours of disembarkation mayhem, as well. If you are heading straight to an airport, stock the outer pockets of your larger suitcases with refills of diapers, wipes, and other items you may need to replenish in your carry-ons and diaper bag before checking in for your flight.

Bringing Along Baby Gear

Car seats and strollers take up extra cabin space—yet having them along may be critical to enjoying your cruise vacation. And having a portacrib provided by the ship may seem like a major convenience—but it may also be a major obstacle. Here are some points to consider when deciding what stays and what goes when packing for your cruise.

- **Stroller** – The stroller may be helpful while visiting your ports, or not. Consider what kind of sights you will see and whether or not it might be easier to use a child carrier instead, or if she'll insist on walking most of the time anyway and the exercise would be beneficial. If you'll be joining a group for organized sightseeing, there may not be room in the bus or van for a stroller. Onboard, however, you may be very glad to have your stroller to help get your child to sleep, to use while feeding her in the cabin, to shade her while napping next to you on deck, or simply to keep her from getting into too much trouble in your un-childproofed cabin as you dress. We enjoyed watching our daughter practice walking while pushing her stroller backwards up and down the ship hallways and across the decks, and it was a comfy, secure place for her to sit (versus crawling and cruising free-range) while we enjoyed coffee on deck. If you do decide to bring a stroller, you will want to bring one that folds very compactly to take up minimal space in your cabin.

- **Car seat** – You may be able to find safe transportation alternatives that don't require a car seat—or be able to rent one (along with a car) for the portions that you do. In many cases, there is no need for a car seat once the cruise begins. You may be able to walk off the ship to explore your port by foot, or join an organized group to travel by bus or minibus—where you most likely wouldn't find seatbelts anyway. In the interest of cabin space, you might consider the Radian folding car seat which folds to a mere 6.5" thick to store nicely in your cabin closet. But if your destinations would most easily be explored by taking taxis, you might want to consider the Sit 'n' Stroll convertible car seat and stroller, or a RideSafer travel vest for older children (both included in Car Seats, Accessories, and Alternatives, pg. 66, and featured in detail at www.TravelswithBaby.com).

- **Travel beds** – Rather than use the portacrib provided by your ship, you may prefer to bring along a travel bed to save floor space in your cabin. Various options exist for infants, toddlers, and even preschool-age children, which can be folded up and stored in your closet or drawer if needed during the day. (See Travel Beds and Sleeping Solutions, pg. 76 and online at www.TravelswithBaby.com.)

Arches National Park, Utah

Afterword
Five Reasons Travel Trumps the Other Gifts I've Given My Children

Originally published in the Travels with Baby Tips Blog,
December 2013

I've always been a fan of "experiential gifts" for family members, when possible—from signing my husband up for singing lessons (a shock to him) which caused a huge transformation in not just his singing but his confidence doing so solo in front of an audience, to a hair-curling seaplane ride with my mother on her 60th birthday (good times!).

As the season of giving is upon us, I'm reminded of how grateful I am for all of the things I am able to give my children besides what comes wrapped in a box with a bow: healthy food, clean water, warm beds, help with homework, music lessons, trips to the library, and ears for listening to all of their stories and concerns rank very high on that list.

While they are still—for the moment—all under 10 years old, I have to say I am impressed by how much they already understand that our travels together have also been a tremendous gift for which we should all be very grateful. As I watch them grow, I am also seeing the value of our travels-so-far compound beyond anything I can imagine putting under the tree this year.

Here are some of the gifts traveling has given us as a family.

The first gift of travel...

Enabling us to give each other more of ourselves than we are usually able to at home, where there are constant distractions of daily busy-nesses, where extra time together is lost to the daily commute, and there are the built-in distractions of TV, computers, telephones, chores, and way too many toys...

The second gift of travel...

Helping us continue to rethink what is "normal" as far as what we are expected to know and understand at each of our ages, what we should be wearing, how much food we need, how far we can travel on our own two feet or paddle in our own canoe, and how we choose to get ourselves around our own hometown.

The third gift of travel...

Forcing us to try new things—even when we don't want to. It can make you glad not only for the extra packets of Top Ramen you put in the corner of the suitcase but for the strange-looking yogurt, salami, cheese, or vegetable you might never have tried if other options were available. And don't get me started on strange public toilets—there could be an entire blog post in that.

The fourth gift of travel...

Introducing us to adults who have managed to follow my children's same young interests through to actual careers, and enabling them to ask how they did so, from dive masters who lead the shark show in the Maui Ocean Center to wildlife rescuers in Costa Rica, and from park rangers in Sequoia National Park to paleontologists at Dinosaur National Monument. My children's ideas of what they might be "when they grow up" are not only fantastic—they are fueled by examples of the work and success of others who have done it themselves.

The fifth gift of travel...

Teaching us all patience. My children continue to amaze me with the patience they can show on long car rides now—of which there are plenty in any given year—and plane rides, and I firmly believe it's because we all know what to expect and how to be prepared (as I always say, start 'em young—before they know any different). It takes a lot of time to cross the United States AND the Atlantic Ocean. Sometimes you have to wait 5 hours in an airport—in between flights that take additional time. Sometimes you get stuck behind a watermelon truck, or learn the hard way that a map is a more reliable source for directions than GPS.

I think that final gift, patience, is perhaps the most valuable of all, and the one that is most easily dismissed. After all, few grownups expect any more of children than that they lose patience during travel Worse yet, adults are excused all the time it seems for having mini-temper tantrums when travel doesn't go their way. Didn't anyone teach them?

Life is full of surprises—not all of them pleasant, and not all of them wrapped in little boxes with ribbons and bows. But that doesn't mean they aren't sometimes gifts wrapped in the disguise of experience, not to mention: opportunity. And oftentimes those are the most valuable, memorable, and meaningful gifts of all.

...

Safe journeys,
Shelly Rivoli

Index

A

Accommodations
  condos and vacation rentals..... 59
  hotel suites with kitchenettes... 52
  large hotels and resorts 49
Air travel
  best seats with........................ 262
  bulkhead seats 261
  CARES "safety device" 303
  carry-on considerations 270
  checking baby gear................ 277
  ear pressure........................... 307
  eating and feeding on aircraft 310
  entertaining chilren in terminal
  296
  flying alone with child........... 315
  germs and air circulation 306
  in-flight entertainment 282
  international adoption............ 321
  lap child................................ 236
  lap child safety 305
  preboarding........................... 297
  purchasing child's seat 237
  purchasing infant's seat......... 237
  required documents for.......... 268
  security screening................. 289
  special needs child................ 321
  TABLE
    A parent's guide to airlines 244
    toddlers and preschoolers 286
    twins, multiples, multiple children
    318
  using car seats....................... 299

B

Baby gear rentals........................... 82
Baby supply delivery service 83
Babysitting
  cruises with........................... 386
  details by cruise line.............. 391
  finding sitters in cities 44
  hotels and resorts with............ 50
Backpack carriers......................... 74
Beach vacations............................ 31
Breastfeeding
  anti-malarial drugs................ 169

choosing airplane seats 262
dehydration of infants and
  children............................. 177
for healthy travels................. 156
immunity 18
on road trips......................... 215
other cultures........................ 138
vaccinations for breastfeeding
  mothers............................. 166

C

Campervan rentals...................... 232
Camping
  Back-country camping............. 39
Camping trips.............................. 35
Car seats
  alternatives to 66
  as carry-ons for aircraft 294
  booster seats on aircraft......... 303
  cruise vacations 411
  for travel................................ 66
  in other countries.................. 197
  in taxis 221
  installation of........................ 204
  laws in U.S. 196
  renting with car..................... 225
  travel-friendly....................... 222
  using in RVs......................... 229
  using on aircraft.................... 299
  using with seatbelts 205
Carsickness................................. 215
Childproofing
  checking-in safety checklist... 182
  on arrival 181
  products for travel 188
City vacations
  city smarts for new parents.... 184
  urban adventures.................... 42
Cloth diapers 214
Clothing, considerations.............. 64
Constipation 179
Conversions............................... 134
Co-sleeping
  co-sleepers, infant bumper beds 77
  on Amtrak............................ 350
  while traveling........................ 89
Cough and congestion 179
Cruises
  babysitting onboard 387
  bringing baby gear................ 410
  minimum age requirements ... 385

pricing for infants and children
....382
programs for children 387
TABLE
A parent's guide to cruise lines
....................................391
Culture, preparing for differences135

D

Dehydration.................................177
Diapers
changing in car 211
changing on trains 353
cloth, on the go 214
on cruise ships 408
Diarrhea......................................178
Doctor, finding one 172

E

Ear infections 173
Ear pressure on airplanes............307
Eating and feeding
on aircraft 310
on Amtrak...............................352
on cruise ships 388
on the road.............................215
preparing for changes 94

F

Food and water safety 158
Friends and family, staying with ..46
Frontpack carriers.........................73

H

Health concerns
common travel ailments 177
constipation 179
cough and congestion 179
dehydration............................177
diarrhea..................................178
food and water safety 158
swimming..............................162
vaccinations and shots...........163
Healthy travels
breastfeeding for....................156
pre-trip tips for 143

I

IAMAT (International Association
for Medical Assistance to
Travellers) 173
iHealth record............................172

J

Jetlag
and eating 159
overcoming during trips 91
with infants and babies............14

L

Letter of consent, sample of 133

M

Malaria prevention 168
Medical help..............................172
Mosquitoes
DEET-free solutions..............151
managing of...........................148
when camping with infants......37

P

Packing
carry-on for air travel 270
for car trips 218
for your cruise 408
Passport
child's first Canadian 130
child's first U.S. 126, 127
taking child's photo................130
Play yards...................................76
Potty training
ages and stages 28
and the unpredictable child....113
products for on the go..............98
Products and gear.........................66
car seats...................................66
child carriers, wraps, slings 72
eating and feeding 78
strollers and accessories 71
travel beds and sleeping..........76

R

Rentals
baby gear................................82

campervans or conversion vans 232
car seat with car 225
condos and vacation rentals 59
RVs 227
RV rentals 227
car seat issues 229

S

Sleeping
and packing for road trips 218
and the very regular child 113
cruise ship staterooms 395
naptime 92
nighttime 88
on Amtrak trains 349
on naptime flights 258
on red-eye flights 259
on trains in Europe 377
on VIA rail 361
travel beds 76
Slings and wraps 72
Strollers
accessories for 72
checking for flight 279
for travel 71
on cruises 410

T

Tables
airlines, a parent's guide to 244
cruise lines, a parent's guide to 391
Taxis 221
Temperament
explanation of 107
more tools for 123
types and traits 108
Train travel
advantages of 326
airports for Amtrak 354
baggage on Amtrak 353
in Canada 358, 366
required documents for U.S. rail 356
with twins or multiples 328
Travel ailments 177
Travel beds 76, 77
Travel insurance 191
Travel kit, your child's 61, 62

Twins and multiples
air travel 318
train travel 328

U

Urban adventures 42
city smarts for new parents 184

V

Vacation rentals 59
Vaccinations and travel shots 163
common travel shots 164
flu shots 167
for breastfeeding mothers 166
travel shots for babies and small children 164

Kauai, Hawaii: A pit stop between beaches at Hanalei.

About the Author

Shelly Rivoli has changed diapers on four continents and several islands, and she is the award-winning author behind the original *Travels with Baby* guidebook, *Take-Along Travels with Baby* companion guide, and the Travels with Baby website and blog. Among other accolades, she received the 2012 Bronze Award in Travel Blogs from the North American Travel Journalists Association (NATJA).

Ms. Rivoli has become a noted family travel expert, whose advice has been sought and quoted by major media and numerous magazines, including *The Boston Globe, L.A. Times, American Baby, Parents, Parenting, Pregnancy, Parent & Child,* and *TimeOut New York Kids.* She has also made multiple radio appearances sharing tips for enjoying travel with young children and was a recurring guest on ABC 7's *View from the Bay.*

When not traveling, she hangs her hat in the San Francisco Bay Area with her husband and three children.

Start your family's next adventure at
www.TravelswithBaby.com

You'll find even more helpful information and advice, a directory of useful links and resources for planning your next trip, plus all the great products and gear mentioned in this book. While you're there, be sure to subscribe to Travels with Baby Tips blog for more tips, updates, helpful reminders, and inspiration for your future travels.

Did this book help you? Help spread the word!

If any part of *Travels with Baby* has helped you in your family's travel planning, please spread the word! I am deeply grateful for my readers' recommendations and reviews. Thank you!

Drop me a line!

I welcome your feedback and suggestions for future editions of *Travels with Baby*. You can send me an email at:

shelly@TravelswithBaby.com

Or send a postcard to:

Shelly Rivoli
c/o Travels with Baby
1831 Solano Ave #8461
Berkeley, CA 94707
U.S.A.

Made in the USA
San Bernardino, CA
30 June 2016